Public Relations in Britain

*A History of Professional Practice
in the 20th Century*

Public Relations in Britain

A History of Professional Practice in the 20th Century

JACQUIE L'ETANG
University of Stirling, Scotland

Routledge
Taylor & Francis Group
New York   London

First published by Lawrence Erlbaum Associates, Inc., Publishers
10 Industrial Avenue
Mahwah, New Jersey 07430

Reprinted 2009 by Routledge

Routledge

711 Third Avenue
New York, NY 10017

2 Park Square, Milton Park
Abingdon, Oxon OX14 4RN, UK

First issued in paperback 2013

Routledge is an imprint of the Taylor & Francis Group, an informa business

Cover design by Sean Trane Sciarrone

Library of Congress Cataloging-in-Publication Data
L'Etang, Jacquie.
    Public relations in Britain : a history of professional practice in the
twentieth century / Jacquie L'Etang.
  p.   cm.
    Includes bibliographical references and index.
    ISBN 0-8058-3804-X (cloth : alk. paper)
    ISBN 978-0-415-65119-6 (Paperback)
    1. Public relations—Great Britain. 2. Public relations—Great Britain—
History—20th century. I. Title.
HM1221.L48 2004
659.2'0941'0904—dc22

                                                2003049455

STUART

(2/8/55–18/5/99)

Il miglior fabbro

Table of Contents

Preface

This book presents a first account of the development of British public relations in the 20th century. The focus is on whether British public relations has managed to professionalise. To a large degree, the story is one of failure, despite the exponential growth of the field. The history of this puzzling contradiction is explored in detail, drawing on previously untapped archives and extensive oral history interviews. My argument is that this apparent paradox is explained by the inability of the would-be professional body to establish control over public relations practice. Thus, one of the key features of this book is its presentation of a counter-history of the Institute of Public Relations to that body's own self-understanding.

Turning to the overall development and growth of the occupation, I argue that one of the most significant features of British developments, especially in the first half of the 20th century, was the large role played by local and central governments and the relatively small contribution of the private sector. Key aspects of British government propaganda in both wartime and peacetime are highlighted, including economic propaganda.

The contribution of the British Film Documentary Movement and the collaboration between its leader, John Grierson, and the Secretary of the Empire Marketing Board (EMB), Sir Stephen Tallents, is presented as considerably significant, particularly in terms of the development of public relations ideology. The discourse and actions of key figures within the public relations industry are also foregrounded in the overall analysis. Themes include relationships between the public relations industry, the media and politics, ethics, and the ultimately vain attempts of the industry to establish the widespread legitimacy necessary for professional status.

The first chapter sets the context for analysing public relations history. Chapters 2 and 3 are historical chapters that relate key developments from 1914 to the 1960s. These chapters establish the broad narrative in terms of the development of the occupation in the political, social, economic, and cultural context of 20th-century Britain. Thereafter, there is a more explicit institutional focus on the public relations occupation and its attempts to professionalise. Chapter 4 addresses the development and expansion of consultancies that changed the basic architecture of the occupation from its bureaucratic origins in the civil service. The effort to establish social legitimacy and to determine expertise is explored through chapters 5, 6, and 7, which focus respectively on the media, ethics, and education. These more introspective chapters contribute both a deeper understanding of occupational mores and the historical detail needed for a consideration of public relations' efforts to professionalise. Finally, chapter 8 summarises the key influences in the evolution of public relations in Britain and suggests reasons why professonalisation has so far failed.

My aim in researching the topic was to establish the basic historical facts about the development of public relations in Britain and to gain some insight into the characters who shaped the occupation. Because there was no previously published work, I was fortunate to be able to interview nearly 70 key figures, many of whom had been active in the crucial post Second World War era. Their immense generosity in terms of the time and insights they gave me enriched this project and brought it to life. Many have since died, but their voices can still be heard.

I was also curious to discover whether the occupational trajectory was similar to that in the United States, because it is often assumed that the typology of practice that is based on American historical developments is applicable to other cultures. I believe that this book calls that assumption into question, as it becomes clear that the understanding and practice of public relations in the UK had some unique features arising from its particular history and culture. This is most marked in relation to some of the early (1920s–1930s) imaginative and broad conceptions of public relations in Britain, which included what would now be described as strategic concepts. However, this is not a comparative history and such a comparison will have to await a separate analysis. It suffices to say that my approach in researching British history was to ignore the American historical model on good historical methodological grounds. Imposing existing frameworks on the past can be unwise because it can restrict researchers' ability to see the empirical evidence in front of them. I was also very conscious of the temptation for historians to colligate and package history into phases and periods (which obviously facilitates the formulation of typologies), whereas I was much more interested in trying to understand rich description, overlapping themes, and contradictions. For me, this meant some exploration of British public relations culture and ideology as expressed through discourse. Consequently, although there is a narrative structure to the book, as is expected of a history, there are also digressions and a fair amount of sociological interpretation along the way. Again, because there is currently very little sociology of public relations published, I was keen to write an historical sociology rather than pure history. Nevertheless, I was conscious of only scratching the surface in terms of some aspects such as issues of class and gender (my focus on the period up until the 1960s meant that this is largely a his-story) and there is clearly much more work to be done in terms of our understanding of the occupation in a British setting. At a broader level, the book engages with some issues that are universal to the public relations occupation, specifically those to do with professionalisation (the main focus) and propaganda, both of which are addressed at conceptual and historical levels.

The book is intended for academics, researchers, and advanced students in the fields of public relations, media studies, political communication, and communication studies. In particular, I hope the book's interdisciplinary and critical focus will appeal to those from both mainstream public relations and media sociology to encourage a wider debate about the role of public relations in society, because I detect a somewhat unhealthy tendency for the two fields to ignore or disparage each other without engagement with the detailed arguments from the alternative perspective. My own approach has been to give a fair hearing to sources from different perspectives, literatures, and paradigms and to draw from these, and the empirical evidence, some overall picture of the occupation and its dilemmas. At the same time, I was conscious of the dangers of fence sitting or the (even worse) danger of producing an anodyne account. Thus, I have tried to engage critically with the complexity of the field and the questions it raises, but also to understand the practice in the context of the times. Readers will have to judge for themselves whether I have succeeded in this.

Some of material in the book has appeared in other forms, as follows:

1. Part of chapter 3 appeared in "State propaganda and bureaucratic intelligence: the creation of public relations in 20th century Britain." *Public Relations Review,* 24 (4) 1998, pp. 413–41.

2. Part of chapter 8 has appeared in "Public relations education in
   Britain: an historical review in the context of professionalisation." *Public Relations Review,* 25 (3) 1999, pp. 261–91.

3. Part of chapter 4 has appeared in Pieczka, M. & L'Etang J. (2001).
   Public relations and the question of professionalism. In Heath,
   R. (ed.). *Handbook of public relations.* Thousand Oaks, Califor-
   nia: Sage.

4. Small parts from several chapters appeared in "Playing Janus:
   what the past can tell us about PR's future," paper presented at
   the International Public Relations Research Symposium, Lake
   Bled, Slovenia, July 2000.

5. "John Grierson and the public relations industry in Britain,"
   *Screening the past: an international journal of visual media
   and history,* http://www.latrobe.edu.au/www/scregthe past,
   July 1999, ISSN 1328-9756.

6. "Organising public relations' identity: an historical review of
   the discourse work conducted within, and on behalf of, the
   Institute of Public Relations in the UK," paper presented at the
   international seminar on *The business of organising identities,*
   Stirling Media Research Institute, June 2000.

7. Grierson and the public relations industry in Britain (2000). In
   Izod, J. & Kilborn, R. with Hibberd, M. (eds.). *From Grierson to
   the docu-soap: breaking the boundaries* Luton: University of
   Luton Press, pp. 83–96.

This project would never have begun without the specific inspiration
of Professor Philip Schlesinger, whose guidance throughout the project's lengthy progress has been invaluable. I am also grateful for the
comments of Dr. Brian McNair, Professor Paddy Scannell, Professor
Kevin Williams, and Peter Meech.

I am indebted to the History of Advertising Trust, Beccles, Norfolk,
for access to the Institute of Public Relations' archive and for photocopying services.

I am also grateful to the archivists of the Modern Records Centre at
the University of Warwick, where I obtained background information
on the Federation of British Industry; the Design Research Centre at

the University of Brighton, which supplied information on the growth of the British design industry; and the Grierson Archive at the University of Stirling, which houses John Grierson's writings on public relations and propaganda.

Thanks are due to Emily Wilkinson, commissioning editor of Lawrence Erlbaum Associates, for her enthusiasm and patience and to Oron Joffe, Alison Cooper, and Art Lizza, who tackled technical problems and also to the senior book production editor, Sarah Wahlert, and the copyeditor, Rachel Anderson.

On a more personal note, I should like to thank Cathy Collinson, Magda Pieczka, Heike Puchan and Brian Whitworth, Fiona and Robert Somerville, and my aunt and uncle for their unstinting support and encouragement. I owe an incalculable debt to my late friend and partner, Stuart Jones, who supported me through the research process and much of the writing up. This book is partly his and is for him.

1

British Public Relations: Definitions and Debates

INTRODUCTION

This book presents a first account of the development of British public relations in the 20th century. The focus is on the sociological concept of professionalisation and, to a large degree, the story is one of failure, despite the exponential growth of the field. The history of this puzzling contradiction is explored in detail in this book, drawing on previously untapped archives and extensive oral history interviews.

This chapter situates the book in the context of previously published research and explains the contribution of this book to existing knowledge about public relations. Because little has been written directly on the development of British public relations, a variety of sources has been used to frame the empirical research. Because the main focus of the book is occupational formation and development, the literature on the sociology of the professions is emphasised. However, invaluable insights are also drawn from the fields of propaganda studies, public opinion, public relations, and media studies. To date, there has been little debate between media sociologists and public relations academics, which has necessarily inhibited understanding about the evolving phenomenon of public relations, even at the level of basic terminology. This book encompasses perspectives from both fields.

The variety of perspectives reviewed illustrate three main paradigms of thought concerning public relations: the critical (arising largely from media sociology), the functional, and the rhetorical. Because the bulk of the work emanating from the academic field of public relations is from the United States, both the functional and the rhetorical have been broadly underpinned by the values of liberal pluralism. It is also the case that the overwhelming motivation behind such work is to improve the practice. This book offers a different approach, focusing on developments in British culture, its interest in public relations as both an occupation and a social process, and its avoidance of apologism.

The present chapter begins with practical, unproblematised definitions of the field before reviewing ideas germane to an historical sociology of the public relations occupation in the United Kingdom. Relevant sources include histories, sociological analyses, ideas from the relatively new academic field of public relations, political perspectives including propaganda studies, and the sociology of the professions.

DEFINITIONS

In practical terms, public relations can be described as the practice of presenting the public face of an organisation (be it a company, educational institution, hospital, or government) or individual, the articulation of its aims and objectives, and the official organisational view on issues of relevance to it. The currency of public relations is information. Much of this work is carried out through media relations: positioning the organisation as an information source on issues relevant to its operation, thus contributing to its image, market position, political clout, and, some would argue, to its economic survival. *Image* is a complex concept, but is used loosely in UK media and nonspecialist literature to refer to the way an organisation is perceived. Public relations serves an educational and rhetorical role by providing the media with timely material packaged in a form that facilitates media use. The symbiotic relationship with the media is crucial and of great sociological significance. Public relations attempts to influence media production and the fact that the major institutions in society (government, finance, corporations, multinationals, the cultural industries) sponsor such activities has considerable implications in shaping communicative space.

In addition to the purely representational role, public relations practitioners are required to manage relationships on a continuing basis with a range of publics or stakeholders such as shareholders, competitors, suppliers, employees, local and central government, and the local community. The public relations function consists of identifying the information needs of various groups and communicating with them using a range of techniques. The overall public relations aim is to encourage target publics to engage sympathetically at emotional and intellectual levels with the organisation in order to encourage publics to take on board the organisation's point of view. Much of the work is at the technical level, planning and designing communications products that will support the overall aim. Public relations practitioners can thus be seen as discourse workers specialising in communication and the presentation of argument and employing rhetorical strategies to achieve managerial aims. It is fair to say, however, that the common perception of public relations (even among some practitioners) is based on the physicality of output (press releases, leaflets, etc.) rather than on their symbolic construction.

Some public relations relies on interpersonal skills, especially networking, for example, in the field of lobbying. Such work requires a behind-the-scenes negotiative approach akin to diplomatic work and, as such, the process is largely hidden from citizens. Related to the diplomatic aspect of public relations is the function of *issues management*, a strategic role responsible for scanning the environment for emerging issues that may affect the organisation. Its portrayal as an intelligence function implies a degree of subterfuge.

Within their organisations, public relations practitioners are responsible for educating the workforce about the organisational *vision* (the aspirations of the organisation encapsulating its future direction) and its *mission* (the formal definition of the organisation's strategic goal). It is the role of public relations to define the organisational mission in symbolic terms so that managers and employees express themselves through organisational culture and adopt the organisational identity as part of their personal identity. The process of defining organisational identity implies a close engagement with the dominant managerial culture, the propagation of that culture, and, implicitly, the subduing of minority cultures and countercultures. In short, public relations is entrenched within the power structures of organisations.

Public relations entails *meaning management*, which has linguistic, psychological, symbolic, cultural, and sociological components. These elements are obscured by a focus on communication techniques that can hide the role of public relations in society. This book aims to fill a gap in knowledge by contributing an historical sociological perspective to the development of the field in the UK, explaining the key evolutionary processes at societal, institutional, and biographical levels. By taking this approach, it is able to demonstrate how public relations emerged in Britain primarily from the sources of political and economic power.

PREVIOUSLY PUBLISHED RESEARCH

Histories of Public Relations

Academic sources on the history of public relations in the UK are scarce. It is the main aim of this book to begin to address that neglect. A rare exception is Grant, who comprehensively covered the history of British government public relations between the two world wars and reviewed the major government publicity campaigns in this period.[1] Her analysis contributed significantly to an appreciation of the growing role of public relations in the exercise of British government and highlighted the roles of some key individuals. However, her work reveals little about the occupation as a whole and the reasons for its development, beyond its support for specific government policy objectives. Important as these are in the story of public relations in the UK, Grant left out much that is interesting about the relationship between public relations and changes in the social, cultural, economic, and political spheres; its role in the private sector; and the point at which public relations activities had become sufficiently numerous to be recognised both by practitioners and clients as constituting a discrete occupation. It is on such unexamined issues that this book focuses.

Accounts of public relations practice written by practitioners reveal many insights, typically in the introductory sections of textbooks written by practitioners. The majority of these depend to varying degrees on an article by Freddie Gillman, a journalist between 1915 and 1939 who moved into public relations for the RAF during the Second World War, where he rose to Deputy Director Public Relations at the Air Ministry.[2] After the war he was Chief Press and Information Officer for British Overseas Airways Corporation (BOAC). Gillman's article itself appears to depend on an earlier article published in 1957 written by Sir

---

[1]Grant, M. (1994). *Propaganda and the role of the state in inter-war Britain.* Oxford: Clarendon Press.

[2]Gillman, F. C. (1978, April). Public relations in the United Kingdom prior to 1948. *International Public Relations Review,* pp. 43–50.

Tom Fife-Clark, Director of Central Office of Information.[3] It also owed something to an article written by the Chief Information Officer of the Ministry of Pensions and National Insurance, F. D. Bickerton, also published in *Public Relations* 5 years after Fife-Clark's piece.[4] The similarity in these accounts was presumably due to the fact that all the authors had civil service backgrounds. All emphasised the benign role of publicity in supporting government policy and informing the public. Although they identified some significant developments such as the establishment of the Empire Marketing Board, and some important names, they did not provide much explanation for the evolution and growth of the practice. Typically, textbooks have made extensive reference to developments in the United States before focusing on the Empire Marketing Board and the establishment of the Ministry of Information in wartime.[5] There is an assumption in much of the literature that public relations was first developed in the United States and was then exported elsewhere, a view that this book challenges. Another feature of historical reviews within public relations literature is the way in which public relations is defined as akin to activities carried out by the Greeks or the Romans, as well as journalists and activists such as Jonathan Swift, Daniel Defoe, Charles Dickens, and William Wilberforce. Such definitions imply that persuasion, rhetoric, sophistry, advocacy, and lobbying are a central part of public relations practice. At the same time, claims are made for the importance of public relations as part of management, a move that suggests a respectable, technocratic, neutral function. The tension between these broad and narrow types of definition is of fundamental importance to the study of public relations, particularly from a sociological perspective, and is now explored in more detail.

Sociological Perspectives

Media sociologists tend to be broadly critical of public relations work and not to engage with its literature. The influence of the German

---

[3]Fife-Clark, T. (1957). The administrator and the PRO. *Public Relations, 9* (2), pp. 7–17.

[4]Bickerton, F. D. (1957). So that the people shall know. *Public Relations, 15* (1), pp. 48–52.

[5]Black, S. (1962, 1976). *Practical public relations.* London: Pitman; Lloyd, H. (1963, 1970, 1980). *Teach yourself public relations.* Sevenoaks, Kent: Hodder & Stoughton; Harrison, S. (1995). *Public relations: an introduction.* London: Routledge.

sociologist, Jurgen Habermas, has been significant in generating critiques of public relations in relation to deep structural changes that have eroded the public sphere:

> The integration of the public and private realms entailed a corresponding disorganisation of the public sphere that once was the go-between linking state and society. This mediating function passed from the public to such institutions as have arisen out of the private spheres (e.g. special interest associations) or out of the public sphere of parties; these now engage in the exercise or equilibrium of power in co-operation with the state apparatus, treating it as a matter internal to their organisations. At the same time they endeavour, via the mass media that have themselves become autonomous, to obtain the agreement, or at least the acquiescence of a mediated public. Publicity is generated from above, so to speak, in order to create an aura of good will for certain positions. Originally, publicity guaranteed the connection between rational-critical public debate and the legislative foundation of domination, including the critical suspension of its exercise. Now it makes possible the peculiar ambivalence of domination exercised through the domination of non-public opinion: it serves the manipulation of the public as much as legitimation before it. Critical publicity is supplanted by manipulative publicity![6]

Habermas' intervention urges us to see the importance of contextualising specific public relations activities such as media relations within broader structures of society, in order to understand their wider implications. Specifically, he identified public relations as supporting the dominance of elites and reinforcing structural inequalities.

In one of the rare, early British sociological excursions into the field of public relations, the dichotomy between the technical and the strategic levels of public relations was noted astutely in Stuart Hall's brief but pertinent critique. Hall suggested that the emphasis placed by practitioners on technique concealed "an empty space. . . . This is the *technics* of public relations: but what is its *praxis*?" He argued that the emphasis on technical expertise and scientific methods could be explained as a rhetorical effort to confer legitimacy and expertise on public relations practice. In a book review, he suggested that one of the basic textbooks of the 1960s and 1970s:

> Diffuses a gentle glow of legitimacy over the field . . . a highly effective public relations exercise for public relations: the elevation of PR into the

---

[6]Habermas, J. (1989). *The structural transformation of the public sphere: an inquiry into a category of bourgeois society.* Cambridge: Polity Press, pp. 177–78.

ranks of the "management sciences." . . . It is impression management raised to the level of ideology, managerial science becoming a reified discourse . . . a walking case-book of the technicisation of culture . . . a Weberian vision of bureaucratic rationality gone mad, the infinitely trivial elevated to the status and impersonality of—science.[7]

Hall argued that it was of sociological importance to focus on the "social tendency of the enterprise [public relations] as a whole," yet until recently there has been little work of this nature. Exceptions have been Sussman, Pimlott, Tunstall, and Hall.[8] Only the last two authors concentrated exclusively on the British phenomenon of public relations (in the 1960s and 1970s). Historically driven contributions were made by Curran and Seaton, and also Ward, who insightfully pointed out that the British Documentary Movement "must be seen in terms of the development of public relations in Britain," and that:

It was the growing movement towards a centralisation of news sources through the Press Association and the location of correspondents in and around government sources which offered the opportunity for the management of news stories by the growing number of public relations departments attached to large firms and government departments.[9]

Tunstall's analysis, published in book form in 1964, was based on ethnographic work. It demonstrated how the pressures on journalistic practice created a dependency on public relations services.[10] Tunstall's book was described by one former president of the Institute of Public Relations as "prejudiced . . . unbalanced. The author clearly has an antipathy to his subject which arises like a stench from almost every page."[11] This response is perhaps the earliest example of the public relations occupation's sensitivity to sociological analysis. The strength of the reaction was probably influenced by the fact that, at that time,

---

[7]Hall, S. (1969, December). The technics of persuasion. *New Society*, pp. 948–9.

[8]Sussman, L. (1948–9, Winter). The personnel and ideology of public relations. *Public Opinion Quarterly*, pp. 697–708; Pimlott, J. A. R. (1951). *Public relations and American democracy*. Princeton, New Jersey: Princeton University Press; Tunstall, J. (1964). *The advertising man*. London: Chapman & Hall; Hall, S. (1969, December). The technics of persuasion. *New Society*, pp. 948–9.

[9]Curran, J. & Seaton, J. (1988). *Power without responsibility: the press and broadcasting in Britain*. London: Routledge, pp. 235–6; Ward, K. (1989). *Mass communication and the modern world*. Basingstoke: Macmillan, pp. 121, 124.

[10]Tunstall, J. (1964); see also Tunstall, J. (1983). *The media in Britain*. London: Constable, pp. 6–7, 40, 146, 187–8.

[11]Crisford, J. (1964). Author versus 'blurb.' *Public Relations, 17* (1), p. 49.

public relations was attracting a large amount of criticism from journalists. The story of this particular conflict is related in chapter 5.

Stuart Hall urged consideration of the wider societal implications of public relations practice when he argued that it "comes of age in an epoch of the modern corporation and the mass media. It is a product of the extreme specialisation of functions which has invaded and recast the social relations of production . . . communication has been more or less severed from its substantive base in production."[12] Thus, for Hall, the advent of public relations was a consequence of capitalism and the growth of the mass media. His book also seems to imply that the specialisation of communications in the corporate context led to a functionalism and instrumentalism that inevitably reduced the authenticity of communications.

Relatively little British research on public relations has taken place since Hall and Tunstall. Insightful theorists, such as Chomsky and Wernick, tended to conflate advertising, marketing, promotion, propaganda, and public relations, whereas others focused specifically on the political sphere and the media or on particular issues such as the environment.[13] Chomsky's "propaganda model" suggested that the media serve the interests of state and corporate power, "framing their reporting and analysis in a manner supportive of established privilege and limiting debate and discussion accordingly," and implied the need for elite networkers and wheeler-dealers, rhetoricians and lobbyists who can put their case across.[14] Likewise, Gandy's notion of information subsidies points to structural inequalities in society that are reinforced by public relations and the media.[15] Media sociologists, notably Hall, Schlesinger,

---

[12] Hall, S. pp. 948–9.

[13] Herman, E. S. & Chomsky, N. (1988). *Manufacturing consent: the political economy of the mass media.* New York: Pantheon Books; Chomsky, N. (1993). *Necessary illusions: thought control in democratic societies.* London: Pluto Press; Chomsky, N. (1998). Propaganda and control of the public mind. In McChesney, R. W., Wood, E. M., & Foster, J. B. (eds.). *Capitalism and the information age: the political economy of the global communication revolution.* New York: Monthly Review Press; Wernick, A. (1991). *Promotional culture: advertising, ideology and symbolic expression.* London: Sage; Parenti, M. (1993). *Inventing the politics of the news media reality.* New York: St Martin's Press; Altschull, J. H. (1995). *Agents of power: the media and public policy.* New York: Longman; Rowell, A. (1996). *Green backlash: global subversion of the environment movement.* London: Routledge; Hansen, A. (1994). *The mass media and environmental issues.* Leicester: Leicester University Press.

[14] Chomsky, N. (1993). *Necessary illusions,* p. 10.

[15] Gandy, O. (1982). *Beyond agenda setting: information subsidies and public policy.* Norwood, NJ: Ablex; Gandy, O. (1992). Public relations and public policy: the structura-

Anderson, McNair, Miller, Dinan, and Davis, have more recently turned their attention to source-media relations and, drawing on Habermas' insight that "public relations . . . techniques have come to dominate the public sphere,"[16] debated the implications for citizen access to the public sphere, work that cuts across political science and communications.[17] Miller and Dinan presented a fascinating account of the growth of public relations consultancy in the UK in the 1980s and 1990s and the expansion in the market for such services. They argued that public relations has been both a symptom of the political domination of free market ideas and also the means to facilitate ideological change.[18] Overall, the substantial critiques emerging from media sociology have not been addressed by the public relations discipline, as is now discussed.

Public Relations Perspectives

Existing narratives of the origins and development of the public relations occupation are largely American. One interpretation still dominates—that developed by J. Grunig and Hunt, which suggests that

---

tion of dominance in the information age. In Toth, E. & Heath, R. (eds.). *Rhetorical and critical approaches to public relations.* Hillsdale, New Jersey: Lawrence Erlbaum Associates, pp. 131–63.

[16]Habermas, J., p. 193.

[17]Hall, S. et al., (1978). *Policing the crisis: mugging, the state and law and order.* London: Macmillan; Schlesinger, P. (1990). Rethinking the sociology of journalism: source strategies and the limits of media centrism. In Ferguson, M. (ed.). *Public communication: the new imperatives: future directions for research.* Thousand Oaks, CA: Sage; Anderson, A. (1991). Source strategies and the communication of environmental affairs. *Media, Culture & Society,* 13 (4), pp. 459–76; Anderson, A. (1993). Source-media relations: the production of the environmental agenda. In Hansen, A. (ed.). *The mass media and environmental issues.* Leicester: Leicester University Press, pp. 51–68; McNair, B. (1996). Performance in politics and the politics of performance: public relations, the public sphere and democracy. In L'Etang, J. & Pieczka, M. (eds.). *Critical perspectives in public relations.* London: International Thompson; Miller, D. (1993). Official sources and 'primary definition': the case of Northern Ireland. *Media, Culture & Society,* 15 (3), pp. 385–406; Miller, D. (1998). Public relations and journalism: promotional strategies and media power. In Briggs, A. & Cobley, P. (eds.). *The media: an introduction.* London: Longman, pp. 65–80; Miller, D., Kitzinger, J., Williams, K., & Beharrell, P. (1998). *The circuit of mass communication: media strategies, representation and audience reception in the AIDS crisis.* London: Sage; Miller, D. & Dinan, W. (2000). The rise of the PR industry in Britain, 1979–98. *European Journal of Communication,* 15 (1), pp. 5–35; Davis, A. (2000). Public relations, news production and changing patterns of source access in the British national media. *Media, Culture & Society,* 22 (1), pp. 39–59.

[18]Miller, D. & Dinan, W., pp 5–35.

public relations has passed through four developmental stages: publicity, public information, asymmetrical communication, and symmetrical communication. Somewhat simplistically, the first two stages are described as "one-way" communication in comparison to the "two-way" types, of which the asymmetrical variety employs research techniques to support its persuasive efforts. The symmetrical type is motivated to achieve consensus between an organisation and its publics. Much of the literature promotes the idea that this evolutionary model is universally applicable both as an historical explanation and as a typology that satisfactorily explains professional practice. Yet it fails to take account of significant cultural and political factors in non-U.S. settings, and its monolithic application in deductive research and status as a worldview has inhibited the development of research grounded in the daily practice of public relations.

The dominant paradigm is broadly liberal pluralist and sees public relations as supportive of democracy, opening up channels of communications in society and facilitating dialogue between organisations and publics.[19] The conception of two-way symmetrical communications entails the use of "bargaining, negotiating and strategies of conflict resolution to bring about symbolic changes in the ideas, attitudes and behaviours of both the organisation and its publics."[20] According to this view, public relations is neutral, benign, and broadly utilitarian. The dominant paradigm therefore chooses to ignore the intrinsic self-interest necessarily present in the representation of an interest and advocacy on behalf of an organisation.

Within the generally instrumental field of public relations, a few academics have begun to explore the rhetorical aspects of public relations and have, possibly inadvertently, begun the process of reconnecting *technic* with *praxis*.[21] The majority of this work is focused on legitimat-

---

[19]Grunig, J. E. (2000). Collectivism, collaboration and societal corporatism as core professional values in public relations. *Journal of Public Relations Research*, 12 (1), p. 24.

[20]Grunig, J. E. (1989). Symmetrical presuppositions as a framework for public relations theory. In Botan, C. & Hazleton, V. (Jr.). *Public relations theory*. Hillsdale, New Jersey: Lawrence Erlbaum Associates, pp. 17–44.

[21]Pearson, R. (1989). Beyond ethical relativism in public relations: co-orientation, rules and the idea of communication symmetry. In Grunig, J. E. & Grunig, L. A. (eds.). *Public Relations Research Annual, 1*, Hillsdale, New Jersey: Lawrence Erlbaum Associates; Pearson, R. (1989). Business ethics as communication ethics: public relations practice and the idea of dialogue. In Botan, C. H. & Hazleton, V. (eds.). *Public relations theory*. Hillsdale, New Jersey: Lawrence Erlbaum Associates; Toth, E. & Heath, R. (eds.). (1992). *Rhetorical and critical approaches to public relations*. Hillsdale, New Jersey:

ing public relations activity by utilising Habermas' theory of communicative action as an ethical justification for the practice, by arguing that public relations can and should facilitate ideal speech communication between organisations and their publics.[22] However, to date, the self-proclaimed rhetorical scholars have not really presented an alternative paradigm in that they still seek the beneficial effects of public relations. The dominant paradigm sees the role of public relations as achieving consensus between organisations and their publics through dialogue and negotiation, and is thus positioned as working in the public interest. Initially, the rhetorical approach appeared to offer an alternative model of public relations as advocacy on behalf of organisational interests, but, subsequently, the model has been transformed into something slightly different that fits within the dominant paradigm. For example, one of the key scholars in the field, Heath, defined rhetoric as "the use of discourse by competing interests seeking to induce one another to accept a mutually harmonious view" and claimed that rhetoric "involves positioning an organisation or issue to gain advantage without distorting the debate."[23] Such definitions imply benign and accommodating motivations and ignore the reality of organisational struggles in the marketplace. Thus, even rhetorical public relations literature tends to be idealistic normative and, in common with the rest of the public relations canon, does not generally engage with critical perspectives. The small amount of critical work within public relations gets short shrift in the United States. Some such work was recently dismissed as "naive" because it failed to conform to the perceived requirement in the field to "construct new and better ways of practicing the profession."[24]

Political Perspectives

The work of Sussman alerted us to both the culture and mores of the public relations occupation and, in exploring public relations ideology,

Lawrence Erlbaum Associates; L'Etang, J. (1996). Public relations and rhetoric. In L'Etang, J. & Pieczka, M. (eds.). *Critical perspectives in public relations.* London: International Thompson Business Press, pp. 106–23.

[22] Habermas, J. (1991). *The theory of communicative action: reason and rationalization of society.* Cambridge: Polity Press.

[23] Heath, R. (1992). Visions of critical studies in public relations. In Toth, E. & Heath, R. (eds.). *Rhetorical and critical approaches to public relations.* Hillsdale, New Jersey: Lawrence Erlbaum Associates, pp. 317–8.

[24] Grunig, J. E. (2001). Two-way symmetrical public relations: past, present, and future. In Heath, R. L. (ed.). *Handbook of public relations.* Thousand Oaks, CA: Sage, p. 17.

revealed the importance of the concept of public opinion to public relations work.[25] This work consequently resonated in the concerns of
media sociologists regarding the manipulation of public opinion by elite
groups, and the decreasing lack of space for citizens to raise issues
because of the increasing domination of the public sphere by corporations and other institutions. Literature on public opinion is extensive,
ranging from the classical works of Locke, Hume, and Rousseau to
Herbst's useful typology, which encompasses aggregative, majoritarian,
opinion formation and reified approaches.[26] Aside from the important
epistemological debates, there have been methodological developments
and the appropriation of the aggregative concept by social scientists
employing survey methods. Nevertheless, within literature on public
opinion there are issues that clearly suggest public relations' dark side
and it is here that the concept of propaganda appears. Cultural theorist
Stuart Ewen reinforced those connections in his study of public relations in the United States. Ewen combined biographical material on key
figures in the public relations field with the analysis of conceptual
developments in public opinion and propaganda, in the context of late
19th- and early 20th-century political, social, and industrial American
history.[27]

In the historical context of this book, it is appropriate to turn to the
American political writers Lasswell and Lippman, who were publishing
in the 1920s and 1930s on the problems of democracy and public opinion. Lasswell expressed serious concerns about the development of propaganda in the First World War and argued, "Discussion about the ways
and means of controlling public opinion . . . testifies to the collapse of
the traditional species of democratic romanticism and the rise of a dicta-
torial habit of mind."[28] It was Lasswell who introduced the Taylorist
metaphor of engineering to public relations work and his compatriot
Lippman introduced another such metaphor—the manufacture of con-

---

[25]Sussman, L., pp. 697–708.

[26]Locke, J. (1979). *An essay concerning human understanding*. Ed. Nidditch, P.H.
Oxford: Oxford Clarendon Press; Hume, D. (1980). *A treatise of human nature*. Oxford:
Oxford University Press; Rousseau, J. J. (1968). *The social contract*. Harmondsworth:
Penguin; Herbst, S. (1993). The meaning of public opinion: citizens' constructions of
political reality. *Media, Culture & Society*, 15 (3), pp. 437–54.

[27]Ewen, S. (1996). *PR! A social history of spin*. New York: Basic Books.

[28]Lasswell, H. D., Casey, R. D., & Smith, B. L. (1996). Propaganda and promotional
activities: an annotated bibliography. In Ewen, S. *PR! A social history of spin*. New
York: Basic Books, p. 174.

sent. (Bernays adopted the engineering metaphor himself in 1955 in the title of his book *Engineering of Consent*. Engineering has remained a managerial metaphor as seen by the 1980s term for organisational restructuring *business process re-engineering*). Lippman's pessimistic view of mass society led him to recommend the creation of a cadre of communication specialists who would be given privileged access to elites and events and who would subsequently be responsible for briefing the media.[29] Public relations, propaganda, and public opinion were intrinsically connected by Bernays, a self-styled public relations "counsel," in his books.[30] In the first part of the 20th century, *propaganda* was an unproblematic term that became initially tarred with the brush of totalitarianism in the 1930s and then further tarnished during the Second World War and the Cold War. Propaganda studies emerged from the field of research that focused on effective persuasion. Common to most definitions has been the idea of partisanship and of communicating a particular set of beliefs. For the aspirant occupation of public relations, such a definition is immediately problematic because it potentially infringes the necessary condition of privileging the public interest, a criterion required of professions. Post-Second World War definitions have tended to include deception or lying as key tactical features of propaganda. These developments help explain why, in public relations literature, the importance of truth telling and the pluralist values of the free market (in terms of competing ideas) are emphasised. However, there is a considerable tension in the public relations literature between universalist and relativist notions of truth.[31] The emergence of professional bodies in public relations has coincided with attempts by its practitioners to separate the practice from propaganda, exemplified in Traverse-Healy's pamphlet written in 1988 for the International Public Relations Association entitled "Public Relations and Propaganda: values compared."[32] The pamphlet is typical of a number of public relations

[29]Lippman, W. (1998). *Public opinion*. London: Transaction Publishers.

[30]Bernays, E. (1928). *Propaganda*. New York: Boni & Liveright; Bernays, E. (1961). *Crystallising public opinion*. New York: Boni & Liveright; Bernays, E. (1947). Engineering of consent. *Annals of the American Academy of Political and Social Science* No. 250, March, pp. 113–20.

[31]L'Etang, J. (1997). Public relations and the rhetorical dilemma: legitimate 'perspectives,' persuasion or pandering? *Australian Journal of Communication*, 24 (2), pp. 33–53.

[32]Traverse-Healy, T. (1998). Public relations and propaganda: values compared, Gold Paper, *International Public Relations Association*.

sources in utilising Jowett and O'Donnell's somewhat didactic framework that classifies propaganda into white, grey, and black, depending on the degree to which the source is revealed and the information communicated accurate.[33] This framework is attractive to public relations because it enables an apparently clear distinction to be drawn between public relations and propaganda. However, the framework is not particularly helpful in dealing with instances where there is room for multiple interpretations, as is the case, for example, with many contemporary scientific and medical debates. In general terms, the academic field of public relations does not engage in conceptual discussion about propaganda, except insofar as it is acknowledged in some texts that propaganda was part of public relations' prehistory and that some practitioners were involved in government propaganda.[34] In this way, academic public relations has acted to support the public relations professional agenda rather than to analyse what is clearly a fundamental epistemological and moral issue.

Public Relations, Propaganda, and Education

The specific connection between public relations and propaganda is most evident in the literature in propaganda studies that focuses on the educative aspects of propaganda. Here we come closer to the *praxis* of public relations. The contributions of the French theorist Ellul and the American Sproule are of particular interest here.[35] Ellul's work remains radical because, even though he was writing some time after the Second World War, he suggested that propaganda was not only intrinsic to, but absolutely essential for democratic society. He rejected the common view that propaganda was intrinsically evil or concerned with peddling untruths. His sociological approach took the study of propaganda beyond that of psychological persuasion to try to identify its essential features. Central to his view was the notion that education was a prerequisite for propaganda, completely opposite to the dominant paradigm, that education guards against propaganda. For Ellul, propaganda was "an indispensable condition to the development of technological

---

[33] Jowett, G. S. & O'Donnell, V. (1986). *Propaganda and persuasion*. London: Sage.

[34] Cutlip, S. M. (1994). *The unseen power: public relations. A history*. Hillsdale, New Jersey: Lawrence Erlbaum Associates.

[35] Ellul, J. (1965). *Propaganda*. New York: Knopf; Sproule, J. M. (1989). Social responses to twentieth century propaganda. In Smith, T. III. *Propaganda*. New York: Praegar, pp. 5–22.

progress and the establishment of a technological condition."[36] Specifically, Ellul included public relations as part of propaganda because such work "seek[s] to adapt the individual to society, to a living standard, to an activity . . . to make him conform, which is the aim of all propaganda."[37] Sproule presented an historically grounded typology identifying four responses to technological change, urbanisation, and the growth of the media: the "humanist" response, which tried to increase citizen participation in politics and provide a counter to government influence as a media source; the "professional" response, which saw propaganda as necessary for a complex society and thus opened up opportunities for a cadre of communication specialists (the Lippman approach); the "scientific" response, which shifted research in the field from qualitative to quantitative, thus avoiding further analysis of critical issues around the propaganda concept; and the "polemical" response, which was openly partisan and discredited the sources of some ideas such as American anticommunism in the 1950s.[38] Sproule's framework is particularly useful in seeing the emergence of public relations as intrinsically connected to the deep structures of society. Within the present book, the focus on professionalisation makes Sproule's second category, that of the professional response, especially relevant because it presents a complete rationale for the existence of the occupation.

The issue of propaganda was also raised separately within the field of education in the 1970s in terms of indoctrination in the classroom.[39] This illustrates the point that discussion of propaganda should not be limited to the domains of politics and the activities of governments, politicians, spin doctors, and journalists. Power does not reside solely at these levels and a serious consideration of propaganda necessitates a fundamental questioning of many aspects of societal communications. Education and its role in society have been central to the work of the sociologist Pierre Bourdieu in relation to the reproduction strategies used by dominant elites.[40] This opens the way to seeing the education

---

[36] Ellul, J., p. x.

[37] Ellul, J., p. xiii.

[38] Sproule, J. M., pp. 5–22.

[39] Degenhardt, M. A. B. (1976). Indoctrination. In Lloyd, D. L. (ed.). *Philosophy and the teacher*. London: Routledge & Kegan Paul; Barrow, R. & Woods, R. (1988). *An introduction to philosophy of education*. London: Methuen.

[40] Harkner, R. (1990). Bourdieu: education and reproduction. In Harkner, R., Makar, C., & Wilkes, C. (eds.). *An introduction to the work of Pierre Bourdieu: the practice of theory*. London: Macmillan, p. 94.

process as clearly linked to propaganda, but is also useful in considering the role that education plays in the process of professionalisation, which is given some attention in chapter 7. It is therefore highly significant that public relations practitioners and theorists have often defined public relations work as a form of education leading to enlightenment and the consequent accommodation of views.

Sociology of the Professions

Sociologists specialising in the study of professions have not yet turned their attention to the public relations occupation as a case study in itself, but identify important features of professionalising occupations that are useful in helping to frame this study. Sociological literature on professions can be roughly divided into: a typology encompassing research on the necessary and sufficient traits for an occupation to be recognised by society as a profession;[41] research that tries to capture the generic stages of the process;[42] ethnographic research;[43] research drawing on Weber and Marx that emphasises the professions' effectiveness in monopolising a field of work and negotiating high status, known as the "power approach,"[44] which also sees professionalism as "a claim to leadership . . . a mechanism of social control";[45] research that focuses on "the professional project" and the transformation of specialist knowledge and skills into social and economic rewards;[46] and, finally, research that takes a systemic approach to looking at occupations as a linked sys-

---

[41]Millerson, G. (1964). *The qualifying associations: a study in professionalisation.* London: Routledge & Kegan Paul.

[42]Vollmer, H. M. & Mills, D. L. (1966). *Professionalisation.* Englewood Cliffs: Prentice Hall; Caplow, T. (1954). *Sociology of work.* Minneapolis: University of Minneapolis Press; Wilensky, H. L. (1964). The professionalisation of everyone? *American Journal of Sociology, 70,* pp. 137–58.

[43]Hughes, E. (1958). *Men and their work.* New York: The Free Press; Becker, H. S., Greer, B., Hughes, E. C., & Strauss, B. L. (1961). *Boys in white.* Chicago: Chicago University Press.

[44]Abbott, A. (1988). *The system of professions: an essay on the division of expert labour.* London: University of Chicago Press; Johnson, T. (1972). *The professions and power.* London: Macmillan.

[45]Elliott, P. (1972). *The sociology of the professions.* New York: Herder & Herder, p. 152.

[46]Larson, M. S. (1977). *The rise of professionalism: a sociological analysis.* London: University of California Press.

tem in which changes in one occupation will have an impact on other occupations. Of particular importance are questions of "jurisdiction," described by Abbott as "the hold a profession established over a set of tasks."[47] The systemic approach seems conceptually linked to Bourdieu's ideas about the dynamic creation of intellectual fields arising from the "system of relations between themes and problems."[48] In summary, the literature on the sociology of the professions has established as the key features of a profession:

> A specialised skill and service, an intellectual and practical training, a high degree of professional autonomy, a fiduciary relationship with the client, a sense of collective responsibility to the profession as a whole, an embargo on some methods of attracting business and an occupational organisation testing competence, regulating standards and maintaining discipline[49]

and the processes through which an occupation must pass to achieve that status: "(1) the emergence of the full-time occupation; (2) the establishment of the training school; (3) the founding of professional associations; (4) political agitation directed towards the protection of the association by law; (5) the adoption of a formal code."[50]

More recent research has shifted away from assumptions that the professions are a neutral and stabilising force in society to the more critical perspective, which suggests that professions form a powerful, self-interested, and often intersecting elite. It is argued that such interest groups operate competitively to achieve the best status possible, to erect barriers to entry, and to gatekeep those barriers. The delineation of a field of practice based on abstract knowledge is seen as crucial to this process and has been articulated in the literature as the process of "social closure" to maintain jurisdiction over specialised tasks. This book utilises these concepts from the literature on professionalisation to elucidate the historical development of the occupation. However, in the case of public relations, it is also necessary to give considerable attention to the gaining of social legitimacy—the precursor to obtain-

---

[47] Abbott, A., p. 9.

[48] Bourdieu, P. (1971). Intellectual field and creative projects. In Young, M. F. D. (ed.). *Knowledge and control: new directions in the sociology of education.* London: Collier-Macmillan, p. 16.

[49] Elliott, P., p. 5.

[50] Johnson, T. (1972). *Professions and power.* London: Macmillan, p. 28.

ing licence and mandate from the state. The benefits to society of the welfare occupations are obvious; those of public relations less so.

Finally, turning to the public relations literature on professionalisation, one can note its functionalism and focus on the acquisition of technical skills and of gaining acceptance by the managerial class in organisations. Research has concentrated on whether the occupation has achieved the requisite traits of professionalism, but has not gone beyond this except in terms of a stream of quantitatively based research into gender roles.[51] Interestingly, the recent insightful work of media sociologist Davis takes as its unit of analysis the concept of "professional public relations," and Miller and Dinan likewise used the term *professional* in relation to public relations, apparently assuming that the description can be unproblematically applied.[52] This may be because, by presenting public relations as professional, they are able enhance their own moral position by arguing that public relations is an extensive and insidiously evil presence in society. Public relations academics are also guilty of using the term *professional* too loosely, but the motivation here is radically different—evangelism to attain desired status.

This book takes as its frame the concept of professionalisation and considers the evolution of the practice in this context. It engages with the key concepts from the sociology of the professions, but particularly emphasises the process, power, and professional project approaches. Because of the focus on the power approach, relevant critical sociological frameworks, other than those from sociology of the professions, are utilised analytically when appropriate. Specifically, an historical sociological approach is taken to facilitate the combination of descriptive narrative and critical sociological analysis. Such an approach facilitates seeing the development of public relations as part of a social process, not in the rather sterile way adopted by those interested in the stages of professionalism, but in the sense recommended by Torstendahl, in which "the temporal dimension [is] much more closely related to the actual development of world history."[53]

---

[51] Pieczka, M. & L'Etang, J. (2001). Public relations and the question of professionalism. In Heath, R. (ed.). *Handbook of public relations*. Thousand Oaks, CA: Sage.

[52] Davis, A., pp. 39–59; Miller, D. & Dinan, W., pp. 5–35.

[53] Torstendahl, R. (1990). Essential properties, strategic aims and historical development: three approaches to theories of professionalisms. In Burrage, M. & Torstendahl, R. (eds.). *Professions in theory and history: rethinking the study of the professions*. London: Sage, p. 57.

CONCLUSION

It is possible from this brief analysis to identify a major gap in our knowledge about the development of public relations in the UK. This book aims to fill some of this gap by pursuing some linked strands. First, it attempts to construct an overall explanatory account of the evolution of public relations in Britain in the 20th century. Second, it aims to take forward issues perspicaciously identified by Lippman, to focus on the professionalisation of such an occupational field, and to consider the implications of such a development. Third, it seeks to ground analysis of interview and documentary sources within the context of an historical review. Fourth, the focus on professionalisation necessitates consideration of self-identity of the professionalising group. Some attention is given to this aspect and the discourse work practitioners have conducted on their own behalf, particularly in relation to key aspects of professionalism. Taken as a whole, the book is an empirically driven project that aims to contribute new insights about the development of the public relations industry in Britain. The approach taken does not fall neatly into existing paradigms, but attempts to construct a balanced account firmly based on original documentary evidence and oral history interviews with those practising public relations in the 1940s and 1950s when the occupation began to professionalise. The main interest is an unravelling of the problems and dilemmas of a new occupation.

2

Propaganda, Information, and Intelligence: 1914–1945

INTRODUCTION

This chapter sketches the main influences on the development of public relations in Britain in the 20th century from the First World War until the formation of the IPR in 1948. The chapter sets forth the development of public relations within the context of the British political, social, economic, and cultural scene in a turbulent period of European history. The contribution made by local government officials is highlighted prior to a review of central government's peacetime and wartime propaganda efforts. This is followed by a summary of developments in the private sector and the chapter concludes with an account of the first steps toward professionalisation. The major argument presented is that developments in local government, both in terms of the growth of public relations work and in terms of the professionalisation of civil servants, constituted one of the key stages in the emergence of public relations more widely in Britain. In particular, the nucleus of public relations officers within the local government trade union, the National Association of Local Government Officers (NALGO), was responsible for the formation of the IPR and for the development of its mission to professionalise the occupation. Thus, the lessons learned in one specific part of the state sector were applied more broadly to the public relations occupation as a whole. This chapter shows very clearly that public relations emerged of its own accord in Britain and was not simply an import from America.

Because the focus of this book is on the emergence of professional public relations, attention is given to those areas that contributed most to that development. Thus, this history excludes those who did not concern themselves with the professional project, such as those in the Government Communication and Information Service (GCIS). Likewise, although attention is drawn to prominent individuals on the public relations scene who became involved in politics, this story does not relate developments in party political communication in any depth.

BUREAUCRATIC INTELLIGENCE

Local government in Britain developed key public relations concepts and contributed in an important way to public relations ideology, particularly in relation to concepts of professionalism and a public service ethos. Local government public relations officers formed the nucleus of those responsible for setting up the IPR, a task for which they possessed appropriate administrative skills.

Local government in the UK entails the provision of a wide range of services for the public, including fire, police, and health services, town and country planning, and state education. Whereas central government determines overall legislation, locally elected bodies implement policy within the constraints of their local budgets (partly raised directly from the local populace in the form of a property tax). Decentralisation was pragmatically motivated by a desire to reduce congestion in central government. Although the system has ancient origins, the constitution and functions of local authorities date back only to the 19th century in response to the problems of the Industrial Revolution. The Reform Act of 1832 and a raft of later social legislation increased the role and responsibilities of local government, which had major implications for the recruitment, training, and qualifications of officials. Nearly a century after the Reform Act had been passed, the main issues facing local government, which were fundamental to its credibility and legitimacy, can be summed up as professionalism, ethics, communication, and democratic accountability.

In the late 19th and early 20th centuries, the head of a local authority was usually a solicitor and at the turn of the century such a legal qualification was generally the most valued in local government. Much depended on patronage and the ability to buy preferment and there were few opportunities for the humble clerk to progress.[1] There were allegations of corruption and criticism of the lack of transparency in advancement, and in 1905 NALGO was founded to lobby for local government officials' rights to pensions, salary scales, promotion by merit, and appointment by open examination, as had existed for civil servants since Gladstone's era.[2] The debates and negotiations that followed signalled the beginning of professionalisation for local government clerical and administrative staff. This was an era in which many such combinations, associations, and societies were formed, described by the early local government public relations officer Spoor as the emergence of "the professional society."[3]

NALGO was quick to turn to the potential of education to help achieve a higher status, but, in addition to developing a curriculum for a diploma qualification, took as its major purpose the responsibility for educating the wider public about local government and its role in society. In particular, there was much public hostility to be overcome, a legacy of the 19th-century form of local government under which officials such as "the sanitary inspector, school attendance officer and health visitor"[4] were feared and loathed. As early as 1906, a NALGO official complained about attacks on local government by rate payers' societies and suggested that "a Press Gang [be formed] to reply to attacks on librarians and library work in newspapers."[5] In the 1920s and 1930s local government suffered from the "odium of administering unemployment relief and the hated means test."[6] The second General Secretary of NALGO (1909–1943), Levi Clement Hill, was quick to appreciate the necessity of public relations and in 1922 suggested that every branch should have a press correspondent and a publicity committee. However, Hill's ideas were resisted and only in 1932, when the Chancellor of the Exchequer proposed immediate cuts in local government spending, was there agreement to Hill's proposal that there

---

[1]Keith-Lucas, B. & Richard, P. G. (1978). *A history of local government in the twentieth century.* London: George Allen & Unwin, p. 242.

[2]Ibid. p. 103.

[3]Spoor, A. (1967). *White-collar union: sixty years of NALGO.* London: Heinemann, p. 3.

[4]Ibid. pp. 131–2.

[5]Ibid. p. 132.

[6]Ibid. p. 132.

should be a full-scale "publicity campaign to counteract the propaganda which is seeking to write down the value of public administration."[7] Hill felt compelled to educate the public about the role of local government and to correct the impression that local government officials worked in a sheltered occupation and were a burden to businessmen. In the economic depression of the 1930s, businessmen argued that rates and taxes had contributed to economic decline and some suggested that local government officials could be sacked and replaced at half the cost by unemployed men. Hill's view was that:

> Centuries of adverse propaganda meant that very few consumers of local government services and perhaps an even smaller percentage of those who were elected to "manage" them, really believed that these services had any virtues. . . . The national executive [of NALGO] gave this problem its most careful consideration and finally embarked upon a new public relations policy in 1932.[8]

The publicity campaign that followed included a range of activities leading up to the centenary of local government in 1935, such as a letter-writing campaign to the press, commissioned articles and pamphlets distributed to the press and Members of Parliament, a centenary book, an essay competition, exhibitions, mentions of "Civic Sunday" in churches, a *Times* supplement, and a series of open lectures on public administration in universities specialising in the field such as Glasgow School of Social Studies, Liverpool School of Social Sciences and Administration, the London School of Economics, Southampton University College, Aberystwyth University College, and Cardiff University College.[9] On the internal communications side, there was a centenary cruise around the Baltic to enable 500 NALGO members to observe how local government operated in other countries.[10]

Such activities, and the analysis and discussion that preceded them, would not have had much impact were it not for the fact that the public relations concept had received substantial attention in the journal *Public Administration* first published in 1923 by the Institute of Public Administration, which had been formed in 1922 as "the leading independent British organisation with expertise in public sector management."[11]

---

[7] Ibid. p. 133.

[8] Hill, L. (1937). Advertising local government. *Public Opinion Quarterly, 1*, p. 64.

[9] Ibid. pp. 67–8.

[10] Ibid. p. 69.

[11] Royal Institute of Public Administration, 1998, p. 10.

Both the institute and the journal were of significance in establishing public administration on a more professional footing. Although the journal covered a wide range of topics, "Publicity and public relations received much attention both in their own right and as issues cited in articles covering many other diverse topics. . . . Between 1923 and 1942 seventeen articles were published dealing specifically with publicity and propaganda, and another twenty-three addressed 'general relations with the public.' "[12]

Those contributing to the journal demonstrated self-awareness of the interest in public relations. For example, in 1935 Simey noted that from the first issue of *Public Administration* in 1923 there had been "a succession of able articles, concerning Public Relations, a subject hot from the oven, or perhaps still in the mixing bowl."[13] The aims of the Institute of Public Administration were the development of local and national public service "as a recognised profession" and "promotion of the study of Public Administration." These implied the necessity for publicity and lobbying activities. More detailed objectives specified included:

> To maintain the high ideals and traditions of the Public Service and *promote* the professional interests of Public Servants. . . . To facilitate the *exchange of information* and thought on administrative and related questions . . . the *creation of a well-informed public opinion* concerning those services, to provide opportunities for the *acquisition and dissemination of useful information. . . . To promote good relations. . . .* To keep members and the public *constantly informed*[14] (emphasis added).

The new institute was charged with the communicative tasks of representing its members and facilitating networking among them. "Public relations," in contrast to "intelligence," was seen literally as relations with the general public and the role that provided rather than collected information. In addressing the theme of relationships between public servants and the public, Finer suggested that an essential aspect of the role of the public servant is "his obligation to stand as the representative of the vast, unrepresented, anonymous public."[15] Concepts of neu-

---

[12]Grant, M. (1994). *Propaganda and the role of the state in inter-war Britain.* Oxford: Clarendon Press, p. 48.

[13]Simey, T. S. (1923). A public relations policy for local authorities. *Public Administration, 13,* p. 243.

[14]Corner, H. G. (1923). The aims of the Institute of Public Administration. *Public Administration, 1,* p. 50.

[15]Finer, H. (1931). Officials and the public. *Public Administration, 9,* p. 30.

trality and the public interest were important in terms of respectability as public relations sought professional status. As can be seen in the following extract, external and internal intelligence performed a rudimentary function of what is now known as issues management:

> The need for an external intelligence service arises as soon as a department realises that it is not necessarily the receptacle of all knowledge, or the embodiment of all wisdom, about the subject it administers . . . an external intelligence service may be a factor in legislation. The nature and sequence of legislative measures are political matters and are for governments to decide, but an effective intelligence service may well result in influencing [the] shape [of policy] . . . intelligence officers should be expert at the art of laying their hands on technical and other information. . . . This function of an intelligence service merges with public relations. . . . Internal intelligence . . . is to secure the ready availability to the department as a whole of all internal information . . . maintaining the articulation of all the several parts of the machine by a free flow of information about policy, progress, decisions and procedures.[16]

The evidence in *Public Administration* suggests that by the 1930s there was an understanding of the importance of good public relations to facilitate smooth administration. Achieving better understanding between the populace and local government began to be seen as intrinsically important to the job of administration and to the improvement of democracy because "a more vivid realisation of the state of public opinion on administrative matters . . . will show how [the administration of government policy] can be better adjusted to the environment in which it must work. . . . Publicity . . . should ensure that the public will be able to contribute informed but constructive criticism."[17] Officials must learn to communicate clearly and to be approachable, as well as capable of servicing the organisation's information needs to support the development of policy. Internal public relations was seen as the "psychology of administration," responsible for developing "good human relations."[18] The term *publicity* appeared to be reserved for specific media or techniques used to promote ideas such as an internal journal or newsletter or, externally, media relations. It seemed that *intelligence* was equated with information management, whereas public relations

---

[16]Wood, S. H. (1936). Intelligence and public relations. *Public Administration, 14,* p. 43.

[17]Cowell, F. R. (1931). The uses and dangers of publicity in the work of government. *Public Administration, 13,* p. 292.

[18]Wood, S. H. p. 46.

was specifically directed to utilising available information to improve relationships. Salesmanship was another strand associated with intelligence and public relations, and it was seen as "Essential . . . to build up public understanding and appreciation of the services rendered to them and thus obtain their goodwill. . . . Flexible and sympathetic contact between the service and the public is necessary to ensure the proper functioning of the service through the understanding of the public's feelings and needs."[19]

It was acknowledged that commerce had successfully adopted advertising techniques but public relations was seen as distinctly different from publicity: "As long as publicity consists in the supply of information and nothing more, it is unlikely to advance the reputation of the administration unless, as is perhaps conceivable, such a result should be thoroughly well deserved, for the information given is supposed to be true. Publicity is not camouflage."[20]

Definitions were important in establishing boundaries of professional expertise and Sir Stephen Tallents (whose role is explored later in this chapter) argued in *Public Administration* for an enhancement of the promotional role and elevation to professional status: "Publicity should be recognized as a professional job, demanding special training and special capacities which, incidentally, do not include a flair for personal boosting, but do include in the broadest sense, artistic capacity."[21]

The Second World War provided many challenges for local government, especially in London and other centres that had to cope with aerial bombardment. Local authorities had to deal with the effects of the bombing on people's lives, the essential public utilities, housing, and hospitals and also had to organise the evacuation and reception of children, provision of shelters, identity cards, ration books, emergency shelter, and clothing. In such a crisis they depended on "the self-sacrifice of . . . volunteers who strove indefatigably."[22] One such volunteer was Alan Eden-Green, later IPR President (1960–1961). A conscientious objector, he was sent to work in a voluntary capacity in Woolwich, London and recalled, "If there was a particularly big incident we would go

---

[19]Whitehead, H. (1933). Salesmanship in the public service. *Public Administration, 11*, p. 272.

[20]Cowell, F. R., p. 292.

[21]Tallents, Sir S. R. (1933). Salesmanship in the public service: scope and technique. *Public Administration, 11*, p. 265.

[22]Calder, A. (1969, 1990). *The people's war 1939–1945*. London: Pimlico, p. 22.

up there and set up a table, just like the local citizens' advice really, advising people who were involved with the incident."[23] In addition to liaising between several citizens' advice bureaux, Eden-Green noted, "I also found myself picking up the press relations part of the organisation . . . that was my first experience of dealing with the press."[24]

During the war, NALGO established "Reconstruction Committees" to consider how to respond to people's needs once hostilities were over and one of these committees considered "Relations between Local Government and the Community."[25] At the national and local levels, a series of reports and commissions reviewed the shape of local government, social services, education, land use, and planning, the most notable being the 1944 Beveridge Act, which laid out a vision of the welfare state.[26] Planning of new houses and new towns was a priority for local authorities and their responsibilities in these areas and education increased, whereas those for hospitals went to health boards.[27] New legislation swept away longstanding arrangements and new rights and procedures had to be explained to the public on a local level. As Eden-Green recalled, "After the war there was a whole lot of new legislation which had to be put into plain language and interpreted to enquirers."[28]

Geoffrey Lewis, who finished his career as Director of Public Relations at the London County Council (which became the Greater London Council in 1965), offered the view that "We had the re-planning of London after the war, lots of places were bombed out. . . . Local authorities found they were needing to tell people what was going on because things needed to be done. . . . We were going through a period when it was necessary to talk to people, simple as that."[29]

Thus, by the end of the Second World War, local government had been forced into a much closer relationship with the communities for which it was responsible. In 1946, two significant steps were taken, the effects and implication of which are discussed further in chapter 4: NALGO achieved recognition that local government officials needed to be trained not as lawyers but as administrators, which led to the

---

[23]Interview. 16 August 1995.

[24]Interview. 16 August 1995.

[25]Gillman, F. (1978, April). Public relations in the United Kingdom prior to 1948. *IPRA Review.* p. 50.

[26]Keith-Lucas, B. & Richards, P. G., p. 47.

[27]Ibid.

[28]Interview. 16 August 1995.

[29]Interview. 24 July 1996.

establishment of a local government examinations board,[30] and 32 public relations posts were created and filled in local government.[31]

FROM WAR TO PEACE

Interest in propaganda was not confined to local government and many of the articles published in *Public Administration* focused on improving the effectiveness of central government administration. Interest in public relations in central government was the result of a number of different historical developments: the rise of totalitarian regimes in Italy, Germany, the Soviet Union, and elsewhere; increasing tensions in international politics; reactions to the increased democratisation of society; technological developments in communications that contributed to the massification of society; and methodological developments in understanding public opinion.

The success of totalitarian politics overseas and the growth of would-be home-grown versions stimulated an ongoing policy debate about the British response to such developments and the necessity of a propaganda policy to respond to the perceived threat. Decisions also had to be taken at the end of the First World War regarding the fate of the wartime Ministry of Information (MoI). Although British wartime propaganda was deemed to have been very successful, there was a strong feeling that such activities were not entirely appropriate for a democratic country and, in particular, that they were somehow "un-English."[32] To take one example, as late as June 1939 *The Times* argued that the creation of opinion by a government was "one of the inescapable necessities of totalitarianism."[33] Wilcox commented that:

> Such public reactions reflected an unease existing within the Civil Service that an excessive attention to propaganda was questionable as a satisfactory preparation for war with Germany, Italy, Russia or Japan. The fundamental issue was whether the British government should build up a propaganda machine with the purpose of competing with totalitarian

---

[30]Keith-Lucas, B. & Richards, P. G., p. 105.

[31]Gillman, F., p. 50.

[32]Taylor, P. (1981). 'If war should come': preparing the fifth arm for total war 1935–39. *Journal of Contemporary History, 16* (1), p. 31.

[33]*The Times* 16 June 1939, cited in Willcox, T. (1983). Projection or publicity? rival concepts in the pre-war planning of the British Ministry of Information. *Journal of Contemporary History, 18*, p. 98.

states or whether this activity should be organized in a way more appropriate to a "democratic" state or "open" society.[34]

The contrary view was that propaganda was a necessary adjunct of diplomacy or even economics and that, furthermore, it had a part to play in assisting an effective democracy at home through facilitating feedback to civil servants from the public, educating and informing the public about political and legislative developments, and winning their cooperation "to ensure that services were properly and effectively utilised."[35] The Ministry of Health had been established in 1919 with the specific responsibility of collecting and disseminating information relevant to the health of the nation and a growing emphasis on public health and preventative medicine led to a number of campaigns.[36] Some were directed specifically at local authorities such as housing legislation and requirements, others were genuinely mass campaigns such as the milk campaign, where costs were equally shared by central government and the Milk Marketing Board.[37] These initiatives required the dissemination of information and the creation of jobs. According to Grant, by 1930 to 1931, 12 government departments were employing around 44 people in publicity or press jobs.[38]

Interest in propaganda grew in response to the international pressures outlined earlier; to technological developments that positioned film as a revolutionary and popular mass medium; and to intellectual developments in understanding public opinion. Many important ideas criss-crossed the Atlantic and at the end of the 19th and beginning of the 20th centuries, the United States and Britain apparently shared to some degree certain *fin-de-siècle* concerns about democratisation of society.[39] In Britain the extension of voting rights in 1918 was feared by some to "open the door to demagogues and Press-power. More likely, it was feared, it would overwhelm the party-political system and . . . break

[34] Willcox, T. (1983). p. 98. In view of the language employed it is worth noting that Karl Popper's *The open society and its enemies* (London: Routledge, 1962) was first published in 1943.

[35] Grant, M. (1994), pp. 49–51.

[36] Ibid. pp. 123–4.

[37] Schuyler Foster Jr., H. (1939). The official propaganda of Great Britain. *Public Opinion Quarterly, 3,* pp. 264–5.

[38] Grant, M., p. 45.

[39] British contributors to the debate included Graham Wallas, the first professor of political science at the London School of Economics, and the writer Norman Angell, according to Mariel Grant.

up the whole political and social structure owing to the simple fact that practically all that mass of people who has not been able to vote before were working men, their wives and daughters or the unemployed."[40]

Scientific Developments in Public Opinion: An Opportunity Lost?

Politicians' sensitivity to public opinion partly developed as a consequence of the necessity for conscription in the First World War, unemployment resulting from the Depression, and the consequent growth of the labour movement, which peaked in the traumas of the General Strike in 1926 and which, in the eyes of many, were sufficiently extreme to threaten revolution.[41] One solution to such fears was to educate the masses, as proposed by the British advertiser C. Higham, who wrote in 1920: "Mass education is badly needed. The wide dissemination of ideas can no longer be left to chance. Uninformed democracies are the greatest danger facing modern States."[42]

A significant development in public relations history was the advent of market research. In 1934 the League of Nations conducted a Peace Ballot in which 11½ million Britons participated as research subjects. As Alan Campbell-Johnson, an eminent public relations practitioner (Lord Mountbatten's press attaché in India 1947–1948; President of the IPR 1956–1957; and long-term associate of Hill & Knowlton) in the UK explained:

> The Peace Ballot was an effort to try and find out what the nation really thought . . . and what they discovered after years of work and enormous research was that the nation's thoughts were ambivalent. [It] was a cause of heart searching and gnashing of teeth because it had been so expensive and caused so much confusion. . . . While this tremendous operation was going on with all the controversy it provoked and involved, sitting in the London Press Exchange [advertising agency] were some men working on the possibility of organising opinion surveys without having to go to 5 million people to find out what they thought. . . . The discovery that you could get the same answer by asking 1500 people what they thought

[40]Pronay, N. (ed.). (1982). *Propaganda, politics and film 1918–45*. London: Macmillan Press, p. 6.

[41]Ibid. pp. 6–10.

[42]Higham, C. F. (1920). *Looking forward: mass education through publicity*. London: Nisbet & Co. Ltd., p. 14; Miller, K. (1999). *The voice of business: Hill & Knowlton and postwar public relations*. Chapel Hill: University of North Carolina Press.

(which they could have done) was the beginning of PR as a professional capability.[43]

A greater understanding of methodology as a tool to understanding public opinion created the potential for public relations (and government propaganda) to go beyond advertising, publicity, and informal feedback mechanisms. The developments in market research presented the public relations occupation with technical knowledge that could lead to professional status, because a key feature of the professions is a defined area of knowledge for which competence is required and a period of training necessary.

At the forefront of this ground-breaking development was Mark Abrams, an influential figure in the advertising and publicity agency London Press Exchange (LPE). Abrams was an economic researcher from the London School of Economics who had also been a research fellow at the Brookings Institute Research Centre for Economics. He joined LPE in 1934 at a time when it was already using research as an aid to marketing. Abrams was involved in readership surveys but then started specialising more in statistics, and in 1939 he carried out the national food survey for LPE when the agency was commissioned to do so by the government. In 1939 he became Head of Propaganda Research at the BBC and then took a similar post at the Foreign Office in 1941, followed by a year's service with the Political Warfare Mission in Washington. He finished the war in the Psychological Warfare Branch at Supreme Allied Headquarters.[44] In 1964 he became a member of Labour's campaign team, having co-authored *Must Labour Lose?* in 1916.

Another development was that of "Mass Observation," a research investigation started in 1937 by Tom Harrisson, anthropologist, Charles Madge, poet, and Humphrey Jennings, film documentarist.[45] The research was intended to analyse responses to films and employed a range of qualitative methods: observation, formal and informal interviews, and a self-selected national panel of 2,000 citizens who were asked about films but also about other topical issues.[46] The research team were employed by the MoI to provide qualitative research that comple-

---

[43] Interview. 20 March 1994.

[44] Mark Abrams: a profile. Editorial, *Public Relations*, 9 (1) 1957, pp. 43–4.

[45] Harrisson, T. (1982). Films and the home front—the evaluation of their effectiveness by 'mass-observation.' In Pronay, N. *Propaganda, politics and film 1918–45*. London: Macmillan, p. 235.

[46] Ibid. p. 236.

mented the government's ongoing statistical survey.[47] One of the motivations behind Mass Observation was to try to access the reality of working class life, though it was used to evaluate the effectiveness of MoI propaganda. It was also influential in alerting a rather wider audience within senior ranks of civil and military service to methodological issues in relation to public opinion.

The British Documentary Movement and the Empire Marketing Board

There are two men in particular whose influence on British public relations was substantial: John Grierson and Stephen Tallents. Grierson's thought encompassed both technological and methodological developments of the early 20th century as well as film as a medium for mass education; Tallents encompassed imperialism and propaganda. Because they collaborated extensively their joint impact was considerable, not least in terms of public relations ideology.

Grierson was a Scot who was educated first at Glasgow University where he studied idealist philosophy and then, after an administrative post at the Newcastle branch of Durham University, at the University of Chicago (having obtained a Laura Spellman scholarship).[48] During his scholarship Grierson heard lectures by Merriam, Park, and Lasswell, and was exposed to a middle class environment influenced by a number of writers pessimistic of democracy and fearful that the massification of society was breaking down traditional religious and social hierarchies.[49]

The influence of psychology and psychoanalysis gained ground after the First World War and had some influence in public relations. The key champion of such an approach was Edward Bernays, one of the most well-known American publicists, whose uncle was Sigmund Freud. Another eminent American public relations consultant, Ivy Lee, told students at Columbia University's School of Journalism in 1921: "You must study the human emotions and all the factors that move people, that persuade men in any line of human activity. Psychology, mob

---

[47] Ibid. p. 235.

[48] Pronay, N. (1989). John Grierson and the documentary. *Historical Journal of Film, Radio and Television*, 9 (3), p. 231.

[49] Aitkin, I. (1993). *Film and reform: John Grierson and the documentary film movement*. London: Routledge, p. 54; Ewen, S. (1996). *PR! A social history of spin*. New York. Harper Collins Basic Books, pp. 131–45.

psychology, is one of the important factors that underlay this whole business."[50]

According to the cultural analyst Stuart Ewen, fear of the mob led to the emergence of a somewhat Platonic view of society in which a limited democracy would be run by elites on behalf of the rest of society. Mediation between the belief that elites must be able to govern and the broader democratic aspirations of the masses created a demand for techniques of mass persuasion. From his contemplation of public opinion and democracy, Grierson turned to film as a mass medium that could help to break down the barriers to an informed citizenship. Recollecting the origins of the Documentary Film Movement, Grierson wrote:

> The British documentary group began not so much in affection for film per se as in affection for national education. . . . Its origins lay in sociological rather than aesthetic aims. Many of us . . . were impressed by the pessimism that had settled on Liberal theory. We noted the conclusion of men such as Walter Lippman, that because the citizen under modern conditions could not know everything about everything all the time . . . democratic citizenship was therefore impossible. We . . . turned to the new wide-reaching instruments of radio and cinema as necessary instruments in both the practice of government and the enjoyment of citizenship.[51]

The term *documentary* was first used in 1926 by Grierson in his review of Robert Flaherty's *Moana*.[52] For Grierson, documentary was intended to be inspiring, representative of reality but with more creative input than a fly-on-the-wall actuality film. But the distinguishing feature of Grierson's approach was his educative mission and commitment to assist the democratic process by informing the masses about a range of social issues. His publicly funded films, created under a Conservative government, celebrated the working man and rather anticipated the populist mood of the post-Second World War era, which brought the Labour government to power. Winston notes that the word *documentary*, coined in 1802, derived from the term *document*, used to imply information and evidence. The word *documentum* evidently entered the language in 1450 when it meant "lesson," which demonstrates its connection to the concept of education and also its potential

---

[50] Ewen, S., p. 132.

[51] Grierson, J. & Hardy, F. (eds.). (1979). *Grierson on documentary*. London: Faber & Faber, p. 78. (Original work published 1946).

[52] Winston, B. (1995). *Claiming the real: the documentary film revisited*. London: British Film Institute, p. 11.

connections with both political propaganda or indoctrination and public relations.[53]

Grierson saw a distinct and important role for film makers in which "an effective, socially purposive cinema must engage and resolve the dreams and ambitions of the public and must provide models for social action."[54] He formed a band of documentary enthusiasts who propounded their beliefs through public lectures, nontheatrical screenings, exhibitions, film libraries, and journals.[55] There are interesting parallels to be drawn between Grierson's ideas and those of John Reith, founder of the BBC, which Reith promoted as a method to create "an informed and reasoned public opinion as an essential part of the political process in mass democratic society."[56] Reith's approach, like Grierson's, aimed to combine education with entertainment, to inform, but also to interpret. There is clearly a good opportunity for further research into the parallels between these two fascinating men.

Grierson did not restrict his vision to the use of film, but argued for a more ambitious role in society for propaganda, which he defined as "the art of public persuasion"[57] and a necessary technique for modern states. This view was shared by Fleetward Pritchard, who, in 1950, declared, "Organised persuasion is necessary to the proper integration of all civilised communities."[58]

Grierson's knowledge of the emerging public relations industry, as opposed to theoretical concepts of pubic opinion, propaganda, education, and democracy, benefited from contact with a number of influential practitioners such as A. P. Ryan, Jack Beddington, and Jock Brebner. All were involved in pre-Second World War government publicity and were important in the development of public relations in the postwar era. Ryan worked at the Empire Marketing Board, the Gas, Light, and Coke Company, was Assistant Controller of Public Relations at the BBC, helped set up the Ministry of Information, and was controller of

---

[53] Ibid. p. 11.

[54] Aitkin, I. (1993), p. 98.

[55] Sklar, R. (1993). *Film: an international history of the medium*. London: Thames & Hudson, p. 244.

[56] Scannell, P. & Cardiff, D. (1991). *A social history of British broadcasting*, Vol. 1. Oxford: Basil Blackwell. In McNair, B. (1994). *News and journalism in the UK*. London: Routledge, p. 28.

[57] Grierson, J. Propaganda: a problem for educational theory and for cinema. *Sight and Sound*, Winter 1933–4; G3A: 5: 1.

[58] Pritchard, F. (1950). 'Persuasion' conference presentation. *Public Relations*, 2 (4), pp. 20–1.

BBC News Services during the war. Beddington headed Shell's Publicity and Advertising Department and was Head of the Ministry of Information's film division. Brebner worked for the Post Office and helped set up the Ministry of Information in 1937. Brebner also wrote the first British textbook on public relations, which was published in 1949 and in which Grierson's influence was apparent, as shown by Brebner's proseletising of "film as an instrument of education."

Another influence on Grierson was S. C. "Clem" Leslie, public relations officer at Gas, Light, and Coke, who advised the Inter-Departmental Co-ordinating Committee on Government Publicity in the late 1930s. Leslie shared his ideas on public opinion formation and domestic morale in a correspondence with Grierson in the 1930s and subsequently recommended that a ministry for democratic propaganda be set up to "bring alive the idea of democracy in the public mind."[59] Leslie was active in helping the Labour Party with its political communication in the 1930s.

Grierson's impact was facilitated by the patronage of Sir Stephen Tallents, a career civil servant who, at the time they met in 1927, was Secretary of the Empire Marketing Board (EMB), established a year earlier to implement imperial preference through market research, supply chain management, and publicity. The purpose of the EMB was to bind the Empire together by "bring[ing] the Empire alive to the minds of its citizens" and "sell . . . the idea of the Empire as a co-operative venture between living persons interested in each other's work, and in each other's welfare. Our task was not to glorify the power of the Empire but to make it live as a society for *mutual help*, a picture of vivid human interest, as well as of practical promise"[60] (emphasis added).

Tallents had developed an enthusiasm for publicity and national propaganda from prior appointments that required an awareness of public opinion.[61] He was an outward-looking man who employed nearly 70% of his staff from industry and the media. According to Aitkin, "Tallents' achievement lay . . . not in the origination of embryonic publicity ideas,

---

[59]Leslie, S. C. The formation of public opinion. October 15, 1938, Grierson Archive G3: 16: 4.

[60]Lee, J. M. (1972). The dissolution of the EMB. *The Journal of Imperial and Commonwealth History, 1* (1), p. 51, cited in Aitkin, I., p. 94.

[61]Administering food rationing in the First World War, as British Commissioner for the Baltic Provinces, as Imperial Secretary for Irish Affairs and secretary to the cabinet committee set up to deal with the General Strike. Swann, P. (1989). *The British documentary movement 1926–46.* Cambridge: Cambridge University Press, p. 23.

but in the establishment of a channel, through which ideas already in circulation could find final expression."[62]

The Projection of England and The British Council

Tallents' ideas were encapsulated in his pamphlet, *The Projection of England*, published in 1932, in which he laid out his concept of a "school for national projection."[63] Rotha suggested that many of Tallents' views had been developed quite early after his appointment as Secretary of the EMB in 1926.[64] Tallents argued that, prior to technological communication such as the telegraph and wireless, a country's reputation was built on interpersonal communication at international and diplomatic meetings. He suggested that new techniques for communication should be fully understood and mastered because they affected how "a nation would be truly known and understood in the world" and that this was even more important at a time when countries were increasingly interdependent.[65] The term *projection* had resonance in both film and diplomatic contexts: "It is essential for England [sic] as a world power that she should be able to make herself known to her fellows. Peace itself may at any time depend upon a clear understanding abroad of her actions and motives. . . . If we are to play our part in the new world order, we need to master every means and every art by which we can communicate with other peoples."[66]

Tallents argued that projection was vital for internal and external trade relations and tourism and that a national school for projection should:

> Be on the watch for material which can be turned to the advantage to England overseas. . . . It must watch for and sometimes create opportunities for using that material . . . be in close touch with . . . channels, at home and abroad, through which the material . . . can be projected. It must work . . . in friendly contact with the press and news agencies . . . be able to distribute its material and sometimes to suggest . . . appropriate modes for its treatment. It may seek to inspire, but must never attempt to regulate them.[67]

---

[62] Aitkin, I., p. 94.

[63] Tallents, Sir S. R. (1932, 1955). *The projection of England.* London: Olen Press, p. 40.

[64] Rotha, P. (1973). *Documentary diary: an informal history of the British documentary film 1928–1939.* London: Secker & Warburg, p. 22.

[65] Tallents, Sir S. R., p. 11.

[66] Ibid. p. 17.

[67] Ibid. pp. 40–1.

Tallents' objective was to support British economic aims through the promotion of culture, technology, and science and an enhanced sense of national identity and core values. Realising these ideals required some careful diplomacy within the civil service: The first film made by Grierson's unit, *Drifters* (1929), about the herring fishing industry, was chosen as a topic specifically to appeal to Arthur Samuel, Financial Secretary to the Treasury, who had published a book, *The Herring: Its Effect on the History of Britain.* The EMB proceeded to communicate its overall concept through a number of documentary films such as *Canadian Apples, Sheep Dipping, South African Fruit.*[68] The EMB's remit expanded to include publicity for trade throughout the Empire and an increased budget facilitated increased production, mostly for films for nontheatrical production. However successful the "hearts and minds" initiative was, the EMB was evaluated by strict financial criteria: The organisation was deemed unsuccessful in off-setting the economic depression and was abolished in 1933. Tallents was awarded a knighthood for his work there and managed to take the film unit with him to his new public relations posting at the Post Office. Subsequently, Tallents claimed to be the first person appointed to a post titled "Public Relations Officer" and said that the title had been chosen by his superior, Sir Kingsley Wood of the Post Office, who had allegedly taken the title from the *Report of the American Telegraph and Telephone Company.*[69] The EMB Film Unit became the GPO Film Unit, making a number of films, of which the most famous has been *Night Mail* about the overnight mail train service from London to Scotland. This was intended partly as an exercise in internal communications as well as external publicity. Throughout this period the GPO Film Unit occasionally made films for external bodies, which it was able to do simply because virtually all the staff were freelance. The unit made films for the Ministries of Health, Agriculture, and Labour. In 1935, Tallents was posted to the BBC[70] and the unit came under the surveillance of traditional civil servants. In 1939, the Post Office successfully argued that the film unit should be absorbed into the MoI, where it was renamed the Crown Film Unit.

Meanwhile, Tallents' ideas percolated throughout the bureaucratic and political spheres and resonated with those of Sir Henry Newbolt

---

[68] Swann, P., p. 37.

[69] Royal Commission on the press. *Public Relations,* 1 (2) 1948, pp. 10–12.

[70] Scannell, P. & Cardiff, D. (1991). *A social history of British broadcasting,* Vol. 1. Oxford: Basil Blackwell.

and Victor Wellesley in the Foreign Office, both of whom wrote reports recommending that Britain develop a cultural propaganda policy. Wellesley argued that cultural propaganda had the advantage of reaching a far wider audience than merely opinion leaders: The Foreign Office "saw cultural propaganda as a long-term policy which, by promoting an atmosphere of international understanding and co-operation would ultimately benefit both the political and economic climate in which British interests could flourish."[71]

At the time, such proposals were considered unaffordable by the Treasury despite arguments that France and Germany were already spending large sums on cultural activity.[72] Nevertheless, the worsening international situation and a growing number of influential voices such as Rex Leeper, Head of the Foreign Office News Department, led to the formation of The British Council in 1934, founded to achieve goodwill through promotional work and exchange of persons. The British Council's stated mission was:

> To make the life and thought of the British peoples more widely known abroad; and to promote a *mutual interchange of knowledge and ideas with other peoples*. To encourage the study and use of the English language. . . . To bring other peoples into closer touch with British ideals and practice in education, industry and government; to make available to them the benefits of current British contributions to the sciences and technology; and to afford them opportunities of appreciating contemporary British work in literature, the fine arts, drama and music. To co-operate with the self-governing Dominions in strengthening the common cultural tradition of the British Commonwealth.[73] (emphasis added)

Although apparently founded on principles of reciprocity and mutuality, an American commentator in 1939 noted that, "As contrasted with the American Division of Cultural Relations, there would seem to be much less emphasis upon the reciprocal nature of . . . cultural contacts."[74] Furthermore, there was a substantial political agenda, according to Taylor, who argued that the Council was:

---

[71]Taylor, P. (1981). *The projection of Britain 1919–39.* Cambridge: Cambridge University Press, pp. 129–30.

[72]Sums of £500,000 by France and £300,000 by Germany are given by Taylor, P. Ibid. p. 139.

[73]White, A. J. S. (1965). *The British Council: the first 25 Years 1934–59.* London: The British Council, p. 7.

[74]Schuyler Foster Jr., H., p. 268.

Created partly to perpetuate the appearance of power in the minds of for-
eigners at a time when hostile propaganda was beginning to expose the
harsh realities of Britain's decline. Although the Council itself would not
have considered itself to be in the business of myth-making, the very fact
that there was felt to be a need to project British achievements abroad
was in itself symptomatic of Britain's declining influence in international
affairs.[75]

Peacetime propaganda emphasised the breaking down of barriers
between social groups through information, education, and persuasion,
often utilising personal relationships as the means to achieve this.
Within governmental circles, propaganda was seen as an appropriate
governmental tool, ostensibly to ensure the smooth working of democracy, but in reality to help maintain the status quo.

WARTIME PROPAGANDA

Modern war and the development of communications technology contributed greatly to the practice of propaganda. The increased democratisation of society necessitated public opinion management in times of
war. Government needed to control and censor unfavourable information that might harm morale, to penetrate enemy communication
networks in order to confuse or demoralise, and to win and maintain
alliances from which political, economic, or military support might be
forthcoming. In wartime the British government made substantial
propaganda efforts both at home and overseas. The distinctions between
propaganda, public relations, information, intelligence, persuasion, and
psychological warfare became harder to draw.

The size and geographical distribution of the British Empire and its
dominions presented a challenge, but also offered opportunities. The
growth of an international network of news agencies connected by electric telegraph in the late 19th century ended governments' ability to
entirely control news and also offered new opportunities for debate and
comment. The British government offered subsidies to cable companies
in order to encourage them to route cables through British territories,
thus giving the British security services the chance to monitor and
censor news as well as to gather intelligence.[76] Their opportunism was

[75]Taylor, P. (1981), p. 173.

[76]Pronay, N. (1982). *Propaganda, politics and film 1918–45*. London: Macmillan, pp.
11–12.

envied and admired by the French, who noted: "England owes her influence in the world perhaps more to her cable communications than to her navy. She controls the news and makes it serve her policy and commerce in a marvellous manner."[77]

Control over technology facilitated British control of news flow. Examples include censorship in the Boer War; the cutting of German cables within hours of the 1914 ultimatum, thus inhibiting Germany's chances of making a diplomatic case to the United States and ensuring that the British view dominated in the American press; and jamming transmissions from the Soviet Union in 1925 and 1926 because it was feared that the general strike of workers in Britain during the Depression might develop into a more comprehensive revolt or even revolution.[78]

Prior to the First World War, Britain and Germany were major trading partners and their mutual loss of trade encouraged both to expand their markets in the United States or "better still, to entice the Americans to join their cause."[79] The Germans tried to build support through existing trading associations, but the British adopted subterfuge in setting up a secret information and intelligence unit under the auspices of the Foreign Office at Wellington House between 1914 and 1917. This source was successfully concealed from the then neutral Americans as well as the fact that its main purpose was to encourage the Americans to enter the war on Britain's side.[80]

Once the Americans had entered the war in 1917, Wellington House became less important, and a Department of Enemy Propaganda was formed at Crewe House under Lord Northcliffe. MoI was formed under another press baron, Lord Beaverbrook, responsible for propaganda in allied and neutral territories. This ministry was formed from the existing Department of Information headed by the novelist John Buchan, whose prewar popular fiction had featured foreign spies.[81] According to Grant:

> The recruitment of the press barons and the successful approach to propaganda which they supposedly introduced have been highlighted and

---

[77] Preamble to the 1890 French Telegraph Act cited in Pronay, N. Ibid. p. 11.

[78] Ibid. pp. 12–13.

[79] Taylor, P. (1990). *Munitions of the mind.* Glasgow: William Collins, p. 164.

[80] Ibid. p. 164.

[81] Balfour, M. (1979). *Propaganda in war 1939–1945.* London: Routledge & Kegan Paul, p. 3.

overrated ever since. Credited with securing the Allied victory, Beaver-brook and Northcliffe were elevated to the status of great propagandists, creating, or perhaps reinforcing the view of the newspaper proprietor as publicity expert. In fact, the appointments and the new administrative structure introduced had a relatively limited impact. Journalists had long been assisting in official propaganda and the ministry did not develop an approach significantly different from that pursued to date.[82]

On the home front, the use of anti-German atrocity stories was rife, especially those that involved the violation of innocents such as babies and nuns. Events such as the execution of the British nurse Edith Cavell, who was shot for spying in occupied Brussels in 1915, received wide publication.

Film was increasingly used as a mass medium for propaganda; examples include *Britain Prepared* (1915), *The Battle of the Somme* (1916), the *Battle of Ancre and the Advance of the Tank* (1917), *Hearts of the World* (1918), and *The Leopard's Spots* (1918).[83] Films relating to a more imperial theme included *The Building of the British Empire* (1917) and *What are we Fighting for?* (1918), which purported to demonstrate a German plot for world domination. A film produced after the armistice, *The World's Greatest Story,* presented the war as a catalyst in the growth and development of Empire and its role in "contributing to progress."[84] The instigation and commissioning of official films came from the War Office Cinematograph Committee and the War Office Topical Committee from 1917 onward. The imperial theme was also pursued in films depicting more exotic locations that dealt with the war in the Middle East and in India, including *The British Occupation of Gaza, With the Australians in Palestine,* and *With the Indian Troops at the Front.*[85]

Leafleting by parachute, balloon, or aeroplane was an activity intended to demoralise German troops, although Michael Balfour argued that the claims made for its impact were exaggerated by North-cliffe and his chief of staff Campbell Stuart for purposes of personal aggrandisement.[86] Balfour cast doubt on whether many of the leaflets even reached their target audience, given that many were delivered by

[82]Grant, M., p. 29.

[83]Taylor , P. op. cit., p. 177.

[84]Mackenzie, J. (1985). *Propaganda and empire: the manipulation of British public opinion 1880–1960.* Manchester: Manchester University Press, p. 75.

[85]Ibid. pp. 75–6.

[86]Balfour, M., p. 3.

short-range balloon. After the war, much of the propaganda effort was discredited, especially in America, which had been a primary target.

Propaganda in the Second World War

Debates over the necessity for, and nature of, propaganda had been conducted during the 1930s in the context of increasing international tension in Europe. On reopening for business in 1939, the MoI suffered from a lack of clarity regarding its brief and scope, a swift succession of ministers (Lord Macmillan, Lord Reith, and Duff Cooper by May 1940), problems in recruiting appropriate staff, and extremely poor reception by the media and the general public, who perceived the ministry as overstaffed, underemployed, and largely incompetent. One example given was the MoI's refusal to release information about the content of leaflets intended for German consumption on the grounds that "we are not allowed to disclose information which might be of value to the enemy."[87] The MoI was also criticised for its "Cooper's Snoopers" (named after its then head, Duff Cooper), who as part of the Wartime Social Survey sought to establish the state of morale; many refused to participate. The MoI was parodied in fiction, as illustrated by Graham Greene's *The Ministry of Fear* (1943) and Evelyn Waugh's postwar *Put Out More Flags* (1948). A typical critique of the MoI was that presented by Hargrave's polemic:

> The Ministry of Information is a slow-motion, muddling machine . . . a warmed-up corpse. Then it came to light that the Ministry had a staff numbering 999! What on earth were they doing? The *Daily Express* led the attack. Here was a department staffed with nearly one thousand people, calling itself a Ministry of Information, yet the daily output of information issued for publication in British newspapers was so meagre that it would hardly fill one typed foolscap sheet. Clearly this Ministry of Information has no conception of its work as a modern war-weapon. Its whole job is to stop information and gag almost every form of effective propaganda.[88]

There was an absence of proper terms of reference, lack of censorship experience, and failure of coordination between the MoI and the sources

---

[87]Taylor, P., p. 177.

[88]Hargrave, J. (1940). *Propaganda the mightiest weapon of all words win wars*. London: Wells Gardner, Darton & Co., pp. 7–8.

of news.[89] Poor communications between the three services, the Foreign Office, and civil servants responsible for home security, war production, and civilian supplies caused the main problems. Balfour noted: "Since the outbreak of war, the numbers of senior public relations officers in the various departments had risen sharply (so much so that in 1943 the Cabinet took steps to rein them back). The MoI failed to appreciate the implications of this trend and did little to bring the PROs in any systematic way into its deliberations."[90]

There was criticism of the crudity of early propaganda efforts designed to exhort rather than to inform. An instance was the poster that urged, "*Your* Courage, *Your* Cheerfulness, *Your* Resolution Will Bring *Us* Victory," which appeared to emphasise the distance between the elite class and the ordinary person and was described, even by *The Times*, as "insipid and patronising."[91]

The 1941 appointment of the former financier and intimate of Churchill, Brendan Bracken, was a turning point (and he stayed in post until 1945):

> The MoI came more and more to the conclusion that the best way of sustaining morale was to provide plenty of factual information and guidance. Propaganda had to be regarded as the natural accompaniment of individual political or administrative policies, not something operating on its own. . . . Bracken told his colleagues in April 1942 that "We must stop appealing to the public or lecturing it. One makes it furious, the other resentful."[92]

Ultimately, censorship operated effectively in Britain because it was applied prior to publication, avoiding the French practice of blanking out material thought to be of use to the enemy. The disadvantage of the French system was that people could see precisely how much material was being censored, whereas the British deleted information at source. This system of precensorship was facilitated by the fact that the Press Association (which supplied the domestic press) was in the same building as Reuters (which supplied the overseas press) and, once released, editors of various newspapers were able to tailor the information to their needs, thus giving the impression of considerably more freedom

---

[89] Noted by Reith when he was appointed and cited in McLaine, I. (1979). *Ministry of morale*. London: Allen & Unwin, p. 18.

[90] Balfour, M., p. 63.

[91] McLaine, I., p. 31.

[92] Balfour, M., p. 70.

of information than in fact existed. This illusion was also supported by the MoI's claims to release as much of the truth as possible following Lord Reith's oft-quoted phrase that "news is the shocktroops of propaganda." The value of self-censorship in total war should also not be underestimated. Despite its shaky beginnings, the MoI news management proved successful and achieved wide acclaim:

> What . . . excited most the admiration of contemporary foreign observers, including Dr. Goebbels, and what was undoubtedly the most vital contribution in Britain to the war on the front of morale, was the way in which the press, the BBC and other organs of "news" managed to maintain the trust of the British public at home and gained a reputation for Britain abroad for having even in wartime an honest, free and truthful media, yet which gave practically nothing away to an ever-vigilant enemy.[93]

The role of the BBC was crucial to the propaganda effort. Novelist George Orwell claimed that the BBC employed members of the intelligentsia to "do its publicity" for the MoI via the empire and foreign-language broadcasts.[94] According to Piette, Orwell resigned from the BBC "sickened by the propaganda he had had to do" and proceeded to write *Nineteen Eighty-Four* (1949) as a response to the experience.[95] The BBC style of propaganda was subtle, never appearing as propaganda but as "straightforward information and news, a certain common-sense manliness and restraint, and deliberate flattering of the listeners' freedom to make up their minds . . . features that were designed specifically to contrast with Goebbels' ranting and triumphalism."[96]

The MoI was not the only body responsible for Britain's propaganda effort. Two organizations were established to conduct subversive activities against the enemy: Section D, which ultimately became the Special Operations Executive (SOE), and the Political Warfare Executive (PWE). Under PWE was SOE1, headed by Sefton Delmer, responsible for black propaganda. SOE1's extensive leaflets were printed by a certain Ellic Howe (who joined the IPR as a full member in 1955),[97] who was then

---

[93]Pronay, N. (1982). The news media at war. In Pronay, N. (ed.). *Propaganda, politics and film 1918–45.* London: Macmillan, p. 174.

[94]Piette, A. (1995). *Imagination at war: British fiction and poetry 1939–1945.* London: Papermac, p. 151.

[95]Ibid. p. 160.

[96]Ibid. pp. 151–2.

[97]New Institute members. *Public Relations,* 7 (3) 1955, p. 37.

operating under the pseudonym of Armin Hull.[98] Delmer, who had been brought up in Germany, and for this reason was considered an expert on the German mind, also established a number of black radio stations via which rumours could be spread.[99] Delmer noted recruitment problems:

> Up to this time the Admiralty in common with other Fighting Services had left Psychological Warfare to their Public Relations Department, and I found that the Public Relations Officers had neither the access to the kind of intelligence material we needed nor did they have the understanding for our indirect subversive approach to the enemy. This was no fault of theirs. For their job was the straightforward one of projecting the splendour and invincibility of the British Navy to the world through newspapers and radio. They were not conditioned for the devious approach needed for deceiving and tricking the Germans.[100]

The intelligence effort was concentrated under the existing Special Intelligence Service (SIS) in the form of a variety of military intelligence units that employed cryptographers and computer specialists on a variety of decoding and intelligence operations, including the well-known unit based at Bletchley Park, where the Government Code and Cypher School and the Enigma machine were based. The SOE was created on 22 July 1940 to coordinate sabotage, subversion, and secret propaganda under the direction of the Minister of Economic Warfare, Hugh Dalton.[101] Most of this work took place in France. Known under a variety of cover names, it was outside parliamentary control and necessarily secretive.[102]

In addition to news censorship, propaganda on the home front included poster campaigns to encourage appropriate forms of behaviour: "Make Do and Mend," "Careless Talk Costs Lives," "Dig for Victory," "Is Your Journey Really Necessary?" Some campaigns cleverly achieved real involvement by the populace as, for example, that triggered by the

---

[98] Auckland, R. G. British black propaganda to Germany 1941–1945. Blatter Catalogue No. 13, 2nd edition, first published by the Psywar Society, January 1977, revised July 1989, pp. 1–2.

[99] See Sefton Delmer's autobiographies Black Boomerang and Trail Sinister.

[100] Delmer, S. (1962). Black boomerang. London: Secker & Warburg, p. 72.

[101] Wilkinson, P. & Bright Astley, J. (1993, 1997). Gubbins & SOE. London: Leo Cooper, p. 75.

[102] Foot, M. R. D. (1981). Was SOE any good? Journal of Contemporary History, 16 (1), pp. 170–1.

"Great Aluminium Scare," in which Beaverbrook appealed to people to donate their saucepans, ornaments, and golf clubs. A leading Jamaican newspaper donated the cost of a Spitfire fighter plane (£20,000), following which a series of similar sponsorships were set up throughout the Commonwealth so that an individual, club, or city could "buy" a new aeroplane or part of an aeroplane. Lists of donations were announced by the BBC at the end of news bulletins and in 1 year over £13 million was received.[103]

Propaganda was directed not only against enemy territories, but also toward neutral countries in Europe: Sweden, Switzerland, Spain, and Portugal.[104] As noted, the United States was the target of an extensive propaganda campaign intended to encourage its participation.[105] After the war there was a substantial propaganda effort in liberated territories through radio, newspapers, and specially written pamphlets. The MoI produced a film on German atrocities for circulation in neutral, liberated, and former enemy countries.[106] The aims of propagandists in such territories included:

> *Enhancing mutual understanding; promoting mutual co-operation . . .* explaining British foreign policy principles . . . *explaining* United Nations' policies and promoting agreement with them . . . countering the lingering effects of Nazi propaganda. . . . Under no circumstances were the propagandists to employ any techniques or styles remotely reminiscent of those once used by the Nazis.[107] (emphasis added)

The discourse of mutuality emerges strongly in this quote and remains important within public relations language, values, and ideology.

Film was also used as a morale booster in the Second World War. Imperial films of the 1930s were reshown and Hollywood produced *The Sun Never Sets* and *Sundown* in 1940, "but they were the last of their kind, for the American Office of War Information declined to allow further films to be made about the British Empire."[108] One of the most famous films made by the GPO Film Unit was *London Can Take It*

---

[103] Calder, A., p. 149.

[104] Cole, R. (1990). *Britain and the war of words in neutral Europe 1939–45*. London: Macmillan.

[105] Cull, N. (1995). *Selling war: the British propaganda campaign against American 'neutrality' in World War II*. Oxford: Oxford University Press.

[106] Cole, R., p. 181.

[107] Ibid. pp. 184–5.

[108] Mackenzie, J., p. 90.

(1940), intended primarily for American audiences, and also Humphrey Jennings' *Listen to Britain* (1942) and *Fires Were Started* (1943). Other films were produced specifically as a propaganda tool such as *Next of Kin* (1942), made to discourage "careless talk," and *Millions Like Us* (1943), praising women working in munitions.[109]

Propaganda in wartime was a diverse activity. One aspect that caused particular controversy was that of the Army Bureau for Current Affairs (ABCA). In 1940, a government committee reported that education was essential to troop morale and the Army Education Corps expanded to meet the demand for lectures, discussions, and correspondence courses. ABCA was founded as a morale booster on the basis that soldiers should know what they were fighting for, and from then on there was compulsory adult education for at least an hour a week during training time. Platoon commanders were expected to introduce political debate as well as educate men about the history that led to the conflict. Talks were wide ranging, as one IPR member R. McLoughlin commented in 1950, "general knowledge and interest in local government increased . . . as a result of ABCA training."[110] But not all officers cooperated in their newly designated role as seminar leaders, as is clear from the comments of one public relations practitioner who was prominent on the UK scene in the 1950s and 1960s, Prince Yuri Galitzine:

> [ABCA] in fact was run by the Labour Party. . . . I was horrified. The Labour Party got hold of the education side of the Army and they . . . got these booklets pushed out all over the world and each unit was told to make an education officer and give instruction to troops based on these different booklets and on the surface it looked like a good thing—and from the Labour Party's point of view it was a good thing. And this was to try and ensure that all the troops voted Labour and lots of people like myself . . . tore them up and threw them in the dustbin. . . . You ask a lot of the Labour people. They will tell you this was a brilliant coup.[111]

Subsequently, the Conservative Party did indeed hold ABCA responsible for its loss of the 1945 election. There were also internal communications initiatives within the services that gave some the chance to develop journalism skills on publications such as *The Union Jack* (the Eighth Army news).

---

[109]Calder, A., p. 368.

[110]Some things they said. *Public Relations*, 2 (3) 1950, p. 5.

[111]Interview. 23 August 1995.

Nor was propaganda limited to activities inspired and financed by the British government to home and overseas states and populations. Once American troops arrived in large numbers in Britain in preparation for the invasion of mainland Europe, they launched a major charm offensive to counteract the "overpaid, oversexed, and over here" tag, particularly in relation to community relations. The Americans also had to explain their segregationist Jim Crow practices to their British hosts.

The wartime experience sensitised civilian and military populations to issues of propaganda, information, and intelligence. Although Britain cultivated notions of media independence and truthful information, there was an extensive internal and external propaganda effort. Black propaganda was considered justifiable in the circumstances and somewhat romanticised. The head of SOE's "F" Section was Colonel Maurice Buckmaster (codename "Colonel Britain"), who had worked for the Ford Motor Company prior to the war. After the war he became Director of Public Relations at Ford in the UK and subsequently went freelance representing the French champagne industry. He became a fellow of the IPR in 1954 and was president from 1955 to 1956.[112] The career of such a man clearly demonstrates the overlap between the apparently distinct occupations of public relations and propaganda. Buckmaster was revered among the postwar generation of public relations practitioners as much for his distinguished (if rather controversial) war record. He was the most public representative of a distinct, if small, phenomenon: the propagandist turned public relations practitioner. That this was apparently regarded as unproblematic by that generation of practitioners is interesting, to say the least. It seems to demonstrate that propaganda for one's own political system and ideology is always justified and that debates about definitions of, and the relationship between, public relations and propaganda are political rather than conceptual or methodological. It perhaps also suggests something about the self-identity of the public relations occupation itself. I sensed that for some of those I interviewed wartime propaganda seemed romantic viewed half a century later and the fact that much remained off the record added to the glamour and mystique. The story was oft told by those I interviewed, often in somewhat hushed tones, as though I was being ushered into hallowed halls or a religious sanctuary. One respondent was keen for me to believe that he, too, had been involved in such activities even though his birth date and academic and linguistic abilities

---

[112]New members. *Public Relations*, 6 (2) 1954, p. 45.

would have ruled him out. But when I tried to substantiate his boastful claims, he was conveniently able to shield himself behind the official secrets act (or so he claimed). How many of Britain's public relations practitioners were involved in such activities? It is impossible to say. I only tried to find the names of those involved in some way with the IPR. Those allegedly involved in intelligence or propaganda included Eric Stenton (joined the Intelligence Corps after leaving Oxford and subsequently worked for the BBC External Services, BBC Bonn, *Daily Herald* as Foreign News Editor, Advertising Association as Information Officer, and finally Director of the London Press Exchange in 1959); Alan Hadden, a Manager at Shell who claimed, "I am an erstwhile journalist, a one-time propagandist"; Sydney Walton; Ellic Howe, who, as previously mentioned, under the pseudonym Armin Hull was in charge of forgery printing and the printing of black propaganda leaflets; John Addey, MD of C. S. Services Ltd.; Gerald Samson, who worked for Air Ministry Intelligence; Denys Brook-Hart, who served throughout the war in Special Operations; Mark Abrams, who was in charge of propaganda research at the BBC and at the Foreign Office and then became Head of Psychological Warfare SHAEF; Allan Ashbourne, who worked for the Ministry of Home Security; Jack Beddington, who was Head of the Film Division at the Ministry of Information from 1940 to 1946; Freddie Gillman, who worked at the Air Ministry; Stuart Chant, who worked at SHAPE; and Arthur Cain, who worked for Special Branch as Detective Inspector.

POLITICAL COMMUNICATION: POLITICAL PARTIES

Although the uptake of marketing and public relations techniques has generally been seen as a postwar phenomenon in Britain emanating in the 1950s, it is the case that politicians have always sought to find new ways to entertain audiences in order to enhance the impact of their ideas. Political speeches, tours, and conferences can all be seen as *special events*—a public relations term that has now rather fallen out of use. Criticism of this aspect of politics is not new and is inspired by a fear of political propaganda whereby ideologues might dupe the populace. Political marketing, as opposed to propaganda, is, however, driven by consumer demand and clearly enhances the largely hidden roles of marketeers and public relations practitioners within the political process in a way that seems detrimental to democracy, even though consumerism itself appears to be grounded in democratic values.

Election experts and personality-based campaigns existed in the Victorian era and subsequently the arrival of new communications technologies, especially radio and film, facilitated the emergence of the media adviser, often a journalist. As Scammell recorded, the care and attention that the Conservative leader Stanley Baldwin gave to learning how to present himself on radio and newsreels in the early 1920s, the Conservative Party's use of propaganda films in the late 1920s, and the use of press advertisements by the Liberals in 1929 were all key moments in the development of political marketing in Britain. However, the greatest changes occurred after the Second World War following the uptake of television and market research techniques.

According to Wring,[113] from whose account the following material is taken, the Labour Party first began to market itself just prior to 1918, the year that universal suffrage was introduced. In 1917 the Party formed a Press and Publicity Department led by a former religious correspondent, Herbert Treacey. He was succeeded by W. W. Henderson. The Labour Party became strongly motivated to combat what they perceived as biased reporting in the mass media. By the 1930s Labour had developed a hostility to the BBC and sought alternative media for political communication, including advertising, film, and design. Its first logo was the result of a national competition in 1924. A key development was the return of a Labour administration at County Hall, London. The Labour leader, Herbert Morrison, established a new approach as part of his mission to overhaul the identity of the authority. Intellectually, a major contribution was that of Sydney Webb, who formulated ideas about the stratification of audiences and the development of specially crafted messages to meet the needs of those audiences. Nevertheless, Labour struggled with its conscience as many influential members felt that it was wrong for the Party to adopt the capitalist techniques of promotion. The Conservatives appointed their first press officer, Sir Malcolm Fraser, in 1906 and a Press Bureau in 1911. The Party Chairman, J. C. C. Davidson, appointed Military Intelligence Officer (MI5) Joseph Ball as Head of Publicity as part of this overhaul of party pub-

---

[113]Wring, D. (1995). From mass propaganda to political marketing: the transformation of Labour party election campaigning. *British Election Party Yearbook*; Wring, D. (1996). Political marketing and party development in Britain: a 'secret' history. *European Journal of Marketing 30*, (10/11).

licity. As such, he may have been the first public relations officer appointed with such a background.

PRIVATE SECTOR PUBLIC RELATIONS

There was relatively little public relations in the private sector prior to the Second World War. Activities in the private sector were generally confined to advertising, but are nevertheless significant in the story of public relations in terms of their relationship with propaganda, the self-image of practitioners, and the structures and terminology adopted in consultancies. Public relations was limited to a handful of press agencies, international companies, and national organisations.

The field of advertising was dominated in the 1920s and 1930s by two major agencies run by Charles Higham and William Crawford, respectively. William Crawford was an establishment figure who carried out advertising for the EMB, the Ministry of Agriculture, and the Post Office, as well as the famous "Buy British" campaign of 1931. Higham was a colourful figure, a "self-made man"[114] with a mission to preach the benefits of advertising to society, particularly business, on whose behalf advertising could stimulate consumer demand and the economy in general. Higham was also an enthusiast for the potential of film for community education and government propaganda. In particular, he argued that advertising had the potential to disseminate ideas and to educate the wider populace about a range of issues, including practical matters of hygiene and health as well as more sociological concerns such as high and low culture:

> The public's knowledge of the importance of vitamins — one of the most valuable discoveries of medical research — is entirely due to advertisements of products that are entitled to make use of the vitamin argument, and hardly at all to the learned dissertations of scientists. . . . The recent rapid development in the taste for music — which was noticeable before broadcasting became a habit — is traceable to the advertising of gramophones and their records. . . . The public taste has been elevated by the art of world-famous soloists and orchestras.[115]

---

[114]Nevett, T. R. (1982). *Advertising in Britain: a history.* London: Heinemann, p. 145.
[115]Higham, Sir C. (1925). *Advertising: its use and abuse.* London: Williams & Norgate Ltd., pp. 16–17.

Higham's interests encompassed marketing and propaganda and he argued that government should adopt an explicitly propagandist role:

> Why not use publicity—*To formulate and inspire a collective aim or national idea?* To epitomise and spread broadcast [sic] H. G. Wells's fine conception of the British Empire? *To create an atmosphere* in neutral and allied countries favourable to the purchase of British commodities? To teach mother-craft to working class mothers? . . . *To win general goodwill* for deserving public services? To inculcate a high standard of civic sense?[116] (emphasis added)

These passages seem to anticipate many of Grierson's and Tallents' views and ultimately the three men inhabited the same milieu, for Higham carried out work for several government departments during and after the First World War. Higham had emigrated from America at the age of 13 and retained strong transatlantic connections in order to keep in touch with developments in American advertising. According to Higham, film was already in use by private companies in Britain for marketing and public relations purposes by the 1920s: "Harrods use a film for the training of their staff in salesmanship. . . . The Dunlop Rubber Company possess a film which demonstrates the making of their tyres in every detail. . . . Vickers Ltd also use the cinema for recording and instructing . . . whatever the leading motif, it can be proved on the film if the factory lives up to its reputation."[117]

Advertising agencies played an important part in the development of public relations as they gradually began to develop specialist sections to prepare information and what is still known as "advertorial" for the media. Examples of agencies that developed in this way prewar were LPE and Pritchard Wood. The director of the latter, Fleetward Pritchard, encompassed advertising and public relations and became public relations adviser to the Ministry of War Transport.

One of the earliest public relations consultants was Sydney Walton, who set up in business in 1920, having previously worked as press officer for Lloyd George. His earlier track record was clandestine, as he was one of a number of public relations practitioners who had experience of being an undercover agent. On behalf of Lloyd George he was responsible for running a propaganda campaign designed to incite hostility

---

[116]Higham, Sir C. (1920). *Looking forward: mass education through publicity.* London: Nisbet & Co. Ltd., pp. 80–2.

[117]Higham, Sir C. (1925), p. 190.

against militant trade unionism. The campaign was financed by industry, largely the Engineering Employers' Federation, and took over the propaganda functions of wartime employer-funded front organisations such as the British Empire League and the British Workers' League. According to Scammell, Walton claimed in 1922 that he could place "authoritative signed articles" in more than 1,200 newspapers and journals.

Another key historical figure credited by some as being Britain's first fully fledged public relations consultant was Basil Clarke, a former *Daily Mail* journalist, who subsequently directed the Special Intelligence section at the Ministry of Reconstruction, and who was transferred to the Ministry of Health when it was created in 1919.[118] Difficulties over the extent and direction of the Ministry's publicity effort finally led to Clarke's transfer to the position of Director of Public Information in Dublin Castle at a time of conflict, a posting for which he was subsequently knighted.[119] In 1924, he left the service and set up his own agency, Editorial Services, which he founded jointly with R. J. Sykes of the LPE and James Walker of Winter Thomas.[120] Campaigns included the promotion of pasteurised milk, opposition to the use of harmful colouring matter and adulterants in preserved foods, promotion of Anglo–Danish friendship and trade, promotion of sea cruising on behalf of Blue Star Line, popularising and making respectable greyhound racing, and, in 1931, a campaign to give advertising a better image.[121]

According to Clarke's son, Editorial Services was "a clearing house for all kinds of people needing a job. Few lasted, but all were given a chance. Fleet Street spongers usually found BC an 'easy touch,'" thus suggesting that the transference of journalistic skills into public relations was already established in the 1920s.[122] Clarke, Jr., also claimed that his father had strong Atlantic connections and that "jointly with his friend Ivy Lee of America he coined the phrase 'public relations' and began to use it about the same time (1924)."[123] But Ivy Lee's son wrote to me in a letter in 1998, "I don't remember ever having heard of him [Basil Clarke]"[124] and "neither my brother nor I have recollection of

---

[118]Grant, M., p. 125.

[119]Ibid. pp. 125–38.

[120]Clarke, A. (1969). The life and times of Sir Basil Clarke — PR pioneer. *Public Relations*, 22 (2), p. 9.

[121]Ibid. p. 10.

[122]Ibid. p. 13.

[123]Ibid. p. 13.

[124]Personal correspondence 15 July 1998.

my father having contact with any British practitioners,"[125] so we must remain cautious of the evidence of a close link between the U.S. pioneer and the British ex-civil servant. Furthermore, although Alan Clarke claimed that his father's consultancy "pioneered and developed modern public relations techniques as opposed to mere press agency services,"[126] Nigel Ellis (author of public relations books and President of IPR 1971–1972) described it as "a straightforward press agency."[127] The influence of the agency was important, however. Among others, the first Vice President of the IPR, Roger Forman, began his public relations career at Editorial Services and then moved to LPE in 1932.[128]

A leading Parliamentary lobbyist consultancy, Watney and Powell, was set up in 1926 and had a considerable reputation: "Chris Powell was the arch lobbyist. Watney had been the political correspondent for the old *News Chronicle* and used to go down to the House of Commons with a brief inside his top hat . . . and take it off and hand people his lobbyist's brief."[129]

Public relations activities were present in the financial world as early as the 1930s. Pioneer Theo Lovell (a colourful figure, now apparently forgotten), recalled one campaign:

> In the . . . mid-thirties, I had some experiences which showed how very easy it would be to become a confidence trick man and general swindler. I had been briefed by a number of unit trusts to win more favourable comment about them in the press. . . . As a news source we established off Fleet Street what we called an information bureau. It did quite well, for I was allowed to employ, part-time, a brilliant statistician. I would tell him what I wanted to prove, and he would come back with authentic figures which proved it.[130]

Frank Pick, Publicity Manager of London Transport, was another revered prewar figure credited with the poster campaign that built a favourable image for the Underground. Sir John Elliot (who became Chairman of London Transport in the 1960s) was a former *Evening Standard* journalist appointed to Southern Railways at the moment

---

[125]Personal correspondence 29 July 1998.

[126]Clarke, A., p. 13.

[127]Interview. 30 August 1996.

[128]Who are these people? *Public Relations,* 1 (1) 1948, p. 14.

[129]Interview. 25 June 1991.

[130]Lovell, T. (1968). The jungle days of PR—methods used to get new business. *Public Relations* 21 (9), p. 22.

they were electrifying the railway in 1924 to what he believed was "the first public relations appointment in Britain."[131] Another early appointee who was a founder member of the IPR was Edward Kingsley, who worked for the Port of London Authority from 1911 to 1948. He began to move into the public relations area in 1925 with his launching of the *Port of London Authority Monthly* and the *Staff Supplement*, and in 1929 he was appointed assistant publicity officer.[132] There were also pre-Second World War public relations departments at the Gas, Light, and Coke Company, ICI, British Overseas Airways Corporation (BOAC), Shell, J. Lyons & Company, Ford Motor Company, Rootes Motors, and Brooklands Racing Track.[133] Those in the private sector in this period often worked alone and appear to have been a rather fragmentary group, not possessing a forum or specialised journal for sharing their ideas about the role of public relations in industry (the trade journal *World's Press News* did not focus on public relations until after the formation of the IPR in 1948).

Nevertheless, there is some evidence that public relations was beginning to be debated as an issue for business. In 1924, an American advertising man made a presentation on public relations to an advertising conference in London and between 1936 and 1937 the London School of Economics ran a series of evening lectures for business people.[134] The lectures were disseminated further through publication in book form and included a contribution by an economist, P. A. Wilson, on "Public Relations Departments."[135] According to Wilson, public relations had then been recently established in a number of large businesses, trade associations, and government departments.[136] Wilson's definition of public relations was economic. He argued that public relations was not a new function as such but that the need for it had become greater with the growth of imperfect markets leading to a more unstable environment. He attributed this to the expansion of the consumer

---

[131]Elliott, Sir J. (1956). Why should we mind what the public think? *Public Relations, 8* (4), p. 25.

[132]McLoughlin, A. (1948). Edward Kingsley Holmes: an appreciation. *Public Relations, 1* (1), p. 3.

[133]Gillman, F. (1978). Public relations in the United Kingdom prior to 1948. *IPRA Review*, April, p. 46.

[134]Tunstall, J. (1964). *The advertising man in London advertising agencies.* London: Chapman & Hall.

[135]Wilson, P. A. (1937). Public relations departments. In Plant, A. (ed.). *Some modern business problems.* London: Longman, pp. 123–52.

[136]Ibid. p. 125.

market (resulting in increased competition) and government interventions in the market (creation of monopolies). Wilson therefore hypothesised that:

> Every business firm, if it is to look after its own interests properly, needs an expert negotiator to speak on its behalf with representatives of the Government, and incidentally with representatives of the organized political parties . . . the qualities of a good advocate and diplomatist are rare and expensive, and there will be substantial saving if those who have a common case to put forward can club together and share the expenses between them. Hence the trade association.[137]

Wilson went on to argue that, because governments change every few years, "Business men . . . who seek favours from Governments are well advised to take precautions beforehand to see that they stand well in the eyes of the general public, upon whom in the last resort the Government depends for its continuance in power."[138]

Wilson argued that media relations was the way to manage public opinion because the media represented the main channel of communication with the public and were a major influence in vote formation. He pointed out that journalists need "new news" that governments "do not want . . . for fear this should entail the taking of new decisions,"[139] and that:

> Consequently if you take the trouble to cultivate [journalists'] acquaintance and to keep them supplied with information that comes up to their standard of reasonableness and interestingness, they will probably accept it in the form in which you give it them, and they will not give themselves the trouble of hunting elsewhere for a different version of the same story. Furthermore, one good turn deserves another, and in return for your kindness to them you may find them ready to do kindness to you, by holding back from publication matter which you would prefer not to see appearing just now, or in the form proposed.[140]

In other words, media relations was portrayed as influencing journalists via personal contacts.

The approach taken by Wilson was substantially more pragmatic than some of the other influences discussed in this chapter. Wilson

---

[137]Ibid. pp. 136–7.
[138]Ibid. p. 137.
[139]Ibid. p. 138.
[140]Ibid. p. 138.

viewed public relations as an advocacy function employed to protect the interests of a given client. In dealing with the media, he argued, "the golden rule for a Press Department must always be to get its version in first."[141] He saw the function as encompassing market research, dealing with letters of complaint, supervision of advertising, publicity (promotional literature), press releases, and negotiations with trade unions, as well as the broader ranging "maintenance of the 'personal touch' between the management and rank of file . . . by attendance at social gatherings of the staff in provincial areas and so forth." He also thought that the public relations officer had "a right . . . to be consulted on any matter which might in any way affect the prestige of the firm," and that therefore he should be "an official of high rank and authority," possessing "the talent required of an official diplomatist . . . the talent for gauging the reaction of the public to every kind of possible development . . . the kind of ability for which men are chosen to become cabinet ministers."[142] Such definitions of qualities and talent are vital to professional status, particularly in a service industry, because of their intangibility. Seniority and notions of calibre have remained of considerable importance to public relations and the self-image of practitioners, especially consultants, because they depend on these in their quest for monopoly in the market and for social status. Professional status was an important issue for the earliest practitioners.

THE ISSUE OF PROFESSIONAL STATUS

The selection of appropriate personnel for public relations or propaganda work was an issue for employers as soon as the function became defined. Although Grant noted that some prominent advertising men were asked to help with First World War recruitment and war bond campaigns, she argued that it is significant that they were not invited to serve in departments, in contrast to various eminent journalists. She maintained that advertisers had a poor reputation and cited the example of their exclusion from the external Advisory Committee on Government Advertising (ACGA) in 1914. When the Incorporated Society of British Advertisers asked permission to nominate delegates to the committee, arguing that the society had "many experienced publicity

---

[141] Ibid. p. 141.
[142] Ibid. pp. 150–1.

buyers among its membership," the Treasury refused and an official reported that this was no guarantee of expertise and that, "The mere fact that a man is an advertiser does not imply . . . that he is an authority on advertising. Unfortunately there are many foolish advertisers."[143] Advertisers' claims to expertise at this time seemed overblown, as Grant pointed out: "The qualifications required of a good agent were not clear. It seemed, so the how-to books of the day implied, that anyone with a measure of common sense and intelligence could be successful in the profession. . . . The most influential practitioners of the day lacked training and/or experience in the field."[144] This remained a long-term problem for public relations that only began to be addressed at the end of the 20th century.

Grant recorded that, in 1939, the government formed the Inter-Departmental Co-ordinating Committee on Government Publicity to the various information services.[145] Although it was agreed that it was desirable to invite commercial publicists to sit on separate committees for each department, it soon became clear that the pool of talent was very small. According to Grant, the most common recommendations were, in order: S. C. Leslie, Gas, Light and Coke Company; W. Buchanan-Taylor of Lyons; Gervas Huxley, formerly EMB;[146] A. P. Ryan, Assistant Controller of Public Relations at the BBC; and Christian Barman, London Passenger Transport Board.[147] A smaller number of advisory committees were formed that met the government criteria, comprising "representatives of firms that had been engaging in dignified advertising in the commercial sphere."[148] There was an equal dearth of genuine press experience within the civil service. Grant noted that, in 1934, that only 7 out of 18 ministries then employing press officers had appointed trained journalists.[149] A distinction began to be drawn between press and public relations work:

> A Press Officer, whose essential qualification was an intimate knowledge of the working of the press and ought consequently to be chosen from the press . . . and the Public Relations Officer who was chiefly concerned with spreading a better understanding of the Civil Service among the

---

[143] Grant, M., p. 32.
[144] Ibid. pp. 32–3.
[145] Grant, M., p. 232.
[146] Huxley, G. (1970). *Both hands: an autobiography.* London: Chatto & Windus.
[147] Grant, M., pp. 232–3.
[148] Ibid. p. 232.
[149] Ibid. p. 234.

general public, a post for which a civil servant was obviously indicated. This distinction was reflected in the degree of responsibility enjoyed by these . . . officials. The Public Relations Officer was expected to display a high degree of initiative and assume considerable responsibility, whereas the Press Officer's work was carefully controlled by his superiors.[150]

This marked the beginning of the process of developing hierarchies within the practice and of negotiating jurisdictional boundaries.

CONCLUSION

By the end of the Second World War, the British State had invested heavily in a variety of propaganda activities to support political, economic, and diplomatic objectives. There was no dismantling of the MoI because it became the Central Office of Information (CoI) postwar staffed by non-politically affiliated "specialist" information officers recruited by the Government Information Service (GIS). Within the civil service, there was a substantial awareness of the importance and benefits of propaganda. It was those employed in local government, and particularly those active in NALGO, who were attuned to the issue of professional status and recognition and likely to bring these to the fore in any discussion among themselves. At a time when a wider range of specialists was being recognised within local government and granted a form of professional status, it was in the interests of public relations staff to cooperate and look to improve their status and opportunities for promotion. As Tim Traverse-Healy (IPR president, 1967–1968) explained, "They were a network . . . they were concerned within local government to have [a] professional position."[151]

The Institute of Public Administration made both a practical and an intellectual contribution to the development of public relations, particularly in terms of its relationship to concepts of intelligence and information brokering. Its own journal, *Public Administration*, published some of the earliest thinking in Britain on public relations by academics and government officers. In practical terms, the role of NALGO members sensitive to the importance of professional status was crucial. Apart from their bureaucratic skills, which made it possible to run the newly formed IPR in 1948, NALGO members replicated patterns of organisation that

---

[150]Scorgie, 3 May 1939, cited in Grant, M., p. 236.
[151]Interview. 13 September 1995.

had already been established in the Institute of Public Administration: a journal, summer conferences, a thesis competition, and other networking opportunities.

The documentary movement contributed an idealism about democracy and the sense of responsibility and mission to educate an organisation's publics. John Grierson made an inspirational address to the IPR in 1950 (discussed in chap. 3).[152] Both documentary and fiction films were used to propagate messages to civilian and military personnel based in Britain during the Second World War, and the documentary genre was commonly used after the war to educate publics. In particular, the sponsored film became a common technique.

Finally, the wartime experience enhanced awareness of political propaganda within Britain and gave practical experience to a few individuals in the fields of intelligence and, to a lesser degree, psychological warfare. This pattern of career progression certainly entered the mythology of the occupation. Others gained experience of journalism during the war, working for services newspapers. However, in 1945 the working population had to restart or find fresh careers in a postwar world. Characteristic of the period were the apparently porous boundaries between public relations, propaganda, marketing, and advertising, and this characteristic worked against the possibility of professional status, which requires jurisdiction over a particular field, a body of knowledge, and the ability to demonstrate and enforce a boundary between those who have the relevant expertise and those who do not. These conditions did not then obtain.

---

[152]Grierson, J. (1950). The scope of film in public relations. *Public Relations, 3* (1), p. 13.

3

Establishing the Profession: 1945–1960

INTRODUCTION

This chapter describes the growth and establishment of public relations in the economically uncertain postwar era. Britain ended the war as the world's largest debtor nation, short of labour and food, with reduced productivity and visible exports down to less than half of the prewar level. Although Herbert Morrison described Britain in 1947 as "an impoverished, second-rate power, morally magnificent, but economically bankrupt,"[1] the country's rulers attempted to maintain an imperial role. In the 1940s and 1950s, the UK was paying up to 8% of its gross national product on defence as the Cold War escalated. A change in administration in 1945 brought increased expenditure on social welfare, housing, and health. Nevertheless, in comparison to other European nations, especially Germany, Britain was better off materially in the sense that "normal" life was more quickly restored and the long-term burden of economic debt was not so apparent to the ordinary citizen, who was more concerned with food shortages in the face of tighter rationing.

In this setting there were several opportunities for public relations to become an established part of the socioeconomic framework; the large

---

[1]Sissons, M. & French, P. (1963). *Age of austerity*. London: Greenwood Publishers, Hodder & Stoughton, p. 247.

amount of new social legislation needed to be explained to citizens. Goods had to be promoted, initially to export markets and then, with the increase of consumer durables, to the home market; finally, the new administration's interventionist economic policies required some explanation and triggered opposition from business in rhetorical campaigns that often appealed directly to the public.

The present chapter begins with an account of the establishment of the IPR in 1948, followed by a rather briefer account of the establishment of the International Public Relations Association (IPRA) in 1955, and the role that British practitioners played in that development. The institutional approach taken here includes commentary on the emerging occupational discourse, as reflected in IPR journals of the period and IPRA documentation. This leads to a consideration of the postwar growth of another relatively new field, that of industrial design, with which public relations worked in tandem to promote British goods, often at international and trade fairs and exhibitions. This is followed by a review of the policies of nationalisation and antinationalisation, focusing on the efforts of the lobby group Aims of Industry. The final part of the chapter takes an international perspective in looking at the role of public relations in the context of decolonisation. The chapter covers the period from 1945 until the 1960s to provide sufficient background for the subsequent chapters, which focus more closely on professionalisation.

A VISION: SETTING UP THE IPR

The driving force behind the formation of the IPR was a group of local government officials. Their efforts bore fruit in the postwar era because of the necessity for public relations work by local government, an increasing number of public relations appointments, and a common desire to make contact and share experiences with others in similar jobs. As Tallents remarked at the inaugural meeting of the IPR, "A year or two ago . . . I attended a conference on [public relations] organised by the National Association of Local Government Officers—a gathering of some 500 people. Two things impressed me—their keenness . . . [and] . . . the isolation and loneliness in which many of them had to work."[2]

---

[2]Tallents, Sir S. R. (1973). The first positive step. *The Institute of Public Relations 1948–1973*. Bedford: The Sidney Press, p. 7.

NALGO's postwar Reconstruction Committee recognised that local government could only work effectively if it became "a partnership between the citizen, the elected representative and the local government officer, each working in full understanding of the needs, wishes and difficulties of the other two partners, for the good of the community as a whole."[3] Thus, NALGO accepted the necessity for a persuasive role and consequently developed a large public relations programme, including an exhibition that caught the popular imagination. The forces bought 1,300 duplicates of the exhibition and The British Council distributed sets throughout the world. However, this, and accompanying initiatives, required new staff.

On 8 August 1946, Norman Rogers, then recently appointed as NALGO's assistant public relations officer, met another new public relations officer (PRO), Kenneth Day, from Erith Town Council. According to Rogers, he asked Day if he would like to meet other newly appointed municipal PROs and Day responded "enthusiastically." Rogers recalled, "The Institute had been conceived. An eighteen months' pregnancy had begun."[4] However, Roger Wimbush, first Vice Chairman of the IPR Council, put forward a slightly different historical version:

> Shortly after the war I found myself presiding over a small but growing group of Public Relations Officers connected with local government. We met at monthly intervals. . . . The group was quite informal. . . . Even so specialised a group found itself discussing matters of Public Relations policy in general, and it was obvious to many of us that an organisation embracing all branches of Public Relations might be of service to this comparatively new profession.[5]

A first meeting of about a dozen municipal PROs was held on 10 October 1946 and a second on 6 November 1946 attracted 16. The meeting was formally constituted as the Standing Conference of Public Relations Officers that would "Invite representative public relations officers in the civil service, industry, commerce, the professions . . . to consult with it on the best means of fostering the interests of the profession."[6] A subcommittee was formed chaired by Bill Viny (Hastings) and including L. W. Bates (Port of London Authority), E. Watson Cole

---

[3] Spoor, A. (1967). *White-collar union: sixty years of NALGO*. London: Heinemann, p. 438.

[4] Rogers, N. (1958). Birth of the Institute. *Public Relations, 10* (2), p. 9.

[5] Wimbush, R. (1948). The birth of an institute. *Public Relations, 1* (1), p. 2.

[6] Rogers, N., p. 10.

(Woolwich), A. A. McLaughlin (Paddington), Roger Wimbush (West-minster), E. K. Fletcher (Rowley), and Terrance Usher (Manchester).[7] They drafted aims and objectives for the putative institute and also dis-cussed the possibility of establishing an examination in public relations, but decided that "detailed consideration at this stage would be pre-mature."[8] Alec Spoor (Chief Public Relations Officer of NALGO and author of a book on the history of NALGO) and Roger Wimbush (Westminster) subsequently met Sir Stephen Tallents to ask him if he would be prepared to become involved in establishing a new association because of his experience at the EMB, BBC, and Post Office and evident interest in the field, but, as Spoor recorded, "While sympathetic towards the project, Sir Stephen was unwilling to sponsor it in the way the sub-committee suggested . . . [because] . . . he was now out of harness as a public relations officer. . . . [He] . . . expressed the opinion that most of the public relations officers in Government departments . . . might need a good deal of persuasion to come into an association."[9] This prophecy was to prove remarkably accurate.

The reservations expressed by Tallents are also interesting because they were characteristic of a number of the prewar generation of practi-tioners who saw the postwar entry as inexperienced upstarts, typically from the services, and trying to make a fast buck. In some ways, such reservations also seem symptomatic of public relations culture in that in every generation the established practitioners decry the standards and "calibre" of new entrants. It became clear to me when I was inter-viewing some of the postwar entrants for this book that they were keen to identify themselves with the prewar generation even though their birthdates indicated that realistically they could not have been working before the war.

Regarding the appropriate scope of the new organisation, it was eventually decided to cast the net beyond local government and practi-tioners from a range of organisations were then informally consulted, including representatives from the British Council, the British Gas Council, the Electrical Development Association, the National Council for Women, the Travel Association, the International Wool Secretariat, the Ford Motor Company, and Royal Mail Lines.[10] The standing confer-

---

[7]Rogers, R. M. (1973). The architects. In *The Institute of Public Relations 1948–1973*. Bedford: The Sidney Press, p. 11.

[8]Ibid. p. 11.

[9]Rogers, N., p. 10.

[10]Ibid. p. 12.

ence appointed an "Investigation Committee"[11] and in May 1947 a provisional definition of public relations was established: "Public relations means the deliberate, planned and sustained effort to establish and maintain, by conveying information and by all other suitable means, mutual understanding and good relations between a firm, undertaking, statutory authority, government, department, profession or other body or group, and the community at large."[12]

The IPR was formally established in February 1948, with aims that included:

> To encourage and foster the observance of high professional standards by its members . . . to act as a clearing house for the exchange of ideas on the practice of public relations . . . to develop and foster relations with other bodies or authorities . . . to issue . . . publications . . . to establish a library . . . to institute a register of members, with details of experience and specialist knowledge or qualifications . . . to consider the institution of examinations or other suitable tests with the object of raising the status of those practising public relations to an agreed professional level . . . to give a united voice to the practice of public relations and to enhance its influence and . . . generally to undertake all such activities as are likely to be of benefit to the practice of public relations and the interests of its members.[13]

Despite his reservations, Tallents agreed to become president and acted in this capacity from 1948 to 1949 and again from 1952 to 1953.

The aims of the new Institute had some similarity with those of the Institute of Administration, not only because there was a line of inheritance in terms of personnel, but also because the organisations were both engaged in defining and formalising an occupation and thus engaging in professionalisation. Both organisations defined their role as a conduit for ideas and information exchange and as a lobbying body and opinion leader on behalf of their respective members to raise their

---

[11]The investigation committee was later known as the interim council. It comprised T. Fife-Clark (Ministry of Health), R. S. Forman (LPE), A. K. S. Gore (CoI), A. Hess (Austin Motor Company), E. K. Holmes (Port of London Authority), A. A. McLaughlin (Paddington Metropolitan Borough Council), E. G. Ogilvie (International Wool Secretariat), J. Pringle (British Medical Association), W. J. Seymour (Vauxhall Motors), A. Spoor (NALGO), C. Taylor (Ford Motor Company), J. Taylor (Coventry Corporation), T. Usher (Manchester Corporation), A. K. Viny (Hastings Corporation), R. Wimbush (Westminster City Council), G. Young (from an organisation the acronym of which was HYELM).

[12]Rogers, N., p. 12.

[13]Hess, A. (1948). Our aims and objects. *Public Relations*, 1 (1), p. 8.

status in society. The emphasis on mutuality in the IPR definition has similarities with those of the EMB and the British Council. Mutuality has remained an important value for the British Council and was the subject of a research report written by the then assistant director general Trevor Rutter in the Council's 50th anniversary year (1984).[14]

A council and committee structure was established. The first committee was the Membership Committee set up in 1948 under Euan Ogilvie. Subsequently, committees were created as the need arose (education, professional practices, general purposes, foundation fund) as were regional groups (the first established in Leeds by Raymond Dean in 1952).[15] By the mid-1970s, concerns were expressed about the proliferation and unwieldiness of the committee system and proposals put forward for streamlining.[16]

The 25-strong local government contingent formed the first special interest group within the Institute in 1948. They organised a range of their own meetings, a programme of events, and activities including a weekend school covering printing techniques, brochure design, exhibition planning and administration, news values and journalism practice, and the production and use of film strips. By sheer weight of numbers they dominated the IPR in the early years. This was sometimes resented, as is suggested by McLoughlin's comments that they "continued to make an invaluable contribution to the institute's progress which some people regarded as tail wagging dog."[17] For example, Tim Traverse-Healy, recalling those years, remarked, "All the early [IPR] meetings were 'On a point of order, Mr Chairman, excuse me you can't vote on that till you've done this.' . . . It was very much like running a sort of Council meeting in the Wigan Town Council."[18] On 8 June 1948 there was an inaugural reception, at which was held a "Brains Trust" presided over by Richard Dimbleby as Question Master.[19] The first Annual Gen-

---

[14]Personal observation during my employment at the British Council 1977–88. I was posted to a specially created temporary post for 18 months as Fiftieth Anniversary Assistant Coordinator (one of two people working with top management responsible for event management).

[15]Firsts in the history of the institute (1973). *The Institute of Public Relations 1948–1973*, p. 14.

[16]IPR Archive (1975). 3/1/4.

[17]McLoughlin, A. A. (1973). See how it ran. *The Institute of Public Relations 1948–1973*, p. 42.

[18]Interview. 13 September 1995.

[19]IPR archive /1.

eral Meeting was held on 30 September 1948.[20] (AGMs were referred to as Annual Conferences until 1953.) The first weekend conference was held in 1950. In 1951 there was a "Public Relations Week," based in London, consisting of a series of talks and visits including trips to the BBC, the British Institute of Management, Reuters, the Port of London Authority, and Arthur Guinness.[21]

In September 1948 the first issue of the institute's journal, *Public Relations*, was produced and was edited by Warren Seymour (Vauxhall Motors) for the first 4 years of the Institute's life. Apart from the first year, when it appeared twice, the journal appeared quarterly until January 1968 and then monthly until March 1976, after which the name changed to *Communicator*. The title *Public Relations* was recovered in 1982 and ran quarterly until July 1993, when it continued with the same issue and number series but became known as *The IPR Journal*. The journal offers rich material on the ideals and aspirations of public relations practitioners. The following section draws on journals published between 1948 and 1955 to record how the first practitioners who were consciously engaged in the process of professionalisation conceived their role and that of their Institute.

ARTICULATING THE VISION AND STAKING A CLAIM: THE EMERGENCE OF A PROFESSIONAL DISCOURSE

The first issue of *Public Relations* was printed only a few months after the formation of the institute. The journal embodied the Institute for all its members, because not all members attended meetings or were involved in committees. Although *Public Relations* might be taken generally to represent official or common lines of thought, it was also the case that it gave a mouthpiece to motivated parties, not least the editors, each of whom imposed his particular style upon the journal and the leaders. There are no remaining records detailing reviewing and editorial processes. Some pieces were very long (5,000 words) for such a small magazine, and the inclusion of some polemical material might suggest a shortage of copy. The presence of typographical and grammatical errors could also imply light editorial control. Due to paper rationing, the

---

[20] IPR archive 2/1/1.
[21] IPR archive 8/1/a.

early journals were text heavy, with narrow margins, headers, and footers, and employed 10-point type or sometimes even 8 point for long articles.

In the first issue of *Public Relations* the opening editorial by Bill Seymour was self-conscious and idealistic: "We who have played a part, each according to his ability, in the creation of the Institute of Public Relations, have been inspired by one increasing purpose. The beliefs we hold are as wide as our shades of political opinion ... [but] *one belief we hold in common—that the proper practice of public relations is of unassessable importance to the future of the world*"[22] (emphasis added). In addition to his emphasis on the importance of public relations as an occupation (thus flattering his readers), Seymour highlighted the key ideal for public relations: truth. He explained that:

> The development of popular education is producing a race of people who can think for themselves. They are beginning to demand that they shall be told the truth in so far as the truth be known. . . . It is the responsibility of the serious practitioner in public relations to make them realise it; to convince those in authority that whatever the objective, Truth is the best weapon.[23]

Seymour suggested that public relations practitioners were appropriate guardians of verity, and the importance of truth as *the* ideal for public relations was emphasised by the choice of logo for the Institute, which was explained by Seymour in the second issue: "The torch symbolised enlightenment, which Pros sought to spread: the 'flame of truth' which should be ever-burning in their breasts: and the fire which consumes evil and corruption. The Latin *Pro Fide* means, freely translated, 'In the interests of Truth.'"[24] Actually, the correct translation is "for faith." Exchanging the concept of faith for truth (*veritas*) seems to downplay the role of public relations as persuasion. Public relations is seen as revelatory rather than about influencing beliefs. The idea of faith suggests the need for believers. The eschatological language suggests a moral crusade. The concept of truth has been important in the rhetoric of public relations, because it is truth that has often been employed by practitioners to distinguish their work from propaganda. The Chief Public Relations Officer of London Transport clearly employed this dichotomy, while at the same time recommending counterpropaganda:

---

[22]Seymour, W. J. S. (1948). An invitation to the critics. *Public Relations*, 1 (1), p. 1.
[23]Ibid.
[24]The first conference. (1948). Editorial, *Public Relations*, 1 (2), p. 4.

Evil propaganda must be met and beaten by Truth. She will always win. . . . Give her wings! Let the air be hers and the press and the film and the posters. . . . Let it not be a question so much of countering communist propaganda but of getting in first. . . . Faith exemplified in our adherence to Christian principles and thought is essential to the preservation of western life as we know it . . . a formidable rampart against the insidious workings of evil propaganda.'[25]

A dominant theme that emerged was of the ideological importance of public relations to the world. Public relations was seen as a conduit for the "right" ideas to prevail in society. A predominant ideal was that of freedom. Public relations was presented both as a source of morally good ideas and as a technique that could be favourably contrasted with either totalitarianism or anarchy. The mission and ideals of public relations are strongly bound up with politics. In the first place, the experience of the Second World War can help explain the dual emphasis on freedom and totalitarianism, but so can a growing consciousness of the Cold War. The Cold War context and the fear of conflict in the newly postnuclear world appeared to some to offer a major role for public relations to contribute to international diplomacy: "[Public relations] is a group of crusaders whose job is to carry the torch of understanding into areas where discord and dissension may be eliminated by information and explanation."[26] Public relations could save the world because it aided communication between nations. The rhetoric of battle against an evil empire was often linked to the active promotion of democracy, but also to notions of Western civilisation (often specifically British or English, sometimes more broadly Anglo-American) and Christianity, as demonstrated in the quotations below:

It was vital to let the rest of the world—particularly the underdeveloped areas—know about the British way of life. . . . [This was of] world importance because knowledge of our democratic principles could be a most potent defence against communism and a powerful weapon in the "cold war."[27]

Parsons have been public relations officers ever since Our Lord sent out the first apostles. One might even go further back and say Moses was

---

[25] Dodson-Wells, G. (1951). Bulwark of freedom. *Public Relations, 4* (1), pp. 6–7.

[26] Lipscombe, E. (1953). Let's get lost: seventh session of the conference. *Public Relations, 5* (4), p. 1

[27] Adam, General Sir R. (1952). Public relations in industry. *Public Relations, 4* (4), p. 2

applying a special public relations technique when he displayed the Ten Commandments.[28]

Faith, exemplified in our adherence to Christian principles and thought is . . . essential to the preservation of western life as we know it.[29]

[Public relations is responsible] for saving the soul of humanity.[30]

The evangelical concept of public relations defined the practitioner's role as an apostle for his or her cause or organisation and thus as an advocate. There was an intrinsic tension between this notion and the view that public relations facilitated discourse in society: "We in this country were lucky to have the two-way interpretation. . . . Russia was not so fortunate. . . . The Institute [was like] UNO where people of all creeds and parties were working together for the benefit of humanity and understanding."[31]

Public relations was seen as a major agent in society that could contribute to its survival by perpetuating bourgeois values through available media such as government-commissioned films or exhibitions, for example: "The coming year will be one of intensive Public Relations activity in—and for—Britain. If we are to derive the fullest benefits from the Festival of Britain, we must project all that is best in our way of life, in our industries and services and in our incomparably beautiful land."[32]

Although public relations was seen as a solution to international tension and a way to promote Western political and cultural values, it was also seen as something that could oppose an internal threat, articulated as "bureaucracy." This appeared to be a response to the postwar growth of the state. Opposition to the NHS had been based on fear of complicated paperwork and there were "letters in the newspapers complaining of red tape, bureaucratic high-handedness."[33] Such fears coalesced with similar worries about other aspects of the welfare state and social service provision and were reflected in the local government-dominated IPR, so that, in his presidential address in 1953, Roger Wimbush

---

[28] Morgan, D. (1952). You make me feel at home. *Public Relations*, 4 (4), p. 16

[29] Dodson-Wells, G., p. 6.

[30] Wimbush, R. (1953). The presidential address. *Public Relations*, 5 (2), p. 11.

[31] What they said at dinner. *Public Relations*, 3 (2) 1950, p. 11.

[32] Hess, A. (1950). Conference speeches. *Public Relations*, 3 (2), p. 5

[33] Jenkins, R. (1963). Bevan's fight with the BMA. In Sissons, M. & French, P. *The age of austerity*. London: Hodder & Stoughton, p. 425.

declared, "The need for public relations in the modern world is self-evident to the most myopic observer of the contemporary world. I have referred to it as the dock leaf growing beside the bureaucratic nettle."[34] In this account, public relations was seen as a soothing palliative.

In proving value to society, public relations as a form of social responsibility in itself emerged as a major theme in the early journals. In part, such an ideal seems to have been a development of the local government public service ethos:

J. A. Brongers and F. Hollander presented an inspiring story of public relations which was done voluntarily in the flooded areas of Zeeland by members of the Dutch Public Relations society....[35]

The principles of public relations represent a policy for civilisation that becomes demonstrably more effective the more it is adopted . . . adds progressive strength to democracy today. . . . The philosophy of public relations is a policy of social responsibility — based on an acknowledgement of human values — actively put into practice and skilfully publicised.[36]

Of course, much charity and generosity have been exhibited in the last few decades — exactly the period since public relations was born. An enormous amount of good deeds: aid, help, assistance, care for others, grants, improvement of living standards, readiness to bargain, voluntary agreements and the general tendency to give more satisfaction — all these were undoubtedly inspired by the ideal of public relations. . . . Independent from religious and ethical movements, public relations follows its own path which also leads to better humanity.[37]

Summing up the purpose and aims of the institute in the first issue, Seymour wrote, "The public relations executive must grow in stature. It was to foster this growth; to control it; to eliminate the charlatan; to establish and enforce professional standards of conduct that the Institute was formed."[38] By the third issue of the journal, members' contributions began to reflect upon and reiterate some of the core values, as illustrated by the following:

We who practise public relations believe in promoting "mutual understanding and goodwill." A hackneyed phrase, but one which most of us

---

[34] Wimbush, R. (1953). The presidential address. *Public Relations*, 5 (2), p. 11.

[35] Riding a hobby horse. Editorial, *Public Relations*, 6 (4) 1954, p. 4.

[36] Galitzine, Prince Y. (1960). Philosophy of public relations. *Public Relations*, 12 (4), p. 51.

[37] Vegrin, Dr. E. V. (1960). Letters. *Public Relations*, 12 (2).

[38] Groom, F. S. (1949). Factory visits. *Public Relations*, 1 (3), p. 14; Seymour, W. J. S., p. 1.

have used at some time or another and to which most of us still subscribe. Mutual understanding and goodwill. Is there any better means,
any more direct or effective way, of achieving these aims than that of
bringing an organisation and its public together?[39]

Grierson's influence is retrospectively apparent in the public relations
discourse of this era. In 1950, he gave a talk to the IPR that was clearly
intended to be inspirational. Throughout the speech he identified himself with public relations practitioners, using the first-person plural
throughout. At the outset, he identified public relations practitioners as
the inheritors of a tradition that included the Roman Emperors and
Machiavelli. He appealed to his audience not to forget this tradition and
suggested that, in the postwar world, public relations had lost its way.
His speech is thus a prime and possibly emblematic example of criticism
of more recent entrants to the field:

> I think we may have come to a point where we are not as deeply rooted in
> our conception of public relations as we might be . . . not as conscious as
> we might be of the larger possibilities which are inherent in the commu-
> nications we make to the public. . . . I can think of no time which was less
> ambitious and less penetrating in its plan for public relations . . . many of
> the forces of public relations are amateur and have come into our profes-
> sion without study of its nature. . . . The techniques of public relations are
> important to study but in the last instance we are more than mere crafts-
> men. We are together living creative participants in the modern scene . . .
> we are short on a philosophy of public relations.[40]

Grierson thus had a more strategic view of public relations, but his
interpretation of this appears to have been related to his pessimism
about democracy and a search for a Platonic leadership elite, rather than
the managerial interpretation that currently dominates. Grierson's talk
was very favourably reviewed in the influential advertising newspaper
World's Press News, which suggested that too much emphasis had
perhaps been given by the postwar generation of public relations practitioners to rational aspects of public relations work such as market research and insufficient emphasis to "exhortation":

> Can it be as Grierson suggests that exhortation is too daring, that it in-
> volves a faith in ourselves and confidence in the future we do not have, or

---

[39]Groom, F. S., p. 14.
[40]Critic. (1950, 16 March). John Grierson gave us something to think about. *World's
Press News*, G5A: 1: 3.

that the inspiration is not there at the authoritative level? Whatever it is, we are missing ... the deeper aspects of public communication, clerkishly skimming the rational surface of public relations and hardly working with revelation at all.[41]

The speech appeared to have had some immediate impact on the then President of the IPR, Alan Hess, whose keynote speech at the next IPR conference pronounced, "A personal sensitivity on the part of a PRO is infinitely more important than even the most methodical application of generally accepted techniques. There is no intellectual substitute for the human approach. Today, there is a tendency for too much intellectualism, too much market research mumbo-jumbo to replace honest-to-goodness exhortation."[42] This is a curious view of social science and its rigorous methods, to say the least. Without any sort of rational or intellectual base, public relations could only be dependent on personal qualities such as charisma (which remains a much-vaunted personal quality among recruiters of public relations staff). Perhaps the creation of mystique was important to the insubstantial discipline that public relations practice was at that time.

Others also responded to Grierson's plea, and in so doing confirmed the idealism and aspirations for status held by many of those active in public relations professional associations. Important examples were Roger Wimbush, Vice Chairman of the IPR in 1948, who declared that "the public relations man or woman must have an understanding of the humanities—and that must not be smothered by technicalities"[43] and Norman Rogers (Honorary Secretary 1951–1954) who argued, "If we are not concerned that we are benefiting humanity, we are wasting our time."[44]

One of the most interesting themes to emerge from the early journals is that of middle-class manners as an important component of public relations work. This was clearly partly a result of seeing public relations as an extension of interpersonal relations, but also shows that some of the early members had clear views about who should go into public relations. In the words of Paget-Cooke (IPR president, 1959–1960):

Most people in business today were brought up in their homes with certain standards of behaviour set before them as right—such things as

---

[41] Ibid.

[42] Hess, A. (1950). Conference speeches. *Public Relations*, 3 (2), p. 6.

[43] The qualities of a PRO. Discussion. *Public Relations*, 2 (4) 1950, p. 15.

[44] Ibid.

kindness, tact, friendliness and fairness. These basic standards have been carried over into adult personal life and have become to all intents and purposes part of most people, and a part that is accepted without question and almost without realisation. . . . Public relations is the comparatively recent expression by business of the old precept "do unto others as you would have them do to you." . . . To say of a man he is "a good chap" means the same thing to all Englishmen.[45]

According to this view, public relations staff were expected to exemplify personal qualities held in the greatest regard by the dominant class. It suggested that the occupation required smooth operators, inoffensive and reliable in a way that meant they would be trusted and therefore, perhaps, more convincing. Key qualities included "a personal sensitivity . . . great understanding, great forbearance, a great spirit of attunement with one's fellow beings;"[46] "the quality of being curious . . . the faith of the possibility of change."[47] Public relations itself was described as "ninety per cent common sense and only ten per cent technique;"[48] and "just good common sense."[49] The common sense theme is interesting from a number of points of view. First, it suggests that, despite the rhetoric and high-flown language, public relations was seen as a fairly basic task not requiring any special education, as exemplified by F. Murray Milne from the Wholesale Textile Association: "I'm not one of those practitioners who have surrounded Public Relations with an aura of mystic symbolism and high falutin' nonsense. . . . To me the job that has to be done is just good common sense."[50] This clearly had implications for any aspiration to professional status (even though some were already claiming that public relations was a profession).[51] However, common sense in the public relations context was not clearly defined and it was implied that it was an intrinsic quality that could not be learnt, so perhaps it was simply a question of possessing the right cultural capital. The emphasis that is put on certain qualities

---

[45]Paget-Cooke, R. A. (1951). Good business. *Public Relations*, 3 (3), pp. 9–10.

[46]Hess, A. (1950). Conference speeches. *Public Relations*, 3 (2), p. 6.

[47]Hornsby, L. (1950). The qualities of a public relations officer. *Public Relations*, 2 (4), p. 4.

[48]Our first discussion: members seek definition of public relations. *Public Relations*, 1 (3) 1949, p. 4.

[49]Murray Milne, F. (1949). Public relations in a wholesale way. *Public Relations*, 1 (3), p. 4.

[50]What they said. *Public Relations*, 2 (4) 1950, p. 2.

[51]Another successful conference. *Public Relations*, 4 (4) 1952, p. 1; Nationalism and public relations. *Public Relations*, 8 (1) 1955, p. 29.

is vital in defining an occupation and its values, and affects access to the occupation.

At the outset of its life, then, the IPR had to establish a vision, a mission, and concrete aims and objectives, but it also had to recruit sufficient numbers to become a viable and visible organisation—and those recruits needed to be apostles. Barriers to entry were established in an attempt to withhold the status of membership from "charlatans." Those employed by press agencies were not able to become members, and prospective applicants were required to demonstrate that their jobs were broadly based, as became clear in an early editorial:

> A press agent . . . is surely one who is concerned solely with getting notices about an individual or an organisation into newspapers, magazines and other periodicals. Whereas a Public Relations Executive is concerned with presenting an individual or an organisation to the public in every possible way, not only with the object of getting them talked about, but to explain policy and help the public.[52]

Two classes of membership were initially established: "Full" for those who met the criteria identified in the preceding quote and "Associate" for those who had an interest in public relations, such as a managing director of a company, but who did not themselves practise. By 1953, membership had grown to 376.[53]

ESTABLISHMENT OF THE INTERNATIONAL PUBLIC RELATIONS ASSOCIATION (IPRA)

A number of British practitioners were involved in the establishment of IPRA. According to the IPRA's own history,[54] the earliest international postwar links were between Hans Herman, Public Relations Adviser to the Dutch Prime Minister, and his opposite number, Francis Williams, Public Relations Adviser to the British Prime Minister. Subsequently there was a meeting at Oddenino's Hotel in Regent Street between IPR members Dick Forman (President), Roger Wimbush (Chairman), Tom Fife-Clark (Director General of the COI and Vice Chairman of IPR),

---

[52] The first conference. Editorial. *Public Relations*, 1 (2) 1948, p. 2.

[53] Annual general meeting. *Public Relations*, 5 (2) 1953, p. 9.

[54] Black, S. & Murdoch, T. (eds.). (1995). A commitment to excellence: the first forty years. *International Public Relations Association*. Sweden: GormanGruppen.

Norman Rogers (Honorary Secretary), and the Dutch representatives Hans Herman and Jo Brongers (Shell).[55]

In 1950, *Public Relations* recorded that the Chairman of the PR society of the Netherlands visited the IPR and gave a talk in which he referred to discussions that had taken place in March 1950 at the Utrecht Fair, which had been attended by representatives from Britain, the United States, Holland, France, and Norway.[56] Also present for the meeting in London was Chopin de Janvry, chairman of the French public relations society.[57] The Utrecht meeting had produced a joint declaration that:

> Having considered the necessity of furthering the skill and ethics of their profession and of a clear understanding of their work and considering further the value of international exchange of information and co-operation, we have resolved that a Provisional International Committee be set up with the object of furthering exchange and co-operation and the eventual establishment of an International Public Relations Association.[58]

By the end of 1950, contacts had been made in America, Australia, Canada, France, Holland, India, Norway, and South Africa.[59] Hans Hermans and Odd Medboe cooperated in writing a plan for an international public relations association.[60] This was reworked by Hermans and became known as "The Hermans Memorandum." The use of diplomatic language is interesting and perhaps suggests that this was the status to which the occupation aspired. The Memorandum included a discussion of definitions and the role and scope of public relations, developing a typology: the press agent securing "by honest but sometimes by dishonest means as much unpaid publicity as his relations with journalistic and other circles enable him to gather thus saving advertising money for his employer," in religious, Griersonian, and almost Nietzschean terms, "the welfare officer within management . . . preaching the gospel of social behaviour . . . the voice of the social conscience . . . a kind of superman, constantly throwing the light of the general interest in and on the enterprise on which he wholly depends," and finally, a type who was all things to all people who:

---

[55] Ibid. p. 22.

[56] Public relations in Holland. *Public Relations*, 2 (4) 1950, p. 26.

[57] Ibid. p. 26.

[58] Black, S. & Murdoch, T., p. 22.

[59] Now for the future. Editorial. *Public Relations*, 3 (2) 1950, p. 1.

[60] Medboe, O. (1951). Developments in Norway. *Public Relations*, 4 (1), p. 25.

[Kept] in mind the social value of his enterprise ... but more as a starting point than something to be provided or proved. Given the social value of his enterprise he has to take away or prevent misconceptions or misunderstandings in all its departments. This is the profound interest of the enterprise itself as well as that of the social community as a whole. ... His task is to further the right understanding of the whole enterprise.[61]

According to Hermans, the last type of public relations is the type practised from the beginning of the 20th century by "the really great public relations officers all over the world," who had recognised "the character of their profession as a useful and noble one ... no less serving the interests of the enterprise that pays them and also of great importance for the social community as a whole, because this community has a keen interest in the smooth functioning of large modern enterprises all over [the world]."[62] As far as public relations in government was concerned, Hermans declared that the information officer should not "Preach a gospel of government propaganda. His task is to give information on the facts and motives of government policy, to avoid misunderstanding and to promote general understanding; not to kill criticism, but to further discussion."[63]

Hermans proposed three alternative organisational concepts: a federal concept in which the international association would be a league of national organisations (rejected because many countries did not then possess national organisations); an international criterion whereby membership would be restricted to those working "in the international field or in the service of commercial, political, military or other corporations of an international character" (rejected as being too limited); and the "brotherhood concept," which was an international association of those "joining personally, exchanging experiences, ideas, explaining their work to the world outside the profession ... but above all forming a kind of rotary in which each member in case of need may be sure of the assistance of his fellow members throughout the world."[64] The term *brotherhood* was eventually substituted by the term *professional*.[65]

---

[61] Herman, H, cited in Fife-Clark, T. (1952). Towards an international public relations association. *Public Relations*, 4 (3), p. 11; Black, S. & Murdoch, T. (eds.), pp. 24–25, which is based very heavily on the original article by Fife-Clark.

[62] Fife-Clark, T., p. 11.

[63] Ibid. p. 11.

[64] Ibid. p. 26.

[65] Black, S. & Murdoch, T., p. 28.

Following discussion with existing national associations, the objectives of the new international organisation were formulated around three key issues:

1) The problem of professional recognition. Combating the misunderstandings and objections existing in international circles, among politicians, directors, advertising managers, journalists as well as the public in general;

2) Professional skills. The problem could be addressed by . . . a journal and a series of booklets recording the most recent results of professional experience and research in all the countries represented . . . conferences . . . the preparation of an international "who's who in public relations";

3) The problem of professional ethics: linking and perhaps completing the codes of professional conduct being compiled in several countries.[66]

Despite espousing international cooperation, there was an assumption that American and European perspectives and experiences could be applied elsewhere in the world. Likewise, the provisional committee of IPRA chose to meet each year on the south coast of England prior to the annual IPR meeting. In addition to the five countries formally involved, there were representatives from Australia, Belgium, Canada, Finland, Italy, and Switzerland. Despite the notion of international brotherhood, IPRA was established as an anglophone organisation in the face of lobbying by other language groups. IPRA's 40th anniversary booklet commented that "fortunately English has become the international language of public relations."[67] Anglophone superiority held sway in *Public Relations*, evidenced by an editorial that complained, "There are times when the foreign tourist finds that English is inadequate to cope with the situation. Even in Europe one finds the uneducated native who does not, or pretends not to, understand English."[68]

IPRA was formed on 1 May 1955. Membership was limited to those responsible for planning and executing public relations in a major role in an organisation that would entail "building and maintaining sound and productive relations with special publics and with the public at large

---

[66]Ibid. p. 27.
[67]Ibid. p. 36.
[68]The printed word. *Public Relations*, 6 (1) 1953, p. 9.

so as to adapt itself to its environment and interpret itself to society . . . provided . . . that these activities are of international significance."[69] In addition to a code of professional conduct, IPRA developed an international code of ethics known as the "Code of Athens" (written by Lucien Matrat) based on the United Nations Charter. This followed IPRA's recognition by the United Nations in 1964. IPRA's president in 1988 was Alain Modoux, who, in 1998, was Director of Communication at UNESCO, a post first held in 1947 by the film documentarist John Grierson.[70]

It is clear from the language employed in IPRA publications that it has always had very high aspirations. Apparently, IPRA was formed "in London in the Cabinet Office at No 10 Downing Street."[71] The use of terms such as "Hermans Memorandum" and "Code of Athens" implied diplomatic status reinforced by IPRA's location between 1984 and 1997 in Geneva. Until 1992 there was a post Secretary General in addition to the President, Council, and Board of Directors. Aspirations have not been purely temporal, but took on a spiritual dimension too in 1965, when members presented a copy of the Code of Athens to Pope Paul VI.[72] The superior positioning of IPRA and the perception that its importance extended beyond public relations practice was reflected by the editor of *Public Relations*, who, in 1956, somewhat pretentiously suggested, "T. Fife-Clark's address on the development of the International Association will undoubtedly stand for a long time as source material in the field of international affairs."[73] Fife-Clark's address acknowledged that the formation of IPRA was another step towards professional status: "We are following a well trodden path of evolution. History shows that when a new profession is beginning to find itself and make a collective approach to both its present and its future, it begins also to offer its hand to colleagues in other lands."[74] However, at the same time that practitioners were reaching out to each other internationally, the new organisation intended to limit entry: "It is not so much a question of who will want to join, but who will be admitted. For this is a club with high standards . . . [to be] . . . highly exclusive, formed by a comparatively

[69] Black, S. & Murdoch, T., pp. 27–8.
[70] Hardy, F. (1979). *Grierson on documentary*. London: Faber & Faber, p. 15.
[71] Black, S. & Murdoch, T., p. 31.
[72] Ibid. p. 38.
[73] Editorial, *Public Relations*, 8 (2) 1956, p. 1.
[74] The history and aims of IPRA: address by Tom Fife-Clark. *Public Relations*, 8 (2) 1956, p. 10.

small number of men [sic]. We do not need or seek a large membership.
... IPRA wants only the best public relations officers."[75]

Despite the elitist aspirations and pompous declarations of the 1950s,
IPRA did not succeed in establishing a clear role for itself. Membership
worldwide was low though it rose to "over 400" in 1976 and "over
1,000" in 1995, but subsequently dropped to 855 in 1997 and 716 in
1998 following a severe financial crisis.[76] Its fortunes have revived
slightly recently and membership in 2002 stood at around 900.

DESIGN AND PROMOTION
FOR BRITISH BUSINESS

According to John Grierson, a major stimulus to the growth of the
design industry was Britain's "dismal showing in the Great Exhibition
at Barcelona at the beginning of the thirties."[77] The Society of Industrial Artists (SIA) was established between 1929 and 1930 by Milner
Gray, a designer recognised as "a founding father of the design profession."[78] Gray established the first design group with Charles and Henry
Bassett. The Bassett-Gray group included a number of freelance artists
(including Graham Sutherland)[79] for whom Grey acted as a go-between
with potential clients, who were mostly advertising agencies.[80] Arthur
Cain, Editor of *Public Relations* in 1955, saw the role of Gray's consultancy as key in the development of design, when he remarked on the
similarities between design and public relations:

> There is much in common between the formation of the Society of
> Industrial Artists and the IPR. ... Design in 1930, like public relations
> today, was a somewhat intangible idea that was not properly understood
> by industry or by the nation at large. Thanks in no small part to the

---

[75]Ibid. pp. 10–12.

[76]Black, S. & Murdoch, T., p. 36; Black, S. Preface. In Black, S. & Murdoch, T. (eds.).
International Public Relations Membership directory and service guide 1997–98,
p. 250; *International Public Relations Membership* directory and service guide 1998–
99, p. 221.

[77]Grierson, J. A review of reviews: notes on a pre-war chapter in British propaganda.
Grierson Archive, University of Stirling G6: 33: 14, p. 1.

[78]Hollis, R. (1997, 6 October). Milner Gray: the grandest old man of British design.
The Guardian.

[79]Blake, A. (1984). *Misha Black.* London: The Design Council, p. 19.

[80]Hollis, R.

efforts of the SIA, design has come to be accepted as an essential part of our modern way of life.[81]

Gray took on Misha Black in 1933 and they remained partners until Black's death in 1977. During the Second World War, Gray became head of an exhibition branch at the MoI, and his staff included a number of refugee designers. He was the overall designer of the exhibition "Design at Home," which opened on VE Day, 1945. Many years later, he spoke to the North West Area Group of the IPR on "Planning the Corporate Image," which was subsequently published in the Institute's journal.[82]

By the mid-1930s, Grey's partner, Misha Black, was beginning to publish his ideas about "Propaganda in three dimensions" and during the war he, too, worked for the MoI as a principal exhibitions officer.[83] In an address to the Architectural Association he declared that, in designing exhibitions: "The approach to the problem is very different from that which normally faces the architect. The primary questions the exhibition designer asks himself must be: what is the psychological effect I wish to create, what is the story I wish to tell, what is the best way of getting it across to the section of the public which I have been commissioned to influence?"[84]

Black was a modernist who became one of Britain's most outstanding postwar industrial designers and was extremely influential, contributing to the Council for Industrial Design and to the development of design education in the context of the popular culture revolution in 1960s art schools. He contributed extensively to the professionalisation of design, wrote the first constitution of the SIA, organised an international body of industrial designers, and was awarded many accolades for his work, including an OBE (1945), an honorary doctorate (1968), a knighthood (1972), and an appointment as Professor Emeritus at the Royal Society of Arts (1975).[85] Black envisaged a management level of university-educated designers who:

> Would not expect to become professional artists or designers; they would be prepared to work as managers and organisers, as entrepreneurs and civil servants . . . not dedicated to canalisation of their talents and under-

---

[81] The development of the industry. *Public Relations*, 8 (1) 1955, p. 2.
[82] Gray, M. (1968). Planning the corporate image. *Public Relations*, 20 (4), pp. 2–4.
[83] Blake, A., p. 21.
[84] Ibid.
[85] Ibid. p. 7.

standing within the confines of specialisation but able to bring an artist's insight and sensitivity to focus on problems of human relations and the human environment.[86]

The Council for Industrial Design (COID) was set up in 1945 as a grant-aided advisory body funded by the Board of Trade to improve the standard of design of British manufacturers, with a view to helping them to prepare for greater competition and the end of the seller's market. According to its deputy director, Paul Reilly, in an article published in *Public Relations* in 1955, the COID had to deal with a degree of criticism, partly because many business people were not aware of the benefits of design. Reilly indicated overlaps between public relations and design when he commented that the COID:

> Has invariably treated its job as one of public relations, whether the relations were to be established with industry, with the distributors, with the public, or with all three at the same time. . . . The Information Division . . . can succeed in its propaganda only if it works with and through other groups and organisations that in turn reach important members of the public. . . . The Council of Industrial Design will remain an advisory, propaganda organisation at the service of British industry and the British public. Improving design must always be a public relations job.[87]

It is interesting that as late as 1955 the concepts of *public relations* and *propaganda* were still being used interchangeably and apparently unproblematically in the IPR journal.

Key postwar exhibitions that entered the public consciousness included the "British Army Exhibition" (1945), "Britain Can Make It" (1946), "Festival of Britain" (1951), and the Brussels Universal and International Exhibition (1958) about which an article in *Public Relations* noted, "the 53 countries exhibiting will be out to show the work, culture and achievements of each country."[88]

In 1955, the COID opened its own design centre in Haymarket, London and Joyce Blow, Assistant Press Officer to COID and member of the IPR, was involved in the launch.[89] By the early 1960s, COID was lobbying for the inclusion of design in management education curric-

---

[86] Ibid.

[87] Reilly, P. (1955). Ten years of public relations for good design. *Public Relations, 7* (3), p. 3.

[88] Black, S. (1956). Belgium at home to the world. *Public Relations 9* (1), pp. 21–4.

[89] Blow, J. (1956). Promoting the design centre: a case history. *Public Relations 9* (1), pp. 5–19.

ula.[90] Because Misha Black was the older brother of Sam Black, a very active member of both the IPR from the 1950s and the IPRA from the 1970s, it is interesting to speculate on whether they shared ideas about the professionalisation processes of public relations and industrial design. There was clearly some cross-over, because Misha made at least one presentation to the IPR in the 1950s on exhibitions and published an article in *Public Relations*,[91] and Sam was the author of an article in *Public Relations* in which he argued that London needed a new exhibition centre.[92]

POSTWAR POLITICAL COMMUNICATION

According to Wring, on whose account I depend, the launch of television broadcasting in the 1950s led to a host of new advertising possibilities. The 1945 Labour election victory spurred the Conservatives to undergo a major transformation in terms of their publicity and promotion and they employed the advertising and public relations agency Colman, Prentice, and Varley. In 1948 they also set up the Public Opinion Research Department, which was the first attempt by a British political party to incorporate polling methods into electoral strategy. Partly because of an inherent ideological resistance to engagement with advertising and public relations companies, Labour focused its efforts more on the development of Party Election Broadcasts (PEBs). In the 1960s Prime Minister Harold Wilson built links between Labour and sympathetic advertising and PR professionals such as Freddie Lyons under the chairmanship of David Kingsley. Prime Minister Thatcher's immensely successful collaboration with Saatchi and Saatchi has been well documented and, ultimately, successive election defeats forced Labour to respond and revise its approach during the 1980s and 1990s under Neil Kinnock, John Smith, and Tony Blair.

Although politicians of both sides have criticised increasing "hype" in the political arena on the basis that it degrades political debate, both the main parties in Britain now depend upon public relations and

---

[90]Letter from Oppenheim, Sir D. Chair COID to Drogheda, Lord (1963, 2 September). University of Warwick CBI Archive MSS. 200/F/3/02/5/39.

[91]Black, M. (1952). The influence of the South Bank and Battersea on public taste. *Public Relations* 4 (4), pp. 9–14.

[92]Black, S. (1959). London needs a new exhibition centre. *Public Relations*, 12 (1), pp. 21–4.

marketing specialists. Each generation has identified a particular turning point in terms of the application of new techniques or technology and it is now unimaginable that any party would not afford the best it could in terms of promotional advice to advance its interests.

NATIONALISATION VERSUS DENATIONALISATION

The role of the state in economic planning was much debated after the Second World War. Opposing views regarding the appropriate extent of government intervention and ownership and policies of nationalisation and privatisation (denationalisation) created opportunities for public relations practitioners to step in as advocates on behalf of business in response to government policy.

Britain has traditionally had less state ownership than other European countries but owned specialised industries such as the Royal Dockyards, which built and repaired warships.[93] Wars in 1914 and 1939 required major economic transformation and resulted in state ownership and management.

It was primarily the Labour Party, together with the Trades Union Congress (TUC), that propounded the concept of public ownership throughout the 1930s and made it a central part of its 1945 party manifesto *Let Us Face the Future,* for which Labour received the electorate's mandate with a landslide victory. Nationalisation was believed to be a way of achieving economies of scale and reducing costs for the consumer through a central planning model. Gourvish argued that nationalisation was in part inspired by scientific management.[94] The ideological underpinnings of nationalisation (public ownership based on principles of fairness and equity enshrined in Clause 4 of Labour's Constitution 1918–1996) and antinationalisation (free enterprise based on principles of efficiency through competition) were sometimes linked to international politics and the ideological conflict of the Cold War.

On election, Labour swiftly nationalised the Bank of England, coal, railways, road haulage, electricity, and civil aviation. Subsequent nationalisations were to include gas and, more contentiously, iron and steel.

[93] Ashworth, W. (1991). *The state in business: 1945 to the mid 1960s.* London: Macmillan, p. 1.

[94] Gourvish, T. (1991). The rise (and fall?) of state-owned enterprise. In Gourvish, T. & O'Day, A. (eds.). *Britain since 1945.* London: Macmillan, p. 111.

The threat of nationalisation aroused a response from private enterprise in the form of special interest organisations that could lobby on their behalf. Some of these organisations were active long before the end of the Second World War, such as the Economic League, established in 1919, the Chamber of Shipping, which set up its press department in 1942, and the National Council of the Road Haulage Association, which set up a "Fighting Fund" for public relations to keep the road haulage industry in private hands postwar on 28 June 1945.[95] Other organisations involved in campaigns of antinationalisation included the Council of Retail Distributors, the Institute of Directors, and the Federation of British Industry (FBI—from 1965 known as the Confederation of British Industry [CBI]). The latter organisation had been formed in 1916, and from 1918 it had a promotion and information directorate that was responsible for press relations, publicity, exhibitions, and the production of the *FBI Review* and other publications.[96] The FBI had a wide remit, including economic affairs, consumer protection, industrial research, overseas trade policy, taxation, technical cooperation, industrial art, and export promotion policy. In 1940 it revived the idea of a body like the EMB that could strengthen "British industrial and commercial propaganda in overseas markets . . . not only for the duration of the war but as a permanent institution."[97]

One of the most well-known and publicity conscious of campaigning bodies was the organisation Aims of Industry, established in 1942 to protect free enterprise and oppose nationalisation and "corporate socialism." It was conceived by Lord Perry, Chairman of the Ford Motor Company in Britain, who was the prewar boss of Maurice Buckmaster (President of the IPR 1955–1956). In addition to Ford, Aims' founders included English Electric, the Austin Motor Company, the Rank Organisation, Firestone Tyres, Bristol Aircraft, and MacDougall's Flour.[98] Early recruits to the management team were Alfred Williams, former advertising man at Selfridges, and Gittoes Davies, a former deputy editor of

---

[95] Rogow, A. A. (1952, Summer). The public relations program of the Labor government and British industry. *Public Opinion Quarterly,* p. 221.

[96] Crookham, A., Wilcox, M., Woodland, C., & Storey, R. (1997). *The confederation of British industry and predecessor archives.* Coventry: University of Warwick Occasional Publications No. 26, MSS.200/F/3/I.

[97] Memorandum on industrial propaganda and publicity (1940, 15 August). CBI Archive MSS.200/F/3/I/1/1.

[98] Kisch, R. (1964). *The private life of public relations.* London: MacGibbon & Kee, p. 28.

the *Sunday Graphic.* The former Director of the Road Haulage Association, Roger Sewell, became the Director of Aims of Industry in 1947.[99]

According to Kisch, Aims of Industry operated a covert strategy of networking and high-level contacts in building support for its cause:

> The old boy network, based on university and public school, social, political and professional affiliations, performed invaluable connecting services by linking individuals of varying degrees of weight and influence in the shaping of public affairs. . . . Politicians and perspicacious advertising men mixed with some of the shrewder industrialists. . . . Major attention was paid [by Aims of Industry] to the development of "selective propaganda." . . . The whispering campaign technique was a speciality of the organisation. . . . The organisation of specialist circles for feeding and distributing news and information . . . press campaigns supported by feeding selected writers and journalists with carefully chosen material. . . . The cultivation, socially, of a wide circle of journalists, publicists, advertising executives and other professional PR influences was equally an essential part of the mechanics.[100]

Aims' techniques had similarities to those adopted by black propagandists in the Second World War. It was not above using "front organisation" tactics such as the material attacking the Labour Party, which "purport[ed] to come from a trade union organisation called 'Workers Forum.'"[101] Kisch's interpretation was supported by Sampson's analysis of Britain in the 1960s, which identified an important difference, that of class, in terms of public relations practice between Britain and the United States:

> Britain has [strong] traditional social networks and communications—the network of schools, universities, clubs, families, or parliament—which public relations persuaders come up against. But this does not necessarily make PR less effective: by operating through clubs, school ties and old boy nets it and does take over traditional networks, and public relations is a lucrative field for the old boy net and the public school proletariat.[102]

Aims' antinationalisation clients included meat and cement industries, but its most publicised success was the prevention of the proposed

---

[99] *Aims of industry* 40th anniversary publication [undated, presumed 1982].

[100] Kisch, R., pp. 29–33.

[101] Wilson, H. H. (1951). Techniques of pressure—anti-nationalization propaganda in Britain. *Public Opinion Quarterly, 15*, p. 232.

[102] Sampson, A. (1969). *The anatomy of Britain.* London: Book Club Associates, p. 640.

nationalisation of the sugar industry in 1947, which largely threatened the company Tate and Lyle. Sewell recruited Ray Hudson to take charge of media relations and Tim Traverse Healy (President of the IPR, 1967–1968) to organise meetings, speakers, and "other forms of direct public relations."[103] There were many elements to the sugar campaign, including the creation of a cartoon character, "Mr. Cube," who appeared on all packets of sugar, alongside captions such as "Tate not State" and "Keeping the 'S' out of State." "Mr. Cube" was primarily used to target consumers (primarily housewives but also retailers, employees, and children) and received a good deal of publicity, generating high levels of awareness, according to research conducted by Aims. Other techniques included educational material for schools, lectures, and speeches, a film in which Richard Dimbleby interviewed Tate and Lyle employees on their reactions to proposed nationalisation, and a sugar consumers' petition signed by 1 million consumers.[104]

In theory, Aims was an educational, apolitical, and nonprofit organisation and had some success in portraying itself in this way. *Public Relations,* for example, described Aims as "a Public Relations Organisation which is maintained by the subscriptions of firms, big and small, throughout the country. It is non-profit-making, has no connexion with any political party, and exists to interpret the part played by industry in our National life."[105] In practice, Aims articulated political ideology and, according to one commentator, "It is rather difficult in many areas to distinguish between Aims of Industry and the activities of the Conservative Party."[106] Traverse Healy described Aims as "a sort of gentlemen's Economic League,"[107] but also admitted, "They were pro-free enterprise, which basically meant anti-nationalisation and therefore anti-Labour Party. . . . I don't think it was necessarily what they were saying were lies, but it was certainly slanted to one point of view. . . . I don't think they were interested in any dialogue, so they were probably just telling the truth as they saw it."[108]

Aims was not the only organisation operating on behalf of business, others being the Economic League (which concentrated on direct contact with factory workers) and the Institute of Directors, which was

---

[103] *Aims of industry,* 40th anniversary publication [undated, presumed 1982], p. 11.
[104] Wilson, H. H., p. 238.
[105] Items of news. *Public Relations,* 1 (2) 1948, p. 12.
[106] Wilson, H. H., p. 232.
[107] Interview. 25 June 1991.
[108] Interview. 13 September 1995.

described by a critical merchant banker, Lionel Fraser, as a "colossus of a Director's trade union—a caucus of Right-wing businessmen—for the protection of directors as a class."[109] There was also a broad free enterprise campaign sponsored by the Institute of Directors in the summer of 1951 that aimed to "put before the people what free enterprise represents."[110]

Although the Labour government had a clear mandate for nationalisation, the policy threatened the established order. In response, opportunities arose for paid persuaders on behalf of private enterprise. As Traverse Healy explained:

> Industry found itself being drawn more and more into the political arena. There were moves to retain a number of the wartime controls, a group of industries were listed for nationalisation. . . . When [an] organisation came to realise that it was better to present their point of view without waiting for the criticism, and that such a job is a skilled job involving imagination and initiative, then frequently a public relations man was appointed or a consultant retained.[111]

The eminent Trevor Powell, for many years Public Relations Manager for Shell, argued more broadly that any company's survival depended on social legitimacy and that this in turn depended on successful persuasion that business was good for society:

> In our own time the need has arisen for us to ensure that our achievements, aims, policies are properly represented to the public and—what is equally important though less often realised—to keep ourselves properly informed about the public's various attitudes towards ourselves. . . . Some industries realised this necessity more quickly than others; in certain cases it has taken the threat of nationalisation or the competition for recruitment to bring about this realisation. . . . The sudden awareness of the need of public relations in industry is one expression only of a very important trend—the awareness in all great industrial organisations of the vast responsibilities and influence they have in the world today.[112]

Evidence of the growing alliance between public relations and business is further demonstrated by the following passage from an article in *Public Relations:*

---

[109] Sampson, A., p. 566.

[110] Editorial *Director,* July 1951, p. 50.

[111] Traverse Healy, T. (1953). Public relations consultancy: what it is and how it works. *Public Relations,* 5 (4), p. 58.

[112] Powell, T. (1953). Public relations in industry. *Public Relations,* 5 (4), pp. 42–3.

Business in this country has been shaken by the political assaults upon it in recent years. Its defence in public debate has generally been poor, not for lack of a case, but for the lack of skilled briefing and speakers. Those who saw something sinister in "big business" won legislative victories for a policy of nationalisation, and psychological victories in the mind of the electorate.[113]

Industrialists "who felt the hot breath of nationalisation on their necks" donated substantial sums to the cause of remodeling the Conservative Party after 1946.[114] Its new chairman, the Earl of Woolton, was assisted by a future IPR president, Colin Mann, who helped set up an organisation of the area publicity officers, as well as advising the Association of Independent Unionist Peers on publicity.[115] Although the Labour Party was strongly criticised for its use of government information officers for political causes by newspapers such as *The Daily Mail* and *The Daily Express*,[116] the party did not succeed in convincing the electorate of the benefits of nationalisation, which was generally perceived as failing to deliver promised economic benefits.[117] On regaining power in 1951 the Conservatives denationalised the steel industry and parts of the road haulage industry and legislated successfully against restrictive practices, although they did not specifically promote competition. The Labour Party returned to power in 1964 and took a much more interventionist approach, renationalising parts of shipbuilding, iron, and steel, and giving substantial financial assistance to these and other industries to improve British economic performance in the face of growing competition within Europe. This forced even the Conservative government in 1970 to intervene and nationalise failing industries, a policy that was continued by the following Labour administration. The Thatcher era reversed this trend with a radical free-market approach marked by substantial privatisation of major nationalised industries, including gas, water, electricity, British Airways, and telecommunications. Orchestrating the sale of these industries required a mass communication effort by the GIS and the establishment of specialised public

---

[113] Miller, H. (1960). A private view of public relations. *Public Relations*, 13 (1), p. 37.

[114] Hodgson, G. (1963). The steel debates. In Sissons, M. & French, P. (eds.). *Age of austerity*. London: Hodder and Stoughton, p. 314.

[115] Eden-Green, A. (1963). Profile of Colin Mann: president elect. *Public Relations*, 16 (1), p. 28.

[116] Rogow, A. R., pp. 202–3.

[117] Jenkins, R., p. 246.

relations companies to establish identities, promote services, and maintain customer, shareholder, and employee loyalty.

A number of public relations practitioners involved with the IPR were active in the antinationalisation campaigns. Mention has already been made of Traverse Healy's employment by Aims of Industry. A number of organisations that joined the IPR in 1948 were under threat of nationalisation, or could have perceived themselves to be so, for example, the British Medical Association, British Overseas Airways Corporation, the British Rayon Federation, the British Waterworks Association, the British Export Trade Research Organisation, the Champion Sparking Plug Co., the Copper Development Association, the Dunlop Rubber Co., Petrocarbon Ltd. and Petrochemical Ltd., the Power-Gas Corporation, Radiation Ltd., the Railway Executive, the Road Haulage Association, the Tea Bureau, and the Wholesale Textile Association.[118] Some of these contributed articles to *Public Relations* about their work. For example, F. Murray Milne, PRO of the Wholesale Textile Association (WTA), stated that its public relations aims were "to educate Government departments, manufacturers, retailers and consumers of textile goods of both a need for, and the economic advantages of a system of distribution though wholesalers."[119] The range of public relations activities included "a propaganda fund which is sustained by voluntary contributions from members."[120] This was utilised in a campaign against the government's plans to cut the clothing ration, which the WTA challenged with statistics showing that there were substantial accumulated stocks of textiles. According to Murray Milne, "The WTA took the British Press into its confidence and asked for help. It got it in generous measure. . . . Instead of reducing the ration the Government finally issued a bonus of 12 coupons. . . . The case was good, the cause was just, the story well told. The trade, the Press, the consumer benefited. Surely good Public Relations!"[121]

One of the founding members and a prominent figure in the institute was Leslie Hardern, a PRO of the Gas, Light, and Coke Co., which became the North Thames Gas Board after nationalisation by the Gas Act in 1948. He explained the rationale for his employer thus: "In this country, the word monopoly has aroused suspicion and hostility for hundreds of years. Any industry, business or public utility which

[118]Firms and organisations represented. *Public Relations,* 1 (1) 1948, pp. 16–17.
[119]Murray Milne, F., p. 6.
[120]Ibid.
[121]Ibid.

enjoys, or appears to enjoy, monopoly conditions has therefore to take special steps to disarm this hostility, or better still to prevent it from forming."[122]

John Pringle, PRO for the British Medical Association (BMA), was another founding member who worked in a controversial area. By the time the IPR had been established in 1948, politicised doctors, led by the BMA's secretary Sir Charles Hill (the BBC's much trusted radio Doctor), had whipped up opposition to the white paper proposing details of the NHS to such an extent that "it was feared that the whole scheme might be sabotaged."[123] Aneurin Bevan was able to exploit divisions within the medical profession, to negotiate with some important representatives such as the Royal College of Physicians, and to appeal directly to general practitioners in such as way as to outflank the BMA General Council. The root of opposition to Bevan was the medical profession's sensitivity to:

> Any change that might in some way intrude upon the doctor–patient relationship, an emotional concept which no doctor could quite define but which was held to be in jeopardy the minute the State appeared upon the threshold of the surgery. A Labour government, particularly a Labour government which included Bevan in its Cabinet, not surprisingly exacerbated the traditional fears of a predominantly middle-class professional group.[124]

Pringle's contribution to the IPR journal shortly after the clash with Bevan makes interesting reading, especially where he claimed, "The setting up of a PR Department was a considered act of policy undertaken before the war. In other words the Department was in existence before Mr Bevan became active or prominent."[125] Pringle was appointed to the post in June 1946 and quickly established an information department supervised by a librarian to answer press queries. The previous incumbent had been A. W. Haslett, who was appointed PRO in 1938 and resigned in 1946 so that he could be "free to embark on adventures of his own."[126] Pringle noted the resistance of some doctors to the concept of public relations and explained that part of his job consisted "in trying

---

[122]Hardern, L. (1949). Work under monopoly conditions. *Public Relations, 1* (3), p. 11.

[123]Jenkins, R., p. 237.

[124]Ibid. p. 425

[125]Pringle, J. (1949). Working for 60,000 employees. *Public Relations, 2* (2), p. 15.

[126]BMA Archive Tavistock House, London [unnumbered, undated material].

to persuade the more conservative members of the profession that carefully chosen publicity on the right subjects can be to their advantage."[127] As far as external perceptions were concerned, he explained, "I have made it my job to try and break down the barriers of suspicion between the medical profession and the organs of publicity, particularly the Press. This tradition of distrust goes back a long way. The Press has in the past found doctors either unco-operative or unintelligible, or both. Doctors tend to find the Press inaccurate or sensational or both."[128]

The NHS stimulated the growth of public relations. On establishment in 1948, the *Hospital and Social Service Journal* declared in a way that was reminiscent of debates in *Public Administration* in the 1920s that:

> Public relations throughout the services will be all-important. Specialised technical skills will be required to organise and direct this at some levels, but it must not be forgotten that every officer coming into contact with the public, in whatever rank or grade he serves, must also regard himself as a public relations officer and act as if the whole system would be judged by his attitude and conduct—as indeed it will be by many persons.[129]

State economic and welfare interventions met with some resistance and required opinion management. Both state and capital began to recognise the importance of public opinion in the postwar world, not only within Britain, but in the former Empire, where new challenges presented themselves.

COLONIAL ASSOCIATIONS

The growth of public relations beyond Britain was, in some cases, stimulated by the process of decolonisation. Such processes illustrate clearly the difficulty in distinguishing between public relations, propaganda, intelligence, and psychological operations. For example, in Malaya there was a well-documented campaign to win over Malayan-Chinese to the British government's side against the communists, following the resumption of British rule at the end of the Second World War. News management by the Malayan government sought to control informa-

---

[127] Pringle, J., p. 13.
[128] Ibid. p. 15.
[129] Editorial. *The Hospital and Social Service Journal* (Vol. LVIII No. 2940) 1948, p. 5.

tion flow, to publicise the promise of independence in 1957, and to support counter-insurgency psychological warfare, utilising a variety of tactics: leaflets, voice aircraft (an idea subsequently utilised by the Americans in Vietnam), and black propaganda newspapers.[130] The Malayan Department of Publicity and Printing was established in 1945 and remained an important element, once Malaysia had achieved independence in developing information campaigns to support government policy initiatives, particularly in the field of development.[131] Within Britain, the Foreign Office Information Research Department (IRD) operated from 1947 to 1977 as a broadly based propaganda and psychological warfare operation and played an active role in former colonial countries including Malaysia, Kenya, Israel, and Cyprus.[132]

One IPR member involved in public relations in Malaysia was Major Alan Simpson MBE, FJI, FIPR, PRO for Northern Command who, in 1954, toured Malaya visiting the 1st Battalion of the East Yorkshire Regiment at Kluang and the 1st Battalion of the West Yorkshire Regiment at Ipoh. Simpson carried goodwill messages from parents and local dignitaries, wrote articles for the Malayan and British press, and also wrote to a number of parents. Of his trip he concluded, "Those young soldiers in Malaya, who bash their way through the jungle, who mix easily with Aborigines and Malays, with Tamils and Chinese, who uphold the good name of Britain in a distant land, are not only Britain's best ambassadors, but the Army's best public relations men."[133] This presents a very different view from that which subsequently emerged about the Malayan campaign of poor morale, massacres of local populations (such as that by the Scots Guards), and even attacks by men on their officers.

Decolonisation did not solely affect the government, as the following passage, from an interview with a practitioner who worked for Unilever in Africa, makes clear:

---

[130]Carruthers, S. L. (1995). *Winning hearts and minds.* Leicester: Leicester University Press, p. 91.

[131]Van Leuven, J. K. (1996). Public relations in South East Asia: from nation building campaigns to regional interdependence. In Culbertson, H. M. & Chen, N. (eds.). *International public relations: a comparative analysis.* Mahwah, New Jersey: Lawrence Erlbaum Associates, p. 209; Van Leuven, J. K. & Pratt, C. B. (1996). Public relations' role: realities in Asia and in Africa south of the Sahara. In Culbertson, H. M. & Chen, N. (eds.), pp. 95–7.

[132]Carruthers, S. L. (1995). *Winning hearts and minds.* Leicester: Leicester University Press.

[133]Simpson, A. (1954). Taking army public relations across the world! *Public Relations, 6* (4), p. 25.

> The Board realised that in post-war black Africa there was going to be a big resurgence of political agitation working for independence from the British Commonwealth. . . . [It was therefore] proposed that we should practise public relations . . . anticipating where African desires were going to lead and what sort of attitudes they were going to formulate. . . . It was a question of impressing people with the idea that we were a good thing for them and their country. Public relations was very restricted because the press was very underdeveloped—radio was in its infancy and television didn't exist. . . . A lot had to be done by word of mouth—our managers mixing with the local community. We ran the first strip cartoon . . . in an African paper, and through it the African reader would learn what capital was, what profit was, what employment was, what training was and all those basic things.[134]

Thus, Unilever reacted to decolonisation by introducing public relations, which began by developing personal relationships in the community to win friends and influence people. The campaign aimed to counteract any latent alienation and preserve company interests in the postcolonial context. Another Unilever employee reiterated the fundamental point of interest more strongly:

> During the war it became clear that our public relations policy must be considered in the light of the need for industry to have regard to the social consequences of its actions. The capitalist system, private enterprise, the profit motive would all be placed on trial and big business, just because it was big, would be suspect in the eyes of many. In many of the countries where we operated, we should meet a growing spirit of nationalism, and if we met it in the wrong way, we would quickly find ourselves in the "foreign devils" class.[135]

Thus, the function of public relations can be seen in this context to have engaged in helping to shore up precolonial economic structures.

Another practitioner with African experience was based in Kenya on behalf of the British Army's East African Command prior to the Mau Mau emergency. He described the role of public relations as one that smoothed over social relationships between different classes and races:

> My main work there was with the *East African Standard* . . . the English colonial papers were like the English provincial papers and they could cause a good deal of trouble—there was a lot of work to be done between

---

[134] Interview. 26 March 1997.

[135] McCrory, P. (1960). Protecting, maintaining and developing a good reputation. *Public Relations 12 (3)*, pp. 20–4.

the settlers and the armed forces who were not always on the most friendly terms because here were these chaps coming out to our favourite land—the Happy Valley crowd. So one spent a lot of time getting people together. The proprietor of the *East African Standard* and a number of Swahili papers was a chap called Eric Anderson, who was a very, very, nice man so of course I got to know him and then one would have him to dinner with the General and that sort of thing, and gradually begin to build relationships, which is what it's all about. . . . If you're a good PRO . . . you should be on Christian name terms not only with the editor but also the proprietor and although it's always said the editor's independent of the proprietor that's not, as you know, wholly true.[136]

The case of Kenya, which I have explored elsewhere, shows that decolonisation stimulated British government propaganda and public relations activities (the government had two sections operating in the field under those separate titles) and that, as Kenya moved from colonialism to independence, substantial public relations was required to attract increased international capital to the country as well as to forge its new identity internally as well as externally.[137]

The colonial experience was written about in *Public Relations*. For example, in 1951 there was an article by a Brigadier Johnson on the qualities required for a PRO "in the Colonies." The skills emphasised were language skills, diplomacy, the ability to create media for communication, and the following:

The sort of intellectual and social background which will enable him to work in a very small community of well educated and overworked officials. . . . The sort of man who can discuss high policy with the Governor over dinner and the next day get down to the composing room of a newspaper in his shirt sleeves and talk to the printer as one old hand to another . . . physically tough . . . .in a climate which is perhaps more trying to the human frame and the human temper than even our own.[138]

The government's role was to: "Guide and tutor the press . . . foster the growth of trade unions . . . guide the co-operative societies . . . so that they [the Colonies] may grow into self reliant and independent organi-

[136]Interview. 14 August 1996.
[137]L'Etang, J. & Muruli, G. (2004). Public relations, decolonisation and democracy: the case of Kenya. In Tilson, D. J. (ed.). *Toward the common good: perspectives in international public relations*. Boston: Pearson, pp. 215–38.
[138]Johnson, B. (1951). You cannot get such men. *Public Relations*, 4 (1), p. 9.

sations for securing better conditions and not into subversive political machines."[139]

In contrast to the colonial press, Johnson heavily criticised indigenous media as "wild . . . editorially and technically absurd and inefficient . . . [and sometimes exhibiting] a virulence and a degree of scurrility that passes belief. . . . [One leader] denounced something or other as 'An attempt to strangle neck and crop the rising tide of nationalism.'"[140] Thus, the nationalist position was viewed as irresponsible and without legitimacy, and public relations was mobilised to act on behalf of the forces of imperialism.

Harking back to earlier days, Tom Fife-Clark (IPR president, 1958–1959, and Controller of COID) reiterated a story told to him by Stephen Tallents about Rudyard Kipling, of whom Fife-Clark said, "Rudyard Kipling . . . was I suppose PRO to the British Empire."[141] Nationality was an unproblematic concept in *Public Relations* as was the assumption of the natural superiority of being White and English or British (the two terms were used interchangeably), as illustrated by the following quotation: "Prince Galitzine said it was difficult to put over public relations for Europeans in the Colonies. There was lots of publicity for the 'blacks' and 'browns' but not for the white men who were responsible for development."[142]

In 1952 the journal published a talk, "Information and the Law," given by Horace White, the Cyprus Public Information Officer at the Police Training School, Nicosia, in which policemen were urged to become expert in public affairs so that they knew the reasons for the laws they were charged with upholding. White also told them, "Next year we hope to have our own broadcasting station, giving regular programmes in Greek and Turkish and we plan to import cheap receivers so that most people will be able to afford to listen. At long last, Government will be able to speak in a voice that can be heard (it is so often drowned now by the clamour of politicians)."[143] White also described his dream that Cypriot children should regard colonial policemen with "the same bond of sympathy that exists in England between policemen and children . . . [where] the policeman has become a sort of uncle or

---

[139]Ibid. p. 11.

[140]Ibid.

[141]Planning a home publicity campaign. Address given by T. Fife-Clark, Controller Home COI. *Public Relations* 3 (3) 1951, p. 6.

[142]Riding a hobby horse. *Public Relations*, 6 (4) 1954, p. 36.

[143]White, H. (1952). Information and the law. *Public Relations*, 4 (3), p. 22.

guardian."[144] White argued that the children should be the prime target audience because "If they grow up to be frightened of, or bitter towards or even indifferent to the police then all these states of mind will be reflected in their attitude towards the government of their country."[145]

The emphasis put on personal relations seems likely to play down the substantial importance (at least to Greek-Cypriots) of the deprivation of power and autonomy necessary to achieve *enosis* (union) with mainland Greece: an aspiration of which the British administration had been aware since 1950 and that was transformed into violent action by EOKA on 1 April 1955.[146] Public relations also played a role maintaining economic links of benefit to the colonial powers, such as a Radio and Electrical Exhibition held in Uganda in 1955. The government had reduced the 22% customs duty on cheap sets, but more was needed to stimulate growth in the market and the Department of Information proposed an exhibition. As Horace White, director of information, reported, "The most encouraging feature was the interest displayed by Africans, and especially African housewives, who stood enthralled by cookers, refrigerators and electric irons while their husbands sampled electric shavers and listened to a bewildering variety of radio sets."[147]

CONCLUSION

The decade after 1945 was of considerable significance for public relations in seeing the establishment of both IPR and IPRA. The formation of professional bodies is an important stage in the natural history of a profession.

Public relations began to be entrenched into the policy-making institutions and to be a necessary accompaniment to the large-scale political and economic interventions by the state that were a feature of the postwar world. Increasing intervention and concentration of capital, as Habermas pointed out, contributed to state expansion and resulted in increased politicisation and a higher public profile for private economic

---

[144] Ibid. p. 24.

[145] Ibid.

[146] Carruthers, S., p. 194.

[147] White, H. (1955). Bringing radio and television to the East Africans. *Public Relations, 7* (4), p. 35.

units.[148] Such macrostructural changes can be seen to have enhanced opportunities for the growth of public relations.

Economic and political policies had to be justified in a postwar world in which the new Labour administration apparently offered a more egalitarian social model that was less dependent on traditional and rigid class structures and authority but consequently more dependent on skills of persuasion.

Overseas, the process of decolonisation required continual government propaganda as well as efforts by companies to protect their overseas interests and investments. Technological developments, some of which had been facilitated by wartime experimentation, led to the development of consumer products whose benefits needed to be explained to consumers. The establishment of an international airline passenger industry facilitated the growth of international markets for business and tourism. Airlines were among the first to establish public relations posts in the postwar era. Thus, public relations in the postwar world started to move away from its local government, public service roots toward a more commercial orientation.

Both government and private enterprise had a need to put across particular views to citizens and the media. At the same time, many recently demobbed ex-servicemen were seeking work. Although many employers had offered employees their prewar jobs on return from the services, this was often impractical. Some jobs had had more than one incumbent during the war and often those returning were perceived to be too old and mature for jobs they had held prewar. Public relations offered many of those returning to civilian life a job opportunity for which no qualifications were apparently required other than self-confidence, a degree of social skill, and an interest in the media. It was doubtless an attractive proposition because salaries were relatively generous, and the jobs had white-collar status.

---

[148]Habermas, J. (1989). *The structural transformation of the public sphere: an inquiry into a category of bourgeois society.* Cambridge: Polity Press, pp. 146–8.

4

The Shape of Things to Come: The Emergence of Consultancy, 1948–1969

INTRODUCTION

This chapter focuses on the development of a new and increasingly viable sector in the economy—public relations consultancies—some of which operated within advertising agencies and some independently. The growth of consultancy was important for the process of professionalisation and eventually culminated in the formation of the Public Relations Consultants' Association in 1969. The chapter begins with a discussion of the connection between jurisdiction, expertise, knowledge, and reputation as a way of framing the empirical detail. It then discusses the relationship between public relations and advertising before identifying the important early consultancies. An exploration of practitioners' perceptions of the nature of public relations services and the management practices of early consultancies follows. Finally, there is an historical review of the development of professional associations for consultancies.

KNOWLEDGE, EXPERTISE, REPUTATION, AND JURISDICTION

The development of a profession requires a knowledge base that can serve to exclude others and, specifically, "prevent other occupations from poaching parts of the market that they believe can be supplied with services based on their knowledge."[1] However, in occupations such as public relations, where abstract knowledge is "fragmentary and poorly developed [with] a weak institutional base in academia,"[2] there is a possibility that "the door is open for other occupations to encroach."[3] This alerts us to the need to take account of developments in related fields, as Abbott pointed out:

> The evolution of professions in fact results from their interrelations [which] are in turn determined by the way these groups control their knowledge and skill. There are two rather different ways of accomplishing this control. One emphasises technique *per se* and occupations using it are commonly called crafts. To control such an occupation, a group directly controls its technique. The other form of control involves distinct knowledge. Here, practical skills grow out of an abstract system of knowledge and control and the occupation is then in control of the abstraction that generates practical techniques. The techniques themselves may be delegated to other workers.[4]

Expertise was defined by Friedson as "Tasks which require either extensive training or experience or both, and, in this case, the performers are true specialists . . . expertise that is distinctly theirs and not part of the normal competence of adults in general."[5]

The possession of craft expertise and knowledge enables distinctions to be made between one occupation and another, and is the basis for enforcing market control. Discourse work is required to develop professional identities that can be communicated within the wider context of work and society. The professional project requires power broking and enforcement because "most professional expertise does not enjoy a natural scarcity and its value has to be protected and raised, first by persuading the public of the vital importance of the service and then by controlling the market for it. . . . Professional bodies are . . . institutions for educating the public and for closing the market and operating

---

[1]Macdonald, K. (1995). *The sociology of the professions.* London: Sage, p. 184.

[2]Pieczka, M. (2000). Public relations expertise deconstructed, *The business of organising identities,* Stirling: Stirling Media Research Institute, p. 3.

[3]Macdonald, K., p. 184.

[4]Abbott, A. (1988). *The system of professions: an essay on the division of expert labor.* Chicago: University of Chicago Press, p. 8.

[5]Friedson, E. (1994). *Professionalism reborn: theory, prophecy and policy.* Cambridge: Polity Press, p. 15.

'strategies of closure.'"[6] It is vital for an occupation that aspires to professional status to establish its exclusivity of service.

The emergence and growth of public relations consultancies marked a distinctive historical development in terms of professionalisation of public relations because it presumed sufficient hold on certain crafts, knowledge, and experience and a sufficiently coherent identity for business to survive, indeed thrive, in the marketplace. Such a development represents a major shift in terms of public relations' place in the British economy and signals the point at which there was a major uptake of public relations services and therefore public recognition of the practice.

PUBLIC RELATIONS AND ADVERTISING

Advertising had suffered a poor reputation since the 18th century, largely as a consequence of exaggerated and untruthful claims made about products.[7] There were many critiques from intellectuals such as Macauley, Carlyle, A. A. Milne, and C. P. Snow decrying the existence of advertising and this stream of writing eventually merged with broader critiques about the role of persuasive communication in society.[8] Advertising had also lacked a cognitive base despite attempts of educators to argue that "leaders [in advertising] had not appreciated how intimately advertising is bound up with a knowledge of the social sciences."[9] A separate occupational identity increased the chances that public relations would find social legitimacy. Nevertheless, as in America, a significant proportion of the early consultants began their careers in advertising agencies that subsequently developed public relations departments or subsidiaries. Public relations was useful to such agencies because it apparently generated free publicity and was therefore a useful selling point for advertising agencies that could offer it as an additional service.

There were some definitional problems, however. Paul Reed (British Council) exemplified confusion over the relationship between advertising and public relations when he suggested that "some of the activity

---

[6]Perkin, H. (1989). *The rise of professional society: England since 1880*. London: Routledge, p. 378.

[7]Nevett, T. R. (1982). *Advertising in Britain: a history*. London: Heinemann.

[8]Ibid.

[9]Pringle, H. W. (1933). Introduction. In *The library of advertising*. London: Butterworth & Co.

called PR today was advertising and some advertising was PR."[10] Others disagreed, such as Matthew Crosse, who argued that "PR was much more important than advertising . . . as was shown by the many PROs in industry and Government departments who were responsible for advertising as a facet of the work for their departments." He saw public relations as "a huge concept covering all kinds of relations with all kinds of publics . . . advertising was only a part of it."[11] Three years later, council member Terence Usher argued rather more clearly that "The advertising man is selling a product; our job is to show the social justification of an enterprise."[12] Forman's distinction between the two activities exemplified the aspiration to senior status and power over the client:

> PR was more professional whereas advertising was more frankly commercial . . . the PRO as a professional man, would not allow his client to call the tune, but would offer his professional advice on policy, which the client could accept or reject. The advertising man, on the other hand, usually accepted his client's views and did his best to give effect to them, even if he disagreed with them.[13]

This has considerable implications for the balance of power between the consultant and the client in the two occupations. As presented by Forman, the advertising consultant was subject to the client, who was presumed to have the knowledge, whereas the public relations consultant claimed the diagnostic skill not apparently possessed by the client.

The period under review was one in which many public relations consultants emerged from their umbrella advertising organisations to establish their own stable of clients. At the same time, others from the armed forces, the information services, and journalism were setting up opportunistically from scratch. Although there was debate about the boundaries between public relations and advertising, this did not in fact develop into a jurisdictional struggle because, on the whole, it was a mutually symbiotic and financially beneficial relationship. There was, however, a struggle over the status and legitimacy of those who had emerged from advertising and those who had set themselves up as public relations specialists in the first instance. Thus, advertising was the background context to an internal struggle within public relations

---

[10]Public relations and advertising. *Public Relations, 2* (2) 1949, p. 11.

[11]Ibid. p. 8.

[12]Usher, T. (1952). The personal approach. *Public Relations, 4* (2), pp. 8–9.

[13]Public relations and advertising. *Public Relations, 2* (2) 1949, p. 7.

over status, legitimacy, and, more specifically, authenticity and identity. Advertising influenced all consultancy practice on a long-term basis in terms of organisational structures and hierarchies, culture, language, and concepts. For example, job titles, expense accounts, and a great emphasis on creativity permeated the "independents" as much as those whose origins lay in an advertising agency. Economic expansion in the late 1950s and early 1960s stimulated the consumer industry, which in turn demanded editorial publicity to support advertising and marketing. Over half a century later, a jurisdictional debate emerged between public relations and marketing.

THE 1948 SHOW

No consideration was given to consultants as a separate category of practitioners in 1948 because so few existed. Indeed, of the 101 organisations listed as founder organisations of the IPR in 1948, only 4 were operating as consultancies: Hereward Phillips Ltd., LPE and F. C. Pritchard, Wood and Partners Ltd., which were prewar consultancies, and F. J. Lyon Ltd.[14] Freddie Lyon joined Pritchard Wood in 1952. Also listed as a founder organisation was the advertising agency Paul Derrick. LPE and Pritchard Wood had started as advertising agencies and then expanded their range of operation. Pritchard Wood's public relations department (which became the agency Infoplan) employed many influential practitioners, including Freddie Lyon, Tim Traverse Healy (who had not yet hyphenated his name at this stage), and Colin Mann (formerly of the British Council). Other advertising agencies that moved into public relations were W. S. Crawford; Foote, Cone, and Belding; Colman, Prentis, and Varley Ltd. (where Jack Beddington was a leading light and which established the public relations company Voice and Vision of which Beddington was chairman in the mid 1950s, known irreverently as "Vice and Vision"[15]); Greenlys Ltd.; Saward Baker and Co; S. H. Benson (whose postwar public relations offshoot was Current Affairs Ltd., later run by Hereward Phillips); T. D. Advertising; and J. Walter Thompson (whose public relations offshoot was called Lexingtons). Many important practitioners were associated with Voice and Vision, including

---

[14]Private correspondence 6/2/97; Firms and organisations represented. *Public Relations*, 1 (1) 1948, pp. 16–17.
[15]Interview. 13 September 1995.

the political lobbyist Sydney Wynne (Ernest Bevin's son-in-law), who originally established the agency on behalf of Jack Beddington, and the educationalist Arthur Cain[16] (whose earlier career in Special Branch ironically included a stint shadowing the British film documentarist and public relations idealist John Grierson).[17] Postwar agencies, begun as public relations specialisms, represented in IPR membership between 1949 and 1953, included R. M. Lester and Associates; Lindsay Shankland, Euan Gilchrist, and Associates (associates included Dick Paget Cooke and Tim Traverse-Healy); Johnson-Cross; Notley's (set up by Lex Hornsby, formerly of the Ministry of Labour); the D. Brook-Hart Company; and Willa A. Moojen.[18]

However, many consultancies were not, and never became, founder organisations, nor did their employees become members: A notable absentee among the roll call of founder organisations was Editorial Services. Not all practitioners joined the IPR, including a number of the prewar practitioners who evidently felt that the institute had been established by upstarts without sufficient consultation with themselves.[19] Among these were Fleetwood Pritchard, Jack Beddington (who had worked in advertising for Shell between 1927 and 1946, where he introduced a film unit and went on to head the film division at the MoI from 1940 to 1946), Claud Simmons (who ran Basil Clarke's agency Editorial Services postwar and who had formerly been Managing Director of an advertising agency called Wynford Thomas, was an early enthusiast of political lobbying, and was Director of Public Relations at the Board of Trade during the war);[20] Rawdon Smith (though he eventually did join); Freddie Lyons (who advised Prime Minister Harold Wilson and was rewarded with a knighthood); Howard Marshall (formerly of the Ministry of Food); Mike Williams-Thompson (formerly of the Ministry of Supply whose consultancy was called Sydney Barton); Michael Romaine, Colin Wintle, and Sydney Wynne; and, pre-eminent among the nonconsultants, J. H. Brebner.[21] E. Hereward Phillips' agency, Cur-

---

[16]Those who were there. *Public Relations*, 4 (1) 1951, p. 2.

[17]L'Etang, J. John Grierson and the public relations industry in Britain. *Screening the past: an international electronic journal of visual media and history*, July 1999, http://www.latrobe.edu.au/www/scregthepast; L'Etang, J. (1999, September). John Grierson: public relations idealist. *Media Education Journal*.

[18]Interview. 13 September 1995; Those who were there. *Public Relations*, 4 (1) 1951, p. 2.

[19]Interview. 9 June 1994.

[20]Interview. 30 August 1996; Private correspondence. 6 February 1997; Interview. 30 August 1996.

[21]Interview. 30 August 1996; Interview. 13 September 1995.

rent Affairs, was a subsidiary of an advertising agency called S. H. Benson, which had nearly 100 staff and whose clients included the National Farmers' Union, British Gas Council, the YMCA, the British Legion, and the "Britain Can Make It" exhibition.[22]

The first description of agency work was given in a talk "Public Relations and Advertising" by the president R. S. Forman who had recently moved from LPE.[23] His talk stimulated an important discussion during which a number of fundamental issues were aired publicly for the first time. He claimed that LPE had been the first large advertising agency to start a public relations department, that only around five agencies had such departments "working on a substantial scale," and that in some cases those departments had been formed as separate companies, identified under a different name.[24] Some other agencies had apparently appointed one or two journalists to obtain editorial publicity. According to Forman, the LPE public relations department had initially been attached to a printing subsidiary and had concentrated on internal magazines, but "within six months the department was engaging in full-scale public relations" and then became an autonomous unit.[25]

Thus, the situation in Britain was very different from that in the United States, where, concurrently, all the big advertising agencies had public relations departments and some were beginning to concentrate almost entirely on public relations with advertising a minority interest. However, there is no doubt that advertising agencies financed the growth of some public relations consultancies. For example, one third of the equity of Alan Campbell-Johnson's first agency, Johnson-Crosse (founded in 1946) was provided by a big advertising agency, Macy and Ferguson. Campbell-Johnson explained that Macy thought that public relations and advertising were separate activities: "related first cousins but not to be tied to the point of owning the other."[26] Campbell-Johnson's agency remained ostensibly independent, although in reality much of his work came from Hill and Knowlton in the United States after he had met John Hill in 1952 and begun a close personal friendship that lasted 25 years.[27] He briefly partnered Tom J. Swarbrick (ex-*Daily Telegraph*), but once they parted company he settled down with his long-term colleagues (Ian Braby, John Foley, Harry Balden, and Trevor

---

[22] Interview. 13 September 1995.

[23] Public relations and advertising. *Public Relations*, 2 (2) 1949, p. 7.

[24] Ibid.

[25] Ibid.

[26] Interview. 20 March 1994.

[27] Ibid.

Russell Cobb), working on a few major accounts including Esso, Procter and Gamble, Gillette, and Coca Cola.[28]

According to Forman, there was no rivalry between agencies and their in-house counterparts and there were clear benefits in hiring an agency where "a team of men and women, each expert in a particular field," contrasted with "one harassed PRO who . . . had to be a Jack-of-all-trades."[29] In discussion, Geoffrey Young (known popularly as "Mr. Selfridge" because he was apparently such an enthusiastic advocate of his employer)[30] challenged this view on the grounds that the "[s]taff man . . . was immersed in the affairs of his organisation: they were his life, and he . . . therefore, gave a better return for his salary. The agency man, on the other hand, inevitably regarded a client as 'just another account.' . . . [If] PR work [was] taken over by agencies . . . that would be a bad thing for PR."[31] Matthew Crosse also raised the issue of standards and argued that these were not consistent in agencies (an issue that has lasted to the present day), suggesting that this threatened the agency system because, if "some agencies did PR well, many were doing it badly and getting it a bad name: there was a danger that clients, once bitten by such an agency, would drop PR altogether."[32]

Already, there was a division of opinion as to whether consultants should be freestanding businesses or attached to an advertising agency. According to Forman, "some people argu[e] that association with an agency must prejudice the newspapers against a PR department, others believe that it must help," though in his opinion the acid test for newspapers was newsworthiness and if material met this criterion, then "it did not matter to the newspapers where it came from."[33] However, he was quick to point out that he was careful never to use the advertising side of the company "in an attempt to influence newspapers."[34] He thought that agencies had some advantages in that, if they had a good reputation and were well known to the press, then material that came on their headed paper "would be recognised and regarded as responsible."[35] In other words, public relations consultancies with a

---

[28] Ibid.
[29] Ibid.
[30] Interview. 20 August 1995.
[31] Public relations and advertising. *Public Relations,* 2 (2) 1949, p. 8.
[32] Ibid.
[33] Ibid.
[34] Ibid.
[35] Ibid.

good reputation could be trusted by journalists to be guardians of the truth.

Even at this stage another long-running issue had already emerged: that of the level of fees that could be charged to clients. It was feared that "there was a lot of profit in advertising but little from PR."[36] Despite this, Forman suggested that "all large advertising agencies [should] start a PR department," a recommendation that was queried by Crosse, who thought it was a surprising line for Forman to take, "when, on his own admission, they [the advertisers] did not understand PR."[37]

THE ROLE AND WORKINGS OF CONSULTANCY

It was not until 1953 that there was a major discussion within the institute about the role of consultancy. This took place at the annual conference held in Hastings, at which Tim Traverse-Healy (one of the postwar generation who had previously worked for Ewen Gilchrist's agency and Aims of Industry) from Pritchard, Wood, and Partners gave a presentation on "Public Relations Consultancy: What Is It and How It Works."[38] The published report of the conference session is unique in the detail it gives about consultancy practice in that era. At the outset of his talk, Traverse-Healy presented a progressivist account in his identification of the development of consultancy as a step in professionalisation: "the growth of consultancy in the field of public relations reveals a pattern of development similar to that which has long ago taken place in the realms of medicine and the law—and more recently in engineering and accountancy."[39] According to Traverse-Healy, there had only been a few "independent advisers"[40] between the wars and the term *public relations counsel* had first appeared in the advertising directory in May 1939 with three entries, and only one further addition by 1947.[41] By 1953, there were 23 entries and 67 members of the institute

---

[36] Ibid.

[37] Ibid.

[38] Traverse-Healy, T. (1953). Public relations consultancy: what it is and how it works. *Public Relations,* 5 (4), pp. 57–67.

[39] Ibid. p. 57.

[40] Ibid.

[41] Ibid.

were "either independent consultants or on the staffs of consultancy organisations" or in the public relations departments of an advertising agency.[42]

Traverse-Healy saw consistency of approach and standards as a major issue. Within the category of independent consultants, he identified:

> the man of wide experience who has won a reputation based on success in solving public relations problems and whose work is now for the most part of an advisory nature . . . there are very few of these . . . those who carry out public relations campaigns . . . [and] a few who whilst claiming to be public relations men only concern themselves with editorial and general publicity.[43]

Within this we see a claim to the important concepts of diagnosis and treatment that require processes of inference from a cognitive base.[44] Although Traverse-Healy distinguished between those at craft level and those at professional level, this distinction could only be based on certain types of accumulated experience, seniority, and cultural capital given the absence of a cognitive base.

Traverse-Healy saw the economic potential of public relations consultancy due to the fact that, "working as a team, the firm's services are enhanced by virtue of additional experience, contacts and specialised skill."[45] However, he devoted most of his attention to the threat to public relations' future should it be placed in an inferior position to advertising because although "The problems of marketing cannot be dissociated from those of building and maintaining general goodwill . . . the prime function of advertising . . . is to assist in the selling of goods and services. . . . Public relations work requires a different attitude of mind."[46]

Consultancy functions, according to Traverse-Healy, fell into distinct, hierarchical categories. The advisory level was the most senior and rather akin to the role of a management consultant, to employ contemporary terminology: "The policy and planning of [a] public relations programme . . . or to carry out an investigation into a particular problem and submit his opinion as to its solution . . . to advise on the setting up of a public relations department . . . or to review the workings of an

---

[42] Ibid.
[43] Ibid. p. 58.
[44] Abbott, A., p. 40; Macdonald, K., p. 164.
[45] Traverse-Healy, T., p. 58.
[46] Ibid. p. 59.

existing department."[47] Traverse-Healy suggested that the advisory and executive level should advise and implement campaigns, the publicity and press relations level should concentrate on promotion, and an "ancillary" level should be retained to advise on the programme and the day-to-day work of the client's existing public relations department as well as to carry out some executive work. Of the latter arrangement it is difficult to imagine a scenario more likely to cause tensions and organisational politics between a consultancy and the full-time practitioners employed in house.

Traverse-Healy defined the role of the consultant as spanning three interests: "the public, the client and the media" and he argued, "he should be someone of independent standing, and so less likely to be influenced by becoming overidentified with his client's viewpoint."[48] Protected economically from dependence on one client by virtue of the fact that he had several, the consultant was able "to take a stand when advocating a course of action which he feels to be right and in the best interests of the client and the public."[49] This raises questions about the consultant's legitimacy and the nature and source of expertise required to make such judgements. According to Traverse-Healy, the consultant's range of clients "enables him to bring a much wider range of experience to the solution of a client's problems."[50] In other words, clients paid to provide the consultant with experiences that, if nothing else, would provide him or her with the necessary gravitas to convince other clients that his or her judgements were grounded in knowledge. This analysis is supported by the consultant Michael McAvoy, recalling public relations practice in the 1960s:

> One of the rub-offs of being associated with the advertising business was that there was the marketing analysis that goes into advertising work applied to PR . . . [for example] . . . the very first client I worked for was Procter and Gamble, and what one had the advantage of there was to assimilate P & G's ways of planning and analysis, which stayed with me all my life—like going to an academy.[51]

Traverse-Healy also outlined some of the key aspects of consultancy organisation and procedure and described how, even at this early stage,

---

[47] Ibid.
[48] Ibid.
[49] Ibid.
[50] Ibid.
[51] Interview. 22 April 1999.

"most consultancy firms are organised along similar lines."[52] The basic consulting procedure was described thus:

> One or more of the board directors together with the public relations manager undertake a detailed study of the client's problems and examine them in the light of all other information that can be gathered concerning his sphere of activity, including on occasions the results of a public opinion poll. After discussion as to the objectives of the campaign, the scope of the operation, the time factor and the budget limitations, the public relations manager formulates a positive public relations policy and in consultation with his staff works out as detailed a plan of action as is possible for submission to the client . . . when agreement of policy and plan has been reached . . . the department [goes] into action.[53]

As described, consultation appears a chimera or mirage because nothing was revealed about thinking processes or how analysis was carried out or objectives set. In other words, there was at this stage no transparency or clear cognitive domain. Although the consultant "has to get to know everything he can about the client's organisation or know where he can find the answers," there was no clear method with regard to analysing information. PR expertise was mysterious, like that of the witch doctor. Emphasis was given to the importance of personal relations between the client and the consultant, who "had to gain the sincere support and co-operation of the client's management and staff . . . ensure that he can always get advice and assistance from the senior members."[54] Managing relations and gaining access to decision makers implies the necessity for some shrewd organisational politics. The additional requirement to "be in a position to demand and get the best from the creative staff of his own firm" suggests the ability to lead or at least the ability to impress one's colleagues in a working context that lacked objective criteria or educational qualifications. According to Traverse-Healy, Pritchard Wood employed a considerable bureaucratic structure to provide advice to clients, which consisted of:

> Two committees . . . a public relations policy committee . . . normally presided over by the chairman or managing director of the client organisation . . . [which] meets quarterly . . . taking decisions on major policy issues, receiving reports, reviewing progress and approving plans . . . the

---

[52] Traverse-Healy, T., p. 62.
[53] Ibid.
[54] Ibid.

second committee . . . meets more frequently . . . and meetings are called by the public relations advisers.[55]

The purpose of setting up these bureaucratic structures was to enable the client's staff to become "actively engaged in carrying out" the programme (thus saving the consultancy money and also some of the administrative drudgery) and to strengthen "lines of communication between the client and the consultant . . . and ensure potentially newsworthy material reaches the consultant."[56] Although these last two points were doubtless true, it could also be the case that the consultant was infiltrated into the organisational structure in a way that might make it difficult for the organisation to dispense with consultancy services. At the same time that a degree of dependency was established, the consultants had the chance to spot opportunities for future work.

Fees were charged on three different bases: annual retainer, based on an estimate of time, administrative charges, profit margin, and other expenses such as postage, telephones, entertainment, printing, and production (with up to a 20% markup); a small annual "availability" fee for advice and planning regularly billed, production costs; and a service charge on a project basis, billed as and when required.[57] Traverse-Healy (1953) went to some lengths to stress the importance of entertainment expenses. These were justified on the basis that "every public relations man" needed to develop "contacts in all fields and at all levels . . . [gain] . . . knowledge of people and the public" and although he acknowledged that such contacts were gained through everyday work, he suggested that "a fresh situation involving his client may arise overnight or a new client approach him with an unusual problem which will test his ability to amass information rapidly or check sectional or public opinion" (p. 64), in which case contacts may have to be made out of working hours. Although Traverse-Healy argued that "a cup of tea and a bun in a cafe may provide the right occasion and bring better results than an expensive meal" and warned that "lavish entertainment . . . linked with a request for advice, assistance or information . . . can be detrimental," it seems unlikely that the topic of entertainment both as an item in his speech and as a budget item would have been given such emphasis if real expenditure did not exceed the modest tea-and-bun scenario. The

---

[55] Ibid. p. 63.
[56] Ibid.
[57] Ibid. p. 64.

reality is implied by Traverse-Healy's final guide that "a consultant should circulate in those business, political and social circles where opinions are held and moulded," which shows the importance of social skills, cultural capital, and networking to public relations consultancy practice at this time. In his discussion, Traverse-Healy highlighted the importance of "flair and instinct," although he also thought that the "application of public opinion research to public relations programmes ... [was] ... a growing necessity."[58] Despite the emphasis on personal qualities, Traverse-Healy expressed concern regarding a likely shortage of "trained staff" and thought there might be "a falling off in the quality of public relations staff."[59]

A year later, René Elvin from Crawfords Public Relations picked up on the theme of the importance of senior level access when he regretted that "public relations consultants have not yet acquired in this country the full status of advisers to management which they enjoy in the United States, where they have contributed in no mean way to the startling development and efficiency of industry."[60] Elvin still saw knowledge of journalism as very important, but also saw sponsorship and the provision of educational materials to schools as ways of improving community relations. He further highlighted investor relations as a field that had yet to be developed and suggested that the public relations consultant, "well versed in the habits and methods of public authorities, and knowing his way about in the labyrinthine maze of ministerial departments, can often save his clients untold time and trouble in their dealings with 'the powers that be,'"[61] in short, the function of lobbying.

At the Public Relations Day conference held in December 1960, the problems of budgeting and cost in consultancy were debated by a panel of consultants: Tim Traverse-Healy, Colin Mann, Denys Brook-Hart, Basil Stebbings, and Colin Hodgkinson.[62] Much of the discussion was directed toward convincing clients of the value of consultancy and devising a system that justified costs. Traverse-Healy suggested that, "[a]s a client 'will not give a blank cheque,' it was necessary to have many more headings than is the case of a normal business organisa-

---

[58]Ibid.

[59]General discussion on consultancy. *Public Relations*, 5 (4) 1953, p. 66.

[60]Elvin, R. (1954). Public relations consultancy. *Public Relations*, 6 (3), p. 23.

[61]Ibid. p. 24.

[62]The problems of budgeting and costing. Conference supplement. *Public Relations*, 13 (2) 1961, pp. xii–xiv.

tion" and he recommended that "operational budgets should be split [into] routine and special projects . . . it was essential to keep an adequate reserve [for the latter]."[63] Hodgkinson, an independent consultant, "described the present system [of costing] as hand to mouth."[64] In contrast, Traverse-Healy disclosed that Pritchard Wood had recently shifted from a set fee plus expenses to a retaining fee plus programme costs charged on a man-hours basis. There was discussion as to whether the speculative and competitive business presentations (*pitches* in current terminology) should be paid for as they took up a great deal of time and expense.[65] Three years later, Dennis Lyons disclosed in some detail the costing method used by Infoplan because "there are still too many firms that have not yet reached this stage of development" and he saw such a system as critical to public relations' credibility with clients' directors and accountants.[66] He argued that consultancies were "selling specialised manpower,"[67] in other words, craft expertise. The component elements of the costing method were "salaries and related expenses: space and facilities: client services (including travel and entertainment): corporate expenses (promotional advertising, new business development, professional services)."[68] Infoplan aimed for an operating profit of 25% and a net profit of 8%. All employees had the potential to generate income for the agency from their annual saleable hours of work (excluding weekends, holiday, and sick leave). However, to cover salaries, expenses, and taxation and to achieve the target profit, employees were expected to generate fee income three times that of their salary, a ratio still in use. Consequently, consultancies employed Taylorist methods of management, requiring their employees to keep careful timesheets recording their daily work. Timesheets became the basis of costing and also a tool for ensuring that the client was not overserviced.

Nearly a decade after Traverse-Healy's talk, consultant Giles Wadham was still urging his fellow members to ensure that they charged enough for advice as opposed to executive action.[69] The intangibility of

---

[63] Ibid. p. xiii.

[64] Ibid. p. xiii.

[65] Ibid. p. xiv.

[66] Lyons, D. (1964). A costing system for public relations. *Public Relations, 16* (3), pp. 9–13.

[67] Ibid.

[68] Ibid.

[69] Wadham, G. (1970). Increasing importance of outside specialist services. *Public Relations, 23* (3), p. 4.

the service posed a considerable problem, not least because of the lack of theoretical underpinning to the practice. The methodology of fee charging was important to consultants not only in terms of their survival, but also in terms of their status. There were discussions as to whether public relations should be charging for the cost of activities undertaken, for advice given, or for results achieved. The latter was seen as controversial and unethical, and was detrimental to professional status in that long-standing professions such as medicine and the law are not paid by results. Even though payment by results was prohibited by the Code of Conduct, such thinking influenced the occupation in the emphasis given to the compilation of media cuttings as a way of proving the value of public relations activities. One way in which these cuttings have been evaluated is by assigning advertising value to the space achieved, even though IPR officials have publicly disapproved of this method for more than half a century. Originally, their disapproval was rooted in the desire to separate the public relations occupation from that of press agentry. In the 1990s, there were increasing efforts to harness computers in order to employ qualitative and quantitative methods to analyse media content. It remains the case that most industry efforts evaluating their work have focused on media rather than public opinion research. Such an emphasis tends to limit the public relations role and, more importantly, perceptions of it, in a way that is detrimental to its bid to achieve professional status.

There was remarkably little published on the working practice of consultancies and the division of labour within them. An article by Alan Eden-Green (a codirector of Infoplan) offered some insights into internal organisation, together with a nicely cynical view of the performative aspects of consultancy not acknowledged elsewhere:

> One sometimes wonders whether the energies which public relations consultancies devote towards acquiring new business are matched by their efforts to retain their clients—and how realistic those efforts are. Most consultants and their clients . . . are all too familiar with the crash programme of lunches, dinners, and window dressing presentations hastily organised to restore the confidence of the wilting client about to receive a bill for the balance of the year's fee.[70]

Eden-Green also described the problem of overservicing demanding clients and the concomitant underservicing of less demanding clients,

---

[70]Eden-Green, A. (1965). Account control. *Public Relations, 17* (2), p. 13.

and the administrative support necessary for accurate accounting and charging: time sheets, contact and action reports, progress checking, and the monitoring by senior staff of individual accounts. Eden-Green described four key support departments: the press room, staffed by professional journalists who undertook all writing; the special events department, which carried out administration for events; the women's section, which again largely employed writers who specialised in "fashion, household goods, beauty treatment"; and the photographic section, which ordered and captioned prints for clients. Such extensive support services raise questions about the unarticulated area of expertise of the consultants themselves. Was their role to flatter and pander to clients' egos while the real work was done in the support sections? In the same issue of *Public Relations*, another senior consultant, Moss Murray, Director of Planning at Voice and Vision, seemed to provide the answer in an article that emphasised the importance of reporting back to the client:

> New clients should receive special attention. You can't spend too much time with a new client. Every discussion or meeting you have with him should be reported in a contact report or confirmed by letter. . . . Reporting regularly to all clients has to be regarded as an essential part of public relations practice by everyone. . . . It is . . . advisable to anticipate the monthly reports whenever you have achieved a successful piece of publicity by sending the newspaper or magazine (the whole issue) to your clients on the day it is published. . . . Clients like to talk about themselves and their successes. They are as vain as public relations men and women.[71]

Murray emphasised the importance of the personal relationship between consultant and client and argued that the "personality of the public relations man or woman is vital to the long term success of any campaign, essential in creating confidence, friendship, and cooperation that could avoid a master-servant relationship and facilitate a more equal relationship."[72] This is an extremely interesting point because it suggests that the consultant should not impose his presumed power (derived from his speciality) over the client, but should adopt a more collaborative approach. In such a case, knowledge about the client's

---

[71] Murray, M. (1965). The importance of reporting to clients. *Public Relations, 17* (2), p. 22.
[72] Ibid. pp. 22–3.

problems and solutions would arise from the relationship, not from a book. Thus, the relationship between client and consultant was not so much symbiotic because in some ways the consultant would be acting almost parasitically.

Turning to the literature of the 1950s and 1960s, one can find an equal and noticeable silence about the processes behind consultancy work. The first brief description was a 6-page chapter written by leading consultant Hereward Phillips in the institute's own textbook in 1958.[73] It revealed almost nothing of the process of analysis beyond the notion that research was essential because "the basis of all public relations must be truth," and that the consultant must know about the product and those income groups likely to buy it. Phillips emphasised the importance of managing the relationship between client and consultant, suggesting that the consultant must "possess the gift of tact."[74] In terms of organisation, Phillips described: a standard pattern of directors or managers responsible for "high level contacts . . . policy, planning and administration" (at this time *administration* tended to mean management rather than executive work); a "co-ordination" function, which supervised research and planning and executed plans; specialist sections for particular media such as news, features, women's magazines, and trade and technical journals; a section to collate and present all cuttings; and secretarial, photocopying, accounts, and library staff. Literature of this era focused on specific techniques of communication rather than the process of analysis that lay behind the technique. It rarely ventured beyond standard definitions of public relations or vague generalities that illustrate the intuitiveness of the process and its basis in networking, such as: "Occasionally a public relations man must consciously act as a catalyst to solve a problem when he has no more than a vague feeling that something is wrong in a given area—an uneasy atmosphere built up by a word here, a rumour there."[75] This description hints at the almost shamanistic role of the public relations consultant: mysterious, unaccountable, yet able to pass judgment. However, in a world in which judgments are expected to be evidence based, such sentiments and beliefs were always likely to be unconvincing and to preclude professional status being granted.

---

[73]Phillips, H. (1958). Consultancy. In *A guide to the practice of public relations*. Institute of Public Relations. London: Newman Neame.

[74]Ibid. p. 239.

[75]Paterson, W. (1968). *Industrial publicity management*. London: Business Books, p. 71.

MORE PROFESSIONALISATION: THE FOUNDATION OF SPECIALIST CONSULTANTS' BODIES

In 1953, there was the first discussion of setting up a group to focus on consultants' interests.[76] In November 1953 and February 1954, there were discussions about the status of consultants at the Shaftesbury Hotel, London, and an ad hoc committee was formed. However, according to Arthur Cain, "it was immediately apparent that some members were opposed to including Advertising Agency PROs . . . and no further progress was made."[77] Already in existence were a number of "Publicity Clubs," and by 1957 it was clear that there was a growing rift within the ranks of consultants and, in particular, "a developing opinion among independent consultants that their point of view, and their status in public relations are not fully appreciated within the Institute."[78] This, and the desire to set up a register of consultants, led to the IPR forming a Committee of Public Relations Consultants of the council in March 1957, headed up by Prince Yuri Galitzine. In April, four nonconsultant members of the council (Maurice Buckmaster, Sam Black, Lex Hornsby, and Bill Vint) met the committee to "discuss with them their proposals for the organisation within the Institute of a properly constituted Consultants Group and . . . make recommendations direct to the Council for the most effective incorporation of such a Group within the Institute."[79]

In January 1960 Denys Brook-Hart carried out a survey of consultant members that showed there was a strong interest among consultants to have specific representation within the IPR.[80] Subsequent meetings of independent and advertising agency consultants revealed that, although the advertising agency consultants had "a desire to maintain a unity of all public relations practitioners within the Institute [and] were not interested in setting up a separate group to represent their

---

[76] AGM. *Public Relations,* 5 (2) 1953, p. 9.

[77] Public relations consultants and the IPR. Notes by Cain, A. (1960). IPR Archive 3/5/3.

[78] AGM. *Public Relations,* 5 (2) 1953, p. 9; Public relations consultants and the IPR. Notes by Cain, A. (1960). IPR Archive 3/5/3; Interview. 25 June 1991; Cain, A. (1957). Editorial. *Public Relations,* 9 (2), p. 1.

[79] Minutes of Council Meeting. (1957, 4 May). IPR Archive 2/2/4. p. 3.

[80] Public relations consultants and the IPR. Notes by Cain, A. (1960). IPR Archive 3/5/3.

interests," the independent consultants argued that those from advertising agencies "would not be acceptable."[81] Despite these entrenched positions, Arthur Cain commented that "it seems that the consultants and the advertising agency PROs have much more in common than the consultants are generally prepared to acknowledge."[82] It seems that the basis of the difference had to do with notions of parity with regard to specialism, advertising apparently casting a taint upon the reputation of public relations.

On 19 May 1960, the IPR formally approved the need for an organisation to represent "consultancy and agency" interests and "to enable the IPR to control the practice of public relations in the consultancy field."[83] This entailed the creation of a new class of membership to be listed in the register. The first list of consultants was made publicly available in 1961, but there was no formal approval process: Consultancies could only be listed if the principal was a fellow or member of the institute. The list included ownership details, clients, and number of employees[84] and included 30 independents and 21 advertising agency firms.[85]

At the same time, the institute sought to address definitions. Denys Brook-Hart suggested that definitions were a thorny area in a paper circulated to the IPR consultancy committee:

> In my view, a "consultant" is a person who gives expert and qualified advice only, for a fee, and is usually bound by some code of behaviour or ethics. A "consultant" is not expected directly to implement his advice, or to have an interest beyond an advisory one in the media employed. This definition would exclude nearly all the existing PR "consultants." It would also exclude all advertising agency PR personnel. I therefore suggest that a new term is needed. Possibly "practitioner" would meet the need.[86]

The Brook-Hart definition was accepted by the committee and 1960 thus marks the date of the formal acceptance of the term *practitioner* in the British context.

---

[81] Ibid.

[82] Ibid.

[83] Minutes of the Joint Committee set up by Council. (1960, 19 May). IPR Archive 3/5/1.

[84] Council minutes 8 May 1958. A list of public relations consultants. Both IPR Archive 3/5/2.

[85] Minutes of the Consultancy Committee. (1961, 17 January). IPR Archive 3/5/2.

[86] Notes sent to the IPR Consultancy Committee. (1960, 6 May). IPR Archive 3/5/3.

The IPR consultancy committee worked hard to negotiate between the independents and the advertising agencies that formed separate discussion groups. Forty-six independents met on 16 June 1960 and in November a working party proposed formal recognition by the IPR of their own society: The Society of Independent Public Relations Consultants (SIPRC).[87] The man behind SIPRC was Prince Yuri Galitzine, who explained, "[We tried] to propagate a slightly more thoughtful image of public relations."[88] Thus, the move was inspired by the motivation to create an elite group within the public relations fraternity. SIPRC encouraged the IPR to see SIPRC's formation as a positive development, arguing that the society "would encourage its member firms to encourage their own staff to apply for admission to the Institute, so that the result of the formation of the Society would more likely be an increase rather than a decrease in membership."[89] IPR president R. A. Paget-Cooke appealed to consultants to join forces for the good of public relations:

> I have been surprised this year that the so-called "independent" consultants have not yet concentrated on joining forces, to ensure that . . . [the] . . . fundamentals of public relations are actively maintained. . . . Consultants and consulting firms, with their range of clients in different fields, can do more good—or harm—to the reputation of public relations than most staff public relations people can do individually.[90]

SIPRC sought to establish its own identity and undertook a range of competitive activities, including publishing its own list of consultants, and indicated that it would not wish entries to appear in both lists.[91] This led to further discussion of the conditions for corporate membership. SIPRC members tended to argue in favour of individual membership, whereas consultancy committee members thought the institute should encompass both individuals and firms, though it agreed to review corporate membership with a view to restricting it to public relations firms.[92]

---

[87] List of the IPR members who accepted the invitation to attend the first meeting of the Independent Practitioners Discussion Group. IPR Archive 3/5/3; Minutes of the Consultancy Committee Meeting. (1960, 2 December). IPR Archive 3/5/2.

[88] Interview. 23 August 1995.

[89] Minutes of the Consultancy Committee. (1960, 2 December). IPR Archive 3/5/2.

[90] Presidential address. *Public Relations,* 12 (4) 1960, p. 23.

[91] Minutes of the Consultancy Committee. (1961, 17 January). IPR Archive 3/5/2.

[92] Minutes of the Consultancy Committee. (1961, 11 April). IPR Archive 3/5/2.

In June 1962 this was approved,[93] a year after 40 advertising agency public relations executives had voted overwhelmingly to form their own grouping.[94]

In late 1962 and early 1963 the public relations business contracted apparently in line with the economy, the most vulnerable being the smaller consultancies. The editor of *Public Relations*, Victor Lewis, suggested that many who had set themselves up were "barely qualified."[95] Shirley Barnett agreed with his analysis but blamed advertising agencies that, as an inducement to their own business, offered public relations services at very low rates or even free, far below the economic level of fees demanded by the independents.[96] According to this analysis, independents could not get work, and because advertising agencies often swiftly appointed an inexperienced public relations department for clients who expressed an interest in such a service, the standard of work was often below par and thus lowered purchasers' expectations of public relations. A different view was offered by Tim Traverse-Healy, who recalled, "Actually some of the best work was being done by PR people in advertising agencies for the simple reason that they had the resources and they invested."[97]

Michael Rice, a leading consultancy figure in the 1960s, suggested that the underlying reason for factional splits among the public relations community was both jurisdictional and economic: "It was obvious that a very important component of the PR consultancy field were the consultancies owned by advertising agencies and a number of people in SIPRC . . . were very jealous of their position as independents and resented (as they saw it) the unfair advantage which the agency-owned businesses had over them and it really collapsed because of that."[98]

Incorporation of the IPR in 1963 was the catalyst to the formation of a separate public relations body for consultants: It was not legally possible for an incorporated institute to retain corporate members because incorporation required membership of individuals, not collectivities.[99] In 1965, a legal association was made between IPR and SIPRC[100] and a

[93]Minutes of the Consultancy Committee. (1962, 27 June). IPR Archive 3/5/7.

[94]Minutes of the Consultancy Committee. (1961, 19 July). IPR Archive 3/5/2.

[95]As the editor sees it. *Public Relations*, 15 (2) 1963, p. 2.

[96]Independents' complaint. *Public Relations*, 15 (3), p. 46.

[97]Interview. 13 September 1995.

[98]Interview. 29 April 1999.

[99]IPR archive. 18 March 1958.

[100]Council Minutes. (1965, 22 February). IPR Archive 2/2/8.

year later an agreement was reached between the institute and the SIPRC ensuring close cooperation and "the interdependence of members between the two bodies. . . . SIPRC is not a competing body, but is both complementary and supplementary to the Institute."[101] It seems that consultants were still not entirely happy, as illustrated by the existence of other organisations such as The PR Club[102] and R. C. Liebman's bitter resolution at the AGM:

> It is moved that the Institute of Public Relations during the ensuing year, 1968, stops playing at being a Millionaires' Club, seriously considers the plight of its small Consultant Members and tries to do something for them in return for the outrageously high subscription of ten guineas, instead of applying a disgusting means test and attempting to extricate from them at least another £15 before their names can even appear on a Register of available PR Consultants.[103]

SIPRC became known irreverently as "Shipwreck" and, according to Nigel Ellis, "died partly because it didn't have any money, partly because it couldn't attract any members and partly because nobody could work out what its members were independent of."[104]

Prince Yuri Galitzine was also important in the establishment of a new consultants' organisation in 1969. In an interview, he remembered:

> I was very disillusioned by the way the IPR was getting swamped with advertising people and one day Denys Brook-Hart and I had a heart to heart talk about SIPRC . . . and the effect we were having if at all on PR and I said "This is quite crazy, we've got maybe 20 members, but there must be at least 10 or 12 advertising agencies with enormous budgets who are actually making a mess of PR and the only way of doing anything about it is to amalgamate SIPRC with another organisation including the advertising agencies."[105]

Galitzine hosted a gathering at his house in Hyde Park Gate, London for all the advertising agencies that had public relations interests and the SIPRC members. Crucially, for the independent status of the public relations occupation, it was decided that members of the new organisation, even if owned by advertising agencies, must have an independent

---

[101] Hardern, L. (1966). Report of Dublin. *Public Relations, 18* (3), p. 19.
[102] Letter from Francis Butters and Nigel Ellis. 9 December 1966.
[103] Council Minutes. (1967, 27 September). IPR Archive 2/2/9.
[104] Interview. 30 August 1996.
[105] Interview. 23 August 1995.

identity and be a limited company. Galitzine had clear views about the importance of the proposed new organisation in terms of professionalisation: "We felt that if we were going to have a new organisation . . . partners must be members of the IPR just like the accountants."[106] Looking back to the formation of the Public Relations Consultants' Association, Galitzine recalled, "Denys [Brook-Hart] and Tim [Traverse Healy] and I were sitting down [wondering who was going to run this thing] and I said 'That chap over there, Michael McAvoy, he's a nice neutral kind of guy'—and that was how he was chosen . . . the idea that he was the father of it all—he actually had a couple of parents!"[107]

McAvoy, who became PRCA's first president/director general, recalled the genesis of the new organisation slightly differently:

> I was . . . a Council member of IPR. . . . Tim Traverse Healy was the President and he produced [a policy document] called "Blueprint for Change" [into which] I had some input . . . and Tim [asked me to] . . . look at what I thought the needs of the consultancy sector were . . . and I came up with the revolutionary and I think unexpected proposal that there should actually be a trade association with completely different terms of reference . . . because the requirements of companies are in my view . . . quite different to [those of] individuals. So that was blessed, not without some resistance from SIPRC group [and] I wrote to twelve of the leading and largest firms . . . [because] we wanted to start from the principles of best practice . . . establish what were the appropriate criteria for membership. . . . Some people thought it was being elitist but I think it has paid dividends and I think we did set a very good foundation and I think it contrasted very very much indeed with SIPRC which was rather a weak grouping of people.[108]

Thus, although the formation of the PRCA apparently healed the traditional split between independents and those in advertising agencies, it also limited recruitment to established companies.

CONCLUSION

Within the context of professionalisation, the establishment of consultancy services is of particular interest because specialists who serve

---

[106] Interview. 23 August 1995.
[107] Interview. 23 August 1995.
[108] Interview. 22 April 1999.

clients represent an essential or concentrated form of the practice. They could be seen as the standard bearers for the occupation and owners of the knowledge systems that underpin practice. In fact, public relations consultants did not exercise this control (and do not do so today), but, as illustrated in this chapter, played a complex role in the separation of public relations from advertising. There was also evidence of tensions arising between consultants and in-house practitioners that remain unresolved. Although consultancy developed as a field of expertise requiring specialised skills (creativity, selling and presentation skills, and client handling) that have been important in developing occupational values and rituals, it has not yet evolved as a separate domain as has happened in other professions (such as law, where there are different career tracks for solicitors and barristers).

Consultancy expanded in the 1960s in response to the overall growth of the economy, particularly in the consumer and retail sectors. Business managers saw public relations as a cheap way of gaining media coverage in comparison to advertising. The establishment of public relations consultancy as a viable business and its increasing influence within the occupation is of interest in the context of professionalisation because it demonstrated that a field of expertise had been defined, however vaguely, and was recognised as such in the marketplace. There is a wider economic significance here: The growth of consultancy signified a clear identity for the practice and symbolised professionalism in terms of a structure that mimicked established professions such as law. It made public relations available to a greater range of organisations because services were available on a project basis, which was more affordable than appointing a post in house. Thus, the postwar era marked the beginning of a new business in Britain, the tentacles of which began to reach into various areas of the economy. This was a profound change from the governmental and bureaucratic dominance of the prewar order. The interplay between consultancies, consumerism, and the economic growth of the 1960s was crucial. With hindsight, we can see the growth of consultancy as foreshadowing the exponential growth of public relations that "played a key role in the transformation of British political and economic life in the 1980s."[109]

---

[109]Miller, D. & Dinan, W. (2000). The rise of the PR industry in Britain 1979–98. *European Journal of Communication, 5* (1), pp. 5–35.

5

Professional Dilemmas: Public Relations, the Media, and Politics, 1948–1970

INTRODUCTION

The expansion of public relations and its gradual consolidation as an occupation after the Second World War took place against a backdrop of rapid change in the media. The end of paper rationing in 1956 meant that advertisers, increasingly informed by market research, were able to target audiences more effectively.[1] Newspapers that could not deliver to either elite or mass audiences lost out and there was a spate of closures as the industry began a long-term process of contraction and increased competitiveness.[2] In addition to benefiting from the newly available market research techniques, the growth of public relations appeared to clients to offer opportunities tantamount to free advertising. Public relations copy that mimicked news source styles was tempting for journalists who were increasingly under pressure, both because there were more pages to fill and because the cost of newspaper production increased due to increased size and salary rises. Economic changes forced increasing dependence on public relations, which challenged the jour-

---

[1]Williams, K. (1998). *Get me a murder a day! A history of mass communication in Britain.* London: Arnold, pp. 213–20 passim.

[2]Ibid.

nalists' role and set in motion a seemingly perpetual tension between the two occupations.

The current chapter explores the history of public relations in relation to the media and politics, partially by employing concepts drawn from the sociology of the professions reviewed in Chapter 1: jurisdiction (professional boundaries), competence or professional expertise, and legitimacy. A focus on jurisdiction is useful in identifying the criteria that had to be met for an individual to be recognised as a public relations practitioner. Consideration of jurisdiction reflects on the problems that emerged from the relationship between journalists and the newly formalised occupation of public relations, in terms of their tasks and the degree to which these overlapped or duplicated each other, and the tensions that arose from this.

One of the issues important in shaping professional values was the pattern of career progression, whereby a significant number of journalists moved on to become public relations practitioners. The evaluation of this phenomenon leads naturally to a consideration of expertise, because ex-journalists had expectations of the occupation and were influential in shaping and focusing the role of public relations on media relations. Competence can be seen as part of the claim to legitimacy, which is linked to the notion of the public interest and is the site of debates about the ethics of public relations practice. Emphasising the importance of media expertise naturally suited the ex-journalists, because it increased their own market value within their new occupation. Ex-journalists could offer clients the ability to demystify the media as well as protect them. They therefore offered more tangible benefits than the other major category that formed the postwar influx into public relations: the ex-Army types, who could generally only offer bonhomie and social contacts.

Media criticism of public relations presented a problem for public relations practitioners, because the IPR was trying to establish the occupation as respectable. Media criticism was directed at the perceived incompetence of practitioners and ethical issues such as attempts to bribe the media with lavish hospitality, the development of parliamentary lobbying, and work carried out on behalf of foreign interests, particularly those that were unsympathetic to the British government. Thus, the connection between the worlds of public relations and politics is given some attention. Some examples of these developments are provided, largely from the 1950s and 1960s, because this was a period of rapid growth in UK public relations and an important transition from government-sponsored or public service diplomacy to market-driven, privatised opportunism. As Gandy pointed out:

> The transformation of the relationship between state and private firms increasingly involves the dual strategies of deregulation and privatisation [sic]. It is the role of public relations to make such changes appear normal and rational—simple common sense. . . . Massive public relations have been used by states in crisis to effect transformation of local public utilities into private global competitors.[3]

This chapter illustrates why public relations is of concern to media sociologists and political scientists, who, like journalists, have taken a largely critical approach to the subject. The links between elite and powerful institutions, governmental, corporate, and financial, are partly facilitated by the public relations occupation, which brokers information via the media or key contacts so that, "through the provision of information subsidies, public relations specialists reduce the costs faced by decision makers in acquiring relevant information."[4] The present chapter emphasises issues bearing on the professionalisation of that process.

POACHERS TURNED GAMEKEEPERS: JURISDICTION

The concept of jurisdiction is crucial to the establishment of a profession, because without delineated boundaries practitioners are less likely to be able to articulate their area of expertise to clients, rendering them unable to define or control the market for their services. As noted earlier, many public relations practitioners were recruited from the ranks of disenchanted journalists. Those with backgrounds in journalism have been favourably contrasted with those who tried to move into public relations from advertising: "Some of the public relations agencies were extremely good because their staff had former journalists, others were staffed by advertising agency people who had absolutely no idea how to service newspapers at all."[5] The reason given for preferring

---

[3]Gandy, O. (1992). Public relations and public policy: the structuration of dominance in the information age. In Toth, E. & Heath, R. (eds.). *Rhetorical and critical approaches to public relations.* Hillsdale, New Jersey: Lawrence Erlbaum Associates, p. 148.

[4]Ibid.

[5]Interview. 29 August 1996.

ex-journalists was their practical skills and ability to network: "The main source [for recruitment] was journalism because they had existing ability, writing, and also contacts and understood the press."[6]

The postwar era was a period of renegotiation of the boundaries and relative status between public relations, advertising, and journalism. By identifying itself with journalism, public relations could more easily separate its practice from that of advertising and there was also the allure of greater professional status, as one journalist argued, "The impact of professional journalists in the world of public relations . . . stepped up the general standard of public relations editorial and press work. It enabled professional PR to keep step with the growth of the state and civil service communication, in which accurate and precise reporting and description were recognised as fundamentally important."[7]

In a study published in the 1960s, media sociologist Jeremy Tunstall suggested that the opportunities for career progression from journalism to public relations created personal pressures for journalists at a time when the industry was contracting:

> Despite their severe criticisms of PR organisations, journalists know they are dependent on them. . . . A further reason for journalists to feel uneasy about public relations is, of course, that many PR men are ex-journalists. Few successful journalists would go into this work by choice; but with the continuing trend to newspaper amalgamations, the number of senior posts in national journalism is certainly not increasing. . . . A young journalist in his twenties may well be wondering, as he is fed information by an ex-journalist twice his own age, whether his career in journalism will end the same way.[8]

The journalist Richard West also suggested a deep-seated and personal tension, though he chose to see career failure rather than opportunism as the motivating factor in journalists moving to public relations posts: "Journalists know in their heart of hearts that they may too become PROs when they fail at their present profession; they tend to see in PROs the embodiment of their own future failure."[9] This view

---

[6]Interview. 23 July 1996.

[7]Kisch, R. (1964). *The private life of public relations*. London: MacGibbon & Kee, p. 37.

[8]Tunstall, J. (1964). *The advertising man in London agencies*. London: Chapman & Hall, p. 178.

[9]West, R. (1963). *PR the fifth estate*. London: Mayflower Books, p. 23.

was shared by some public relations practitioners active in the 1940s and 1950s, two of whom acknowledged in interviews in 1996: "Most of them were failed journalists . . . and all they did was to write pieces that would get into the papers, so there wasn't a great deal of strategic thinking"[10] and "You'll find the NUJ sneers and says that the PR profession is made up of failed journalists; in other words they couldn't make it in Fleet Street so they ended up doing PR."[11]

Examples of the move from journalism to public relations work were Richard Dimbleby, who in 1957 formed the company Information in Industry with past president of the IPR Alan Hess[12] and television personality Peter West, who in 1969 established his own public relations company under the advertising agency John Chesny and Associates Ltd. West implied the similarities between the two occupations, when he declared confidently, "I have been connected with PR in one form or another for 25 years. . . . This new enterprise seems a logical development."[13] It seems that the traffic was largely one way—from journalism to public relations, rather than the other way round.

Although the route from public relations to journalism is still a common career path, the picture is now more complex, with revolving doors between journalism, public relations, think tanks (whose public relations and lobbying role has been somewhat neglected in the literature), and, increasingly, high-level posts in the civil service, especially in those parts that now operate as semiautonomous agencies.[14] The pattern of career paths of those in public relations indicates the difficulty of establishing a clear jurisdiction for the practice, both in the past and for the foreseeable future. There are also implications for what counts as expertise in the field, and it seems that chameleon-like qualities are required in terms of occupational identities in addition to the news-gathering and communication skills. Before proceeding to a more detailed discussion of the competitive aspects of jurisdictional struggle and expertise, it will be useful to review the NUJ's response to the growth of public relations.

---

[10]Interview. 30 August 1996.

[11]Interview. 9 August 1995.

[12]Alan Hess and Richard Dimbleby join forces in a public relations organisation. Editorial, *Public Relations,* 10 (1) 1957, p. 56.

[13]The PR scene. *Public Relations,* 22 (7) 1969, p. 19.

[14]I am indebted to my colleague Magda Pieczka for this insight.

PUBLIC RELATIONS AND THE NUJ

An important point of difference between public relations and journalism is that public relations has never been a unionised occupation. Its only engagement with unionism has been in the context of a small section within the NUJ, the Press and Public Relations Branch (PRB), formed to meet the needs of journalists who had moved from journalism to public relations. Wariness between public relations and journalism apparently manifested itself: "there was a tendency for newspaper journalists to be suspicious of those who had 'gone over to the other side.' "[15]

The PRB contributed public relations advice to the NUJ to support its objective to achieve acceptance from employers that "white collar unions were coming to stay,"[16] conducted salary surveys, and gave advice on pay and conditions, welfare, and education.[17] The PRB established its first house agreement with the Infoplan consultancy in the late 1950s and achieved major success with the British Travel and Holiday Association in 1962, when chapel members achieved rises of between £200 and £400 per year.[18] A number of cases were won over pay and severance conditions, but approaches to the PRCA "to persuade management in PR of the advantages to both employers and employed of having an employers' organisation operating on the same basis as in other industries" and to eliminate some of the small agencies' more extreme malpractices failed.[19] The PRB had, by 1967, "accepted that it was unrealistic to pursue the traditional NUJ approach of a minimum salary for given age and experience," so public relations services were thus aligned at an early stage with the vagaries of the market.[20] Such a development goes some way to explain the importance of "selling skills" in public relations, particularly those directed toward obtaining "new business" in the consultancy world. The continued absence of unionisation in public relations, despite ever-increasing workloads and a gender imbal-

---

[15]*Press and Public Relations Branch: the first 21 years.* Pamphlet published by the NUJ 1978, p. 2.

[16]Ibid. p. 6.

[17]Ibid.

[18]Ibid. p. 11.

[19]Ibid. p. 12.

[20]Ibid.

ance where men are very much in the minority, has tended to lead to depressed salaries, particularly at the lower levels. There exists, therefore, the potential for exploitation, particularly of young women, because it is they who largely inhabit the lower levels of the PR industry in a broadly patriarchal society.

JURISDICTIONAL BATTLES: EXPERTISE AND COMPETITION

The importance of journalism skills as a prerequisite to a career in public relations was an area for debate over a number of years. On 1 February 1950 the IPR hosted a meeting of "friendly frankness,"[21] at which editors of *The Times*, London Counties Newspapers, and *Gas World* addressed "Press Relationships in Public Relations." Pitt-Robbins from *The Times* commented that:

> The PRO system had come to stay and that, properly conducted, it could be of great benefit to the Press. . . . The danger was the system might be abused. Already there was the tendency for unimportant organisations to take on gentlemen who adopted the title PRO. *Some of the results of their work were really ghastly.* . . . If the PRO stuck to facts and the journalist to accuracy, both should benefit without conflict of interest.[22]

Other criticisms included: "PROs serving government were merely obstructionists. . . . Obstructionist PROs with an 'off the record' complex were prostituting what could develop into a very helpful partnership with the Press."[23]

However, broader criticisms were raised regarding the impact of public relations on communications channels, as explained by Dick Paget-Cooke (IPR president, 1959–1960): "It is said that the existence of PROs forces all the news into one narrow channel of their own department. Secondly, the Press complains that the public relations systems slows down the getting of news. Thirdly, there is the criticism that the PRO system has the effect—whether deliberately or not—of concealing activities and news in general instead of revealing them."[24] The *Lan-*

---

[21] Ibid. p. 8.

[22] Seeing themselves from another angle. *Public Relations*, 2 (3) 1950, p. 8.

[23] Ibid. p. 8.

[24] Paget-Cooke, R. (1950). The press and public relations officers. *Public Relations*, 3 (1), p. 10.

cashire Evening Post commented in 1951: "Sight is never lost of the real danger of the modern public relations system. . . . Hand-outs and prepared statements are never critical of the source from which they come. They also occasionally hide the real story. . . . This is a matter on which the Press is naturally sensitive, and the live newsman is ever on his guard against being merely a purveyor of official 'dope.' "[25] Nevertheless, as one practitioner of the era pointed out: "The NUJ man would never admit they got any benefit from PROs, but given a good PR press release the NUJ man will go through that like a pig and will truffle and make jolly good use of it!"[26]

IPR members responded with a range of reciprocal criticisms of journalists, such as:

> The gross butchering of stories after PROs had gone to endless trouble at the request of the newspaper to supply and check technical points; a suggestion that the Press needed to set up Public Relations to explain itself to its readers and to public relations people; a criticism that "news value" was fluid and, as interpreted by some newspapers, did not make the grade with responsible people; a rejection of the contention that Government PROs are obstructionists, and a declaration that the Press itself was sometimes guilty of obstruction.[27]

This quote reveals the expectations practitioners had that their material should be regarded as sacrosanct and also shows their resentment of a role subordinate to press power. Indirectly, it was acknowledged that public relations was the function that brokered information, and such a definition enabled practitioners to see themselves as helping rather than hindering the media. Alan Hess (IPR President, 1950–1951) argued:

> Once we lose respect of editors . . . we simply cannot carry on. But just to be honest with them, although essential is by no means enough. Every good PRO has it in his power to render a service to them and to give help as well as to seek it. Every good PRO steeps himself in a thorough knowledge of his subject and is glad to act as an animated Reference Library — a kind of cornucopia of Facts.[28]

As journalists responded to the growth of this new occupation, there was almost a sense of hurt that emerged from the public relations prac-

---

[25] Telling the tale. *Public Relations,* 4 (1) 1951, p. 18.

[26] Interview. 19 August 1995.

[27] Seeing themselves from another angle. *Public Relations,* 2 (3) 1950, p. 9.

[28] Hess, A. (1950). The conference speeches. *Public Relations,* 3 (2), p. 7.

titioners, as evidenced in a 1954 editorial, which included the key elements of the defences made by practitioners on behalf of the occupation over the course of half a century: that journalists misunderstood public relations practitioners, who were well-intentioned individuals who wished only to "help" journalists; that these PROs were not partisan and did not impede access; that many public relations practitioners were in an excellent position to assist journalists, because so many of them had previously been journalists themselves; and that only lazy journalists were dependent on public relations copy. In fact, it was claimed that:

> There appears to be a deliberate attempt to deny the value of public relations and public relations officers ... newspapers frequently criticise public relations officers, especially those working in the government service, but do not fail to make use of their help as much or even more than other papers. . . . The criticism appears to be based on a persistent failure to appreciate that the main function of public relations officers is to help the press obtain information and not to apologise for official actions ... the Commonwealth Press Union recently [made] a similar error ... [where] they stated that the public relations officer is becoming more and more of a barrier. . . . Is it really believed that a reporter would have better access in the absence of a public relations officer? ... A good reporter will make the maximum use of public relations officers but will regard their help as a stepping stone for further research and investigation. If some reporters are too indolent to do this why should the public relations officers be blamed? The majority of men and women engaged in public relations in this country have spent some time in journalism and are very anxious to work in friendly co-operation with all sections of the press.[29]

In the postwar era, public relations officers saw their role as one of helping the press, although it was stressed that media relations was only one side of the work. The idea that public relations was not solely concerned with media relations was an important part of public relations' claim to status. Public relations practitioners were keen to acquire managerial status as part of the professional project to ensure solid middle-class status for the occupation in society. It was also a way of distinguishing between the fields of journalism and public relations, thus resolving aspects of jurisdictional struggle. Because public relations was subject to much criticism from journalists, it provided practitioners with some ammunition to retaliate, as illustrated by the following quotes:

---

[29]Black, S. (1954). The need for mutual understanding. Editorial, *Public Relations* 6 (4), p. 2.

Journalism experience is certainly not essential and it should not be regarded as the transcending qualification for a PR post. . . . I have never understood why newspapermen believe they have some right to prior consideration for public relations appointments. . . . The mere fact of having been a journalist does not presuppose that one is unusually well-informed, particularly literate, meticulously accurate, able to assess how the public really think, able to achieve a cast-iron reputation for personal integrity in the public or, very importantly, organise and administrate.[30]

Journalists in my experience are not natural managers—they are by instinct and training individualists—and one knows of colleagues who have been failures as PRO's [sic] simply because they have tended to interpret management structures from a narrow journalist standpoint.[31]

Class appeared to motivate practitioners and inform debates. Managerial status in the 1950s was much more respectable than advertising (associated with selling and trade and clearly nonprofessional) and journalism (seen by some as a rather grubby occupation—one practitioner referred to journalists as "ghastly people"). It was claimed public relations practitioners had the intuitive capability to understand the influence of public opinion and the media on organisational reputation. Public relations was supposed to offer advice that was moral and in the public interest. This has remained an important feature of public relations ideology, as Pieczka pointed out in her study of contemporary practice.[32] Claims to the moral high ground were vulnerable to journalists' criticisms that focused on the new occupation's legitimacy, a crucial element in achieving "license and mandate,"[33] which sets up the legal authority for an occupation and formally establishes its area of jurisdiction.[34] Because the benefits of public relations to society are not immediately obvious, much discourse work—the public relations of public relations—has been required throughout the occupation's history in the UK.

---

[30]Is journalism experience necessary? Letters page, *Public Relations*, 22 (5) 1969, p. 25.

[31]Ibid.

[32]Pieczka, M. 'Public relations expertise deconstructed.' *The Business of Organising Identities*, symposium hosted by Stirling Media Research Institute 21–22 June 2000.

[33]Hughes, E. C. (1958). *Men and their work*. New York: The Free Press.

[34]Friedson, E. (1994). *Professionalism reborn: theory, prophecy and policy*. Cambridge: Polity Press, p. 70.

LEGITIMACY: THE PUBLIC RELATIONS
OF PUBLIC RELATIONS

The legitimacy of public relations was challenged by the media in two key areas: perceived attempts to influence media coverage through public relations hospitality and undue influence in the political sphere. Reviewing media critiques in relation to legitimacy includes some necessary repetition relating to issues of expertise and jurisdiction, but is useful in elucidating the relationship between these concepts at an empirical level.

According to Victor Lewis, Editor of *Public Relations* from 1959 to 1969, "Writing snide and pitifully uninformed articles about public relations is becoming a popular sport with the unqualified. Among the latest ... was an effusion ... in that chi-chi socialite scrap album called *The Tatler*."[35] There was a major debate within the IPR after the airing of a critical BBC *Panorama* programme in January 1959, which, according to the editorial in *Public Relations*, "was not a credit to anyone concerned."[36] The editor called for "public relations for public relations."[37] This resulted in a number of efforts to woo the media at meetings and conferences, and in January 1955 the president, A. A. McLoughlin, reported, "this year we are pleased to report far less criticism of public relations than previously."[38] McLoughlin confirmed that the institute would continue its policy of responding to criticism by meeting "the various journalistic, newspaper and advertising organisations in order to foster happier relationships."[39]

At the 10th AGM on 29 November 1957, the new president, Alan Campbell Johnson, alerted members to the publication of *The Hidden Persuaders* by Vance Packard, of which he said, "Our flesh ... is made to creep." He went on to refer to the existence of detractors of the public relations enterprise: "We occasionally hear from the more vociferous purveyors of prejudice that our role is parasitical."[40]

Retiring as president in 1960, Dick Paget-Cooke declared that this had been the year in which "'visibility" was thrust upon public rela-

---

[35] As the Editor sees it. *Public Relations*, 13 (1) 1960, p. 3.
[36] Public relations for public relations. *Public Relations*, 11 (2) 1959, p. 1.
[37] Ibid.
[38] McLoughlin, A. A. (1955). The presidential address. *Public Relations*, 7 (2), p. 18.
[39] Ibid.
[40] Presidential address. *Public Relations*, 10 (2) 1958, p. 5.

tions. In national newspapers, in weeklies, on radio and television, public relations [has] been subjected to scrutiny,"[41] and he, too, remained concerned about the "public relations of public relations."[42] His concern was echoed by the next president, Alan Eden-Green, who warned that public relations officers should be "wary of the limelight," even though it was necessary to "correct misguided writers and broadcasters who find some strange delight in denigrating something which they plainly do not begin to understand."[43] However, not all media reporting of the rise of public relations was negative, as the subsequent president, Tom Fife-Clark, Director General of the COI, reported:

> There is no doubt that the standing of the Institute has risen steadily . . . and is still rising. . . . The editor of a national newspaper said to me the other day: "I used to be very suspicious about the Institute—a queer sort of body, it seemed to me, not at all clear what it was out to do. But now I am satisfied that they are a good lot of fellows, genuinely determined to work for high standards in their own business and that we in journalism have a common interest in this work and we ought to help it along."[44]

This suggests that at least some public relations practitioners had been able to demonstrate possession of appropriate cultural capital to some journalists. The Commercial Editor of *The Financial Times* wrote such a favourable account of public relations activities that the institute reprinted it in full in *Public Relations*, as well as issuing it as a pamphlet under the institute's name. Shortly afterward, *Public Relations* reported with some delight that the City Editor of the *Daily Express* "has seen the light and in public print *admitted* not just the existence of, but the value of, public relations."[45] Nevertheless, by the early 1960s there was a groundswell of media criticism, according to Katherine Whitehorn: "Every now and then you got waspish little articles in the *Spectator* . . . sort of sneering chat . . . and I think you got a culture of disparagement of them even from people who were using them quite heavily."[46] Despite many scathing comments about the public relations practice throughout her career, Whitehorn appeared to have undergone a Pauline conversion by the 1990s, following board-level experience in a

---

[41] Still a vast job of explanation to be done. *Public Relations*, 13 (2) 1961, p. 5.
[42] Ibid.
[43] By their works. *Public Relations*, 13 (2) 1961, p. 5.
[44] The Institute is growing up. *Public Relations*, 12 (1) 1959, pp. 1–2.
[45] As the editor sees it. *Public Relations*, 13 (1) 1960, p. 2.
[46] Interview. 12 September 1997.

number of companies, when she told the IPR journal that "Public relations ... is needed to tell the company when it is about to do something that will get mud thrown at it, which the company often doesn't realise. PR is quite often the way morality creeps into the boardroom."[47]

A key development was the formation, around 1960, of the Society for the Discouragement of Public Relations, comprising a small, but influential, group of journalists. One of its members, Michael Frayn, recalled in an interview in 1998:

> I think the Society was Nicholas Tomalin's idea ... we gathered like-minded people, Robert Robinson, Bernard Levin, Cyril Ray and we set up this society as a joke society and we'd meet and have dinner. The first was in a private dining room of a pub in Fleet Street, then we moved to Bertorelli's in Charlotte Street. When we started there was half a dozen of us and later thirty or forty. There were no speeches or anything. They were genial occasions. It didn't have any real structure. . . . We just . . . [met] regularly . . . for two or three years [and] things used to be written about it in the trade press.[48]

This rather anodyne account is perhaps a little disingenuous given the degree of influence that those particular journalists had.

The complaints continued and by 1965 Bernard Levin had invented a new name for public relations practitioners: "creepers,"[49] Nicolas Tomalin referred to them as "nasty people,"[50] and a letter writer in the *Sunday Times* as "prostitutes."[51] Stung into self-defence, *Public Relations* editorials openly referred to the anti-public relations journalists as "jackals" and the "School of Bias."[52] David Willis, manager of the well known Crawfords agency, made an unpleasantly personal attack on Michael Frayn that demonstrates how tense the relationship was becoming: "Frayn in his attempts to be the poor man's Levin has yet to make even a scratch upon the sharp edge of real journalism."[53]

In January 1963 several members of the IPR appeared on an edition of *That Was The Week That Was*, in which they were interviewed by Bernard Levin. According to one IPR member, the performance of

---

[47] Having the same thoughts as everyone else. *Public Relations*, 12 (4) 1993, p. 5.
[48] Interview. 12 January 1998.
[49] As the editor sees it. *Public Relations*, 17 (3) 1965, p. 3.
[50] Ibid. p. 2.
[51] Ibid.
[52] Ibid.
[53] West, R., p. 99.

various "distinguished" members of the institute had been less than bravura:

> For the umpteenth time public relations received a verbal good hiding on the television screens of the nation, and I, for one, am growing tired of having to sit in anguish and embarrassment while public relations officers fail completely either to justify themselves or to defend our activities from ridicule. . . . The image of public relations came out of the interview considerably worse than it went in, especially when it is remembered that our spokesmen were not inexperienced novices at the game, but a galaxy of Fellows and Presidents, past, present and future.[54]

Another media embarrassment followed in 1968, when a *Man Alive* documentary was screened by the BBC entitled "Men with Tin Trumpets." It was poorly received by the editor of *Public Relations*, Victor Lewis, who wrote with considerable vitriol that "this is public money being used apparently to satisfy the whims of a coterie of closed minds who want to pontificate on a subject about which they clearly know no more than does a backward dachshund. . . . The programme was . . . ludicrous, and the performance of a Mr Robert Robinson . . . shamelessly full of ignorance."[55] Lewis criticised the editorial process and its apparent lack of objectivity. The IPR executive committee sent a copy of the editorial to the Director General of the BBC under a letter from the general secretary, Mrs. Aileen Wood, in which she wrote, "[Members] feel bitterly disappointed at what appears to be the current official attitude of the Corporation towards public relations. Anything you can do to bring about a better relationship between the BBC and the profession of public relations would, I am sure, be very much appreciated."[56] In reply, the director general, Hugh Greene, wrote, "I have long felt that the members of your profession are far too sensitive. It would probably be fair to say that the BBC, week by week, is exposed to much more attack than the profession of public relations. For us to resent this would in my opinion be very wrong."[57]

It would be truly fascinating to know who represented the PR industry in those television programmes. Sadly, the programmes themselves were not retained in broadcasting archives, and the participants are either coy or dead. I was certainly unable to find anyone prepared to

---

[54] Fawcett, J. (1963). I'm no Levin lover but... *Public Relations, 15* (3), p. 46.
[55] Men with tin voices. *Public Relations, 21* (10) 1968, p. 2.
[56] The Institute and the BBC. *Public Relations, 22* (1) 1969, p. 20.
[57] Ibid.

"dish the dirt." Although this is disappointing, it is probably unsurprising in an occupation that is ever sensitive of its image. Media critiques of public relations became an established routine. For example, David Johnson (ex-*Evening Standard*, *The Daily Telegraph*, and *The Sunday Times*) saw public relations in the 1970s as "a motormouth profession that has always attracted silly people with no understanding of the media and no vision."[58] Polly Toynbee argued in the mid-1980s that "the real battle between the press and PRs comes in trying to get information out of them when it is needed. . . . Information Officer often means Disinformation Officer or even Downright Liar, but certainly not Truth Teller. . . . We are indeed natural enemies."[59] Finally, in the late 1990s, Jenny McCartney noted in *The Spectator*, "PR and journalism are locked in a love-hate relationship: an embrace here, a rebuff there, an occasional genial waltz around a story together."[60]

This brief review of media criticism shows how it consistently undermined the legitimacy of the public relations occupation and revealed journalists' fears and defensiveness about their own occupation. Underlying the criticism of "pufflicity" and deception was a jurisdictional struggle over who should define the news and how access was gained to news sources. The attacks also explain public relations' sensitivities and the occupation's growing obsession with its own self-identity, public image, and the public relations of public relations.

FLESHPOTS AND UNDUE INFLUENCE

Many journalists perceived the provision of entertainment by PROs as attempts to undermine their integrity by disposing them favourably toward the cause represented by the practitioner. As Ian Waller, Political Correspondent of *The Sunday Telegraph*, suggested:

> It has become a fashion these days to assume that the only way of getting news across, or of projecting an organisation favourably to the press, is by dispensing lavish hospitality. . . . I am frequently astonished that [clients] are prepared to waste money in this way. . . . I have enjoyed many an excellent party at your clients' expense. I cannot ever recall

[58]Coren, A. (1976, 17 July). A matter of trust or tricks. *The Times*, p. 23.

[59]Toynbee, P. (1984, 5 November). Information officer often means disinformation officer, or even downright liar. *The Guardian*, p. 12.

[60]McCartney, J. (1998, 10 January). *The Spectator*, p. 8.

being impressed or influenced as a result. It has often struck me that the more lavish the entertainment the flimsier the story. The truth is that if you have a good news story to tell, you don't have to pour bottles of gin down journalists to sell it. . . . It certainly does nothing to enhance the reputation of your profession.[61]

However, as Michael Frayn recalled in 1998:

All the journalists at the time were feeling guilty that they were such easy targets for public relations people. Journalists went along [to press conferences] and had a drink, often several drinks and often more than several drinks and then came back with the press release in their pocket and wrote their story from that and nothing else [so] reporters were not as resistant to the blandishments of public relations as they ought to be.[62]

Media criticism of hospitality public relations continued, as illustrated by Liz Jobey of *The Observer*, who wrote in 1982, "The PR lunch is a gruelling affair . . . under cover of polite smiles and forced friendliness, to withstand the pressures of the PR who is determined to drag out some assurance of a mention. One can be plied with wine and exhausted by useless conversation. . . . For the PR, this lunchtime scenario is conducted almost daily."[63] Journalist Richard West suggested that entertainment was a necessary part of the public relations occupational culture because it was based on personal contacts and networking: "Some PROs swear by personal contacts as a way of getting their clients or products mentioned in the press. They will foster friendships with drinks, lunches and the rare exclusive news story. Many PROs . . . drink every lunchtime at Fleet Street public houses such as El Vino's and the Cock Tavern, followed by lunch at a nearby club."[64]

The existence of a strong expense account culture and the importance that alcohol played in it was acknowledged by the public relations industry itself as evidenced by the following:

Maurice Buckmaster [IPR President 1955–1956] . . . commented on the need for PROs to have a good knowledge of the subject [of wine].[65]

---

[61] Waller, I. (1962). I do not condemn public relations—BUT. *Public Relations*, 14 (2), p. 27.

[62] Interview. 12 January 1998.

[63] Jobey, L. (1982, 24 January). Promotion and the art of puffery. *The Observer*, p. 42.

[64] West, R., p. 13.

[65] Talking of food and wine. *Public Relations*, 5 (2) 1953, p. 28.

One must be perfectly capable of appearing to eat two luncheons and several teas, trying to give each party the idea that theirs is the only one that counts.[66]

There are fewer more rapid or effective ways of putting over an idea to a client than by inviting him to lunch. . . . It pays dividends . . . the client can be placed rapidly in the most receptive of moods and ideas presented as naturally and as smoothly as the courses follow the aperitif. . . . We all have to eat and if overworked journalists . . . receive a gay [sic] and novel invitation from a well-known public relations firm to come to a fork-buffet . . . where they can not only make the acquaintance of the new product . . . but also eat amusing food and drink appropriately chosen wines, they are not only very likely to accept but to be favourably impressed. . . . [Hospitality] is a most valid means of establishing that atmosphere of goodwill and understanding.[67]

There are some public relations people who cannot open their mouths unless they open a bottle of champagne at the same time.[68]

Drinking gin can be hard work! Particularly if you go back and clear the in-tray afterwards! Which you do.[69]

These examples also illustrate the importance of class and the necessity for public relations practitioners to achieve an appropriate veneer if they did not already possess the right cultural capital. The appearance of various articles in *Public Relations* on wine, manners, and social graces indicates that the institute saw its role partly as educating its members about values and appropriate behaviour in certain contexts. It is questionable whether journalists were in a strong position to criticise public relations practitioners, given that the media occupational culture was equally entrenched in pubs and clubs, at least until the advent of new technology and the decline of Fleet Street as Fleet Street.

The 1960s were the years when the personal and professional relationships between public relations and journalism developed into patterns of distrust, dislike, and dependence that have lasted to the present day. Much can be put down to territorialism, competition, and jealousy. The emergence of public relations changed the way that journalists were used to working and they resented that. Furthermore, public rela-

---

[66]One man's week: a PRO in industry. *Public Relations*, 6 (1) 1953, p. 8.

[67]Dunn, S. (1956). Hospitality in PR. *Public Relations, 8* (4), p. 28.

[68]Eden-Green, A. (1961). The presidential address: responsibility to society. *Public Relations, 13* (4), p. 31.

[69]Interview. 30 October 1996.

tions practitioners tried to influence journalists' perceptions, often by networking and exerting personal influence in a social context. In one sense, public relations practitioners can be seen to have successfully infiltrated journalism culture. Most difficult of all for journalists was ceding control of news definition. Even more galling, perhaps, was the public relations practitioners' insistence that they were providing helpful, neutral information and facts, whereas the journalists' perception was that they were trying to sell stories. The struggle for authority and power can be understood in terms of Bourdieu's notion of distinction, as well as in terms of jurisdictional conflict. A great deal of effort has been spent by both parties analysing the relationship and articulating criticism and, on the public relations side, defensive self-justification. Revealing though these are of structural changes in information flows, there were more specific issues raised in relation to the political domain that remain of contemporary relevance.

PUBLIC RELATIONS IN THE POLITICAL DOMAIN: DEFINITIONS AND DEBATES

The story of public relations in the political domain is muddied further by another set of definitional debates and jurisdictional struggles between public relations and lobbying. Whereas lobbyists of some sort or another have always hovered around centres of power (there were complaints about harassment of MPs at Westminster in the 16th century), the evolution of the distinctive occupation of public relations occurred in the same period that lobbying activity increased. In the present-day context, many lobbyists recoil from the term *public relations*—Maloney called it "a ritualised term of disapproval."[70] The influential lobbyist Charles Miller dismissed public relations as "lightweight"[71] and claimed that lobbying is based on the law.[72] The comparison illustrates aspiration to the status of one of the most elite and least accessible professions in the UK and, as such, is amenable to a Chomskyan analysis of the way elites link and collude with each other. There is jurisdictional conflict between the specialist lobbyists, who do not want to be defined as public relations practitioners, while at the same time public relations

---

[70]Moloney, K. (1996). *Lobbyists for hire.* Aldershot: Dartmouth Publishing Co., p. 7.
[71]Ibid.
[72]Ibid.

consultancies are increasingly taking on the type of work that demands access to the upper echelons of society. This raises broader issues of structural inequality in relation to a public sphere in terms of access to power being increasingly dominated by those who can employ lobbyists. As Gandy pointed out, "Although PR resources may occasionally be brought to bear in a debate on behalf of the interests of citizens, consumer, corporate and government bureaucracies are the primary clients and beneficiaries."[73]

A common media perception of the lobbyist is of "a somewhat shadowy or sinister figure working furtively behind the scenes."[74] Within the public relations literature lobbying is also in the shadows, described euphemistically as government relations, parliamentary relations, issues management, and public affairs—all important-sounding terms that conceal the real activity going on.[75] Controversies over sleaze exposed some notorious and nefarious lobbyists, as well as the tension within the public relations' occupational psyche between the public face (impression management, media relations) and the behind-the-scenes activity (negotiation, power broking). Media frustration with public relations arises because PROs can limit access to the sources of power. The semimerged identities of public relations practitioners and lobbyists is symbolic of a fundamental problem in public relations: the tension between truth (factual information) and rhetoric (persuasive interpretation). Lobbying as an activity is necessarily about advocacy and is possibly adversarial (hence the applicability of the legal model and the relevance of liberal pluralism), but public relations' bid for professional status has partly depended on arguments suggesting it is a neutral go-between for an organisation and its publics (a public service model). Clearly, these positions are incompatible and, to date, the professional bodies have not considered the implications of this for their professional project.

POLITICS AND PUBLIC RELATIONS: THE ROYAL COMMISSION 1948

The launch of the IPR in February 1948 almost coincided with a Royal Commission on the Press, which invited the IPR president, Stephen Tal-

---

[73]Gandy, O. (1992), p. 135.

[74]Greer, I. (1985). *Right to be heard*. London: Ian Greer Associates, p. 119. Cited in Moloney, K. (1996). *Lobbyists for hire*. Aldershot: Dartmouth Publishing Co., p. 3.

[75]Moloney, K., p. 3.

lents, to answer questions and criticisms about the role of governmental public relations. Concerns had been expressed by journalists that "PROs stand between the Press and contacts with the Ministers and senior civil servants . . . that PROs tend to put a rather rosy colour on the programmes of Departments [and that they put over] the point of view of the Government in power."[76] Tallents responded that "You have to canalise the journalists' approach to Ministers . . . because . . . Ministers are very busy people. . . . In my own practice I always tried to stick to the truth but to make it interesting . . . one does suspect cases in which there is occasionally a tendency to exalt a person rather than the work of a Department."[77]

Tallents' defence is of interest not only because it was re-articulated many times by others, but also because of the line that is taken. Tallents argued in favour of public relations on functional grounds at the same time that he justified the practice on the basis of morality. He deflected the point about the potential for public relations to become full-blown political propaganda on behalf of the government in power by suggesting that only individual politicians might benefit, and he certainly did not deal with the implied criticism behind the query: whether civil servants, in theory bound to serve any government, might become politicised. Tallents also justified the practice on the basis that "the increasing complexity of the processes of government, scientific research and the need to get the co-operation of the public . . . necessitate some arrangement such as the PRO system."[78] Here one can see a harking back to Griersonian ideas as well as an argument partly based on technological determinism.

In 1952, Charles Curran of the *Evening Standard* (later Director General of the BBC) argued against the necessity for government PROs, although he appeared happy that corporate and financial institutions should gain increased influence through their employment of public relations staff:

[He had] no quarrel with public relations officers employed by capitalist concerns for if their shareholders were satisfied then there was nothing more to be said by anyone. With Government and other public relations officers paid out of public money it was a different matter. . . . Only if you agree that the Government should control everybody's lives should

----

[76] Royal Commission on the press. *Public Relations*, 1 (2) 1948, p. 10.
[77] Ibid.
[78] Ibid.

Government PROs be accepted. . . . The PRO is one of the manifestations of a total state.[79]

In June 1956, there was a debate on public relations in the House of Commons arising from a motion put forward by Anthony Wedgwood Benn MP urging the government to "set up a Commission of Inquiry to study the relationship now existing between . . . public authorities and private individuals within the framework of existing policy and to make recommendations."[80] Wedgewood Benn's main interest was the public relations of local and central government civil servants, which he saw as socially beneficial because it facilitated communication. He had nothing but admiration for the IPR and suggested that the institute should be encouraged in its work and that, furthermore, "we should have a committee of enquiry to push their ideas." Ian Harvey MP MIPR followed up with a supportive speech in which he defined public relations as "a new phrase for question of behaviour. . . . Public relations is concerned with the putting of people in the picture . . . an expression of policy . . . an interpretation of leadership."[81] He argued against professionalisation of the occupation because "propaganda is a good name gone wrong . . . public relations might equally go wrong if it were to be thought . . . that it was something confined to a cult of specialists only."[82] Overall, according to *Public Relations*, "The debate was a highly successful one for the profession."[83] The honeymoon was not to last. Nomenclature has remained a contentious issue in the field of public relations as exemplified by the euphemistic job retitling to "corporate communication," "communication manager," and "public affairs" in the 1990s.

In 1956, William Deedes, the Parliamentary Undersecretary for the Home Office, spoke to the IPR on the issue of "how far should government enter into the public relations business?"[84] He argued that party politics "can and does mix publicity, policy, politics, propaganda, pretty freely" and that the neutrality of civil servants was an essential principle in a democracy. He suggested that "relations between a government and the press should not be so good" and that increasing publicity led to

---

[79]Curran, C. (1952). What I think of PROs and why. *Public Relations*, 4 (4), p. 5.

[80]Public relations debate in the House of Commons. *Public Relations*, 8 (4) 1956, p. 50.

[81]Ibid.

[82]Ibid.

[83]Blow, J. (1957). PR through the press cuttings. *Public Relations*, 9 (3), p. 24.

[84]Deedes, F. W. (1956). Government and public relations. *Public Relations*, 8 (4), p. 5.

increasing caution on the part of officials and a diminution in the quality and depth of news coverage.

In April 1957, *Public Relations'* front-page editorial gleefully announced the appointment of IPR member Dr. Charles Hill, an MP and Chancellor of the Duchy of Lancaster (formerly responsible for the public relations of the BMA and subsequently Chairman of the BBC and ITA) to the post: "Officially responsible for the British Government's public relations. . . . One essential result of the Government's fresh top level approach to public relations . . . will be to give further recognition to public relations throughout the world. . . . This wider recognition can only yield a worthwhile result to all the parties concerned and contribute towards peace in the world."[85] But "Rab" Butler, Lord Privy Seal, saw the role of public relations as supporting the British Government and countering other governments' propaganda:

> When you reflect on the effect on a nation's mind overseas, in the Arab World for example, of the incessantly dripping propaganda which goes on from many sources, you will see . . . the importance of your work is greater than that of any that can be done in the world today as long as it is done in the spirit . . . that is not personal or selfish, but in the national interest, and for the national good.[86]

Such overtures suggest that the government hoped that public relations could be harnessed in the same way as the BBC External Services then required to "plan . . . broadcasts in the national interest"[87] and to "play an important part in the 'projection of Britain' and in bringing British goods and British 'know-how' to the notice of other countries, as well as in spreading general knowledge of this country and contributing towards international understanding."[88] The following year, Ian Harvey MP also emphasised the potential of political communication for influencing overseas domestic publics, citing "diplomacy of the Sputnik" and arguing:

> The lesson of all this is that those who are concerned with overseas diplomacy, both politicians and diplomats, must be prepared to study these

---

[85] Editorial, *Public Relations,* 9 (3) 1957. pp. 1–2.

[86] Butler, Rt. Hon. R. A. CH MP. (1957). The government and the public. *Public Relations,* 9 (3), p. 15.

[87] Jacob, Sir I. (1957). The BBC—a national and international force. *Public Relations,* 9 (3), p. 15.

[88] Earley, E. (1960). Telling the world about British industry. *Public Relations,* 12 (4), p. 47.

techniques and use professional advice of those trained in information work. We are in an age in fact not so much of "open diplomacy" as of "public diplomacy" where the influencing of public opinion is of intense importance.[89]

This theme was developed further by Herbert Morrison MP in his talk to the annual conference of the IPR at Brighton in April 1958 on "World Understanding—Can We Achieve It?," in which he criticised Western bloc policy toward communications,

> We are witnessing an intensive public relations campaign on a world scale. It aims at influencing or capturing the minds of men and women everywhere—the peoples of the Communist countries, of the uncommitted nations, and of the West. The contribution of the West in this world public relations campaign is poor in quality, unco-ordinated and largely ineffective. Despite the horrors of their political system—so much like Hitler's—the Communist Powers are winning the campaign particularly in the backward and uncommitted countries. They are even persuading many people in the West to believe things that are not true. Most of the time they have the initiative.[90]

The convergence between public relations and diplomacy has not received much attention,[91] though within political science and international relations attention has been given to the way in which nation-states "manage their communicative relationships with their foreign publics."[92] As public relations developed as a discrete occupation, so did its role in national policies. This attracted attention from the media, which became aware that increasing unseen, paid-for interventions by public relations practitioners were taking place within the political process. It also became apparent that some public relations practitioners were becoming involved more directly in international diplomacy, and not always in the British interest. These developments were seen as controversial by the media and, to some extent, within the public relations field itself.

---

[89] Harvey I., MP. (1958). Information—instrument of policy. *Public Relations, 10* (2), p. 58.

[90] Morrison, H. (1958). World understanding—can we achieve it? *Public Relations, 10* (3), pp. 14–15.

[91] Signitzer, B. & Coombs, T. (1992). Public relations and public diplomacy: conceptual convergences. *Public Relations Review, 18* (2), pp. 137–47; L'Etang, J. (1996). Public relations as diplomacy. In L'Etang, J. & Pieczka, M. (eds.). *Critical perspectives in public relations.* London: ITBP, pp. 14–35.

[92] Signitzer, B. & Coombs, T., p. 138.

LOBBYING AND WORK FOR OTHER GOVERNMENTS 1960–1970

The practice of lobbying first attracted criticism from the media in the 1960s. Two aspects are highlighted in the following discussion: the association between MPs and public relations consultants for organisational gain, and lobbying on behalf of other countries. The focus is on events in the 1950s and 1960s and does not extend beyond 1970, when the IPR established a register of parliamentary public relations interests. But the debates have endured until the present day, as seen in the scandals and sleaze of the 1990s.

Although the relationship between government and public relations had been discussed on various occasions, it was not until 1961 that the IPR journal published an article that directly addressed parliamentary lobbying. The author of the article, Claude Simmons from Editorial Services, was well known as a successful lobbyist, described in the citation for his Fellowship as having "a particular enthusiasm for Parliamentary public relations and the importance of PR as a bridge between the world of commerce and industry and that of Westminster and Whitehall." He was described by contemporary practitioner Reggie Watts as:

> One of the great doyens of that early period . . . very keen on the low profile and took tremendous care. I mean we had a law [in CS Services — later merged and taken over by Burson-Marsteller] that any meeting with an MP or anybody at that sort of level. . . . He forbade anyone to mention the name of an MP even in the contact report . . . tremendous discretion . . . if he was talking to MPs or journalists it was always done very discreetly in clubs and things like that.[93]

This insight reveals the underhanded nature of such work and a role for public relations more akin to that of a secret agent working on behalf of largely commercial and corporate interests and potentially contributing to the institutional domination of the public sphere. It also shows that some of this work has taken place in the context of the privileged and, until very recently, sexist environment of gentlemen's clubs (membership often determined by public school education, Oxbridge, or certain occupations and always by the recommendation of existing members).

---

[93] Fellowship for man who started Board of Trade PR. *Public Relations*, 22 (7) 1969, p. 12; Interview. 10 January 1997.

Simmons argued that in a "much-governed" era public relations was a tool "to ensure fairer play for all and to remove the scales which can dim even Parliamentary eyes."[94] Simmons even went so far as to imply that parliament might not have the public interest as its priority and that public relations should "place the facts fairly and objectively before our rulers."[95] Simmons also displayed some sensitivity about the practice: "the cynical can call this lobbying . . . [but] I don't think bad names are bad publicity"[96] and argued that "our task is to achieve recognition for PR as one of the prime lubricants of the modern world."[97] Simmons' remarks were seen as disingenuous by journalist Richard West, who commented:

> PR firms . . . find it valuable to have contacts with members of Parliament. They are useful for their connections with Ministers, civil servants and back bench pressure groups. With support from an MP in the House, the PRO can back his campaign with letters written on House of Commons notepaper, with hospitality in the Commons' private dining room and the prospect of further support from other MPs.[98]

In 1961, there was a turning point in the relationship between politics and public relations and also in perceptions of public relations. In June, Harold Wilson, MP, drew the House's attention to lobbying methods employed by industrial concerns who wished to amend the Finance Bill in relation to the taxation of hydrocarbon oils.[99] Seemingly, a lunch party was held in the House to which a number of MPs were invited in order to table a new clause. This was considered an inappropriate use of the House facilities, and a letter that encouraged those who had not attended to add their names to a clause on an order paper to be too aggressive. Wilson referred to "Highly improper measures which I think are being put on Hon. Members on both sides of the House of Commons by some public relations firms. We are seeing far too much evidence of it, in relation to both domestic and international and colonial affairs."[100] At this point, another MP interrupted and called the practice "corrup-

---

[94] Simmons, C. (1961). Parliament and public relations. *Public Relations*, 13 (4), p. 41.
[95] Ibid.
[96] Ibid.
[97] West, R., p. 77.
[98] Ibid. p. 73.
[99] Wilson, Rt. Hon H., MP. (1962). Public relations and parliament. *Public Relations*, 14 (3), p. 5.
[100] Ibid.

tion," to which Wilson famously replied, "It is an extremely degrading profession. I think that corruption is too strong a word. It is a rather squalid profession which is developing."[101]

There followed an exchange of letters in *The Times*. Alan Eden-Green, IPR President, defended public relations on several grounds: first, that governments employed practitioners in their departments; second, that public relations work was essential to various worthy causes such as "diphtheria immunisation, World Refugee Year, the restoration of Westminster Abbey" and that, when "Harold Wilson ... lumped all PR men into a 'degrading profession,' [it was like] calling all doctors abortionists"; and third, that an advocacy model of public relations was needed to supply the facts on which particular arguments could be built. Finally, he declared, "My Institute is as anxious as Mr Wilson to prevent malpractices in the name of public relations. If Mr Wilson will give us the tangible evidence on which he bases his accusation, we will undertake to investigate and, if it involves any of our members, to take the disciplinary action which our constitution allows."[102] Then, according to an interview Eden-Green gave in 1996, Malcom Muggeridge "saw my letter in *The Times* and he wrote a letter and said he wouldn't actually have public relations people abolished [but] he would call for them to carry a clapper and a bell so that people knew when they were coming and could avoid them."[103] Muggeridge did indeed conclude his letter with this flippant suggestion, but the main substance of his argument was:

> Persuasion is obviously a legitimate and necessary social activity . . . public relations men are only engaged in doing, on behalf of their employers, what lawyers do for their clients. . . . Where, however, PR persuasion differs . . . is in being, more often than not, hidden behind a camouflage of objectivity and hospitality. It is, as it were, wrapped in slices of smoked salmon, aromatic with cigar smoke, and delivered, not as a sample but as a gift package. . . . The PR man . . . seeks to infiltrate news and editorial columns. He operates in a no-man's land between advertisement and argument. His message is fed into the sausage machine of public affairs in the hope that it may reach the public stomach as normal nutriment.[104]

---

[101] Ibid.

[102] Bringing facts to light: role of public relations. (1961, 23 June). Letter to the editor, *The Times*.

[103] Interview. 16 August 1995.

[104] Persuasion. (1961, 27 June). Letter to the editor, *The Times*.

The exchange between Eden-Green and Muggeridge points up the perennial tension between public relations conceived as advocacy and public relations conceived as information provision in the public interest.

In April 1962, Harold Wilson wrote an article in *Public Relations* in which he criticised those practitioners:

> Who have been commissioned by overseas Governments or other interests for the purpose of promoting their sometimes unwholesome doctrines not only by the usual methods of political advertising and suborning of unwary journalists, but even by direct pressures on Members of Parliament and Ministers. . . . If Portugal feels she has a case on Angola . . . let [her] deploy arguments in the full light of day, in the public press, through full-time Embassy or company spokesmen . . . or at the United Nations, not by under-cover pressure.[105]

The response to this and some of the other criticisms came in the next issue of the IPR journal in a printed speech made by chairman of the council, Colin Mann:

> What on earth does he [Harold Wilson] think Members of Parliament and Ministers are for? I submit that MPs exist precisely in order that they *shall* be exposed to "pressure"—by information and advocacy— from any section of the public which has a case to present. . . . It is, in my view, a perfectly legitimate and democratic procedure for Sir Roy Welensky, for example, to invite MPs of all parties to see for themselves what is going on in Central Africa; and to employ a consultant to make the arrangements and advise him about the invitations.[106]

Thus did public relations practitioners seek to legitimate their lobbying function, to get close to sources of power to enhance their own occupational position, and also to compete with the media in terms of defining and articulating issues. Consequently, it was not too surprising that *Public Relations* took pleasure in pointing out in its April 1963 issue that "Mr Wilson's party has now engaged the services of a public relations company to act for it, and thus for him, in selected constituency areas."[107] Increasingly, the political and public relations spheres have merged with the advent of spin doctors and more politicians running their own public relations consultancies or advising them on parliamentary matters.

---

[105] Wilson, Rt. Hon. H. MP, pp. 7–8.

[106] The unhidden dissuaders. *Public Relations*, 15 (3) 1962, p. 10.

[107] As the editor sees it. *Public Relations*, 15 (3) 1963, p. 7.

A rather different view of the role of public relations in politics was put forth by Sir Edward Boyle MP, who believed that "while there is no means whereby public opinion can force a decision on the Government" and that there was nothing "wrong in principle about the power to communicate ... being something that can be bought with money ... everyone in a democratic society, is entitled to proclaim his own opinions — or to pay someone else to proclaim them for him."[108] George Brown, MP, put forth the opposite view to Sir Edward Boyle, arguing that "deep pockets" would distort political debate and that more openness was needed about payment to political parties: "Money talks, and the more money available the more talking can be done ... rendering nugatory laws which exist to prevent rich people, rich parties, rich groups triumphing over others merely because they are richer ... [also] we don't know in this nation today whose money is talking."[109]

Invited to speak at the 1962 winter conference, Ian Waller, Political Correspondent of *The Sunday Telegraph*, also raised a number of questions about ways in which public relations entered the political sphere. He questioned the consultancy practice of offering retainers to MPs and asked:

> When does the MP begin to become the indirect representative of the public relations firms' clients? Who knows for what he is speaking or whose interests he is promoting? It would surely be a serious thing if Parliament became a collection of hired representatives of outside interests, or if retainers became a recognised perk for an MP. . . . [There is] a small minority in public relations who set out to be what I call "the fixers." They profess to smooth the path to Government departments, to be able to project a favourable image of their clients' interests to the right people.[110]

This passage has an extremely contemporary feel and is equally applicable to the scandals and sleaze of the 1990s. Apart from the cash-for-questions scandal, which revealed extensive bribery and corruption at the seat of power in Westminster, there were other issues such as unofficial privileged access given to clients at back-bench committees, lobbyists masquerading as researchers, and obscurity over links between MPs' and lobbyists' financial interests. Although a parliamentary register of

---

[108] Boyle, Sir E. MP. (1962). Politics, public opinion and public relations. *Public Relations*, 14 (4), pp. 23–4.

[109] Ibid. p. 27.

[110] Waller, I. (1962). I do not condemn public relations — BUT. *Public Relations*, 14 (2), pp. 28–9.

interests was set up in 1974, it was bedeviled with vague and synoptic entries for decades, although it tightened up following the Nolan Committee Report.

In 1969, the IPR set up the President's Special Committee on Political Public Relations and in 1970 it established a register of parliamentary public relations interests, and members were required to specify "an interest" when speaking on any matter in which they had a financial stake. It was thought, "[it] should be sufficient to protect the integrity of debate" and that the application of the rule should be left to the House of Commons.[111] Lobbying was seen as "a perfectly legitimate—indeed, essential—part of the democratic process: provided always that it is conducted an open and honest manner."[112] This has many resonances with recent sleaze scandals in Britain, particularly those involving the lobbyist Ian Greer and the MP Neil Hamilton in the late 1990s. However, although Greer has been pilloried, it seems the corruption was systemic and it is arguable that Greer was a symptom rather than a cause. Recent and continuing criticism of spin doctors also has resonance with the historical events of the 1960s.

PUBLIC RELATIONS AND DIPLOMACY

As already noted, an important focus for criticism of public relations by parliamentarians and journalists was work that was done by consultants for other countries. Both diplomats and public relations practitioners have interpretive and presentational roles, and both attempt to manage communication and public opinion about issues, often through the media. So in some ways, it is not surprising that public relations practitioners of the burgeoning industry of the 1950s and 1960s should have branched out in this way to take advantage of commercial opportunities offered by decolonisation and other political events.

Possibly the earliest example of a public relations consultant working for an overseas country was before the Second World War. Basil Clarke, of Editorial Services, worked for the Danish government to promote Anglo-Danish friendship and trade and was made a member of the Dannebrog, a high honour in Denmark, for his services.[113] In 1955,

---

[111] PR and Parliament: the official (IPR) view. *Public Relations*, 22 (4) 1969, p. 8.

[112] Ibid. p. 9.

[113] The life and times of Sir Basil Clarke—a pioneer. *Public Relations*, 22 (2) 1969, p. 8.

Hereward Phillips acted for the Ethiopian Embassy on the visit of Ethiopia's Imperial Majesty to the UK. Phillips recruited J. R. Hyslop "a well-known journalist with a first-hand knowledge of Sudan and neighbouring countries," and within 2 days they were issuing daily bulletins. The first 3 days were a state visit and arrangements were coordinated with Buckingham Palace. Following this period, the agency liaised with the Foreign Office and the Central Office of Information and afterwards Phillips commented:

> From a propaganda point of view it was remarkable how much was achieved in less than a fortnight.... The general public received a geography and history lesson, while industrialists were reminded that in Ethiopia there is a country with great possibilities.... The hospitality shown to the Emperor by Her Majesty, the Government, and many authorities was a source of gratification not only to all Ethiopians, but to coloured races throughout the world.... This State visit as a whole was a first-class piece of public relations on the part of both His Imperial Majesty and the British Government.[114]

A number of prominent practitioners were involved in work for a variety of overseas, and sometimes controversial, governments. Toby O'Brien, who had worked for Conservative Central Office, was a supporter of Franco from the start of the Spanish Civil War and of Salazar in Portugal, and took on accounts to promote Spanish tourism and to act as PRO to the Portuguese Embassy in the UK after the Angolan troubles began.[115] However, he turned down an account for Yugoslavia, because he "didn't like Commies."[116] Sydney Wynne, son-in-law of Ernest Bevin, represented Sir Roy Welensky's Central African Federation, and Anglo-American Pat Dolan worked for Obafemi Awolowo, Premier of Western Nigeria, for a brief that required him to "create a climate of opinion abroad to encourage foreign investments in Western Nigeria . . . to create an image of Western Nigeria in the eyes of the world that reveals a forward-looking, progressive country with a host of remarkable achievements to its credit."[117] Michael O'Shaunghgun worked for President Senghor of Senegal, Condor Public Relations worked for the Federal Republic of Cameroon, and Kenneth Kaunda

---

[114]Phillips, H. (1955). Public relations for an emperor. *Public Relations, 7* (2), p. 25.
[115]West, R., p. 79.
[116]Kisch, R., p. 78.
[117]West, R., p. 84.

sought and obtained the services of two eminent public relations men Sam Cotton (previously Head of Public Relations at the Ministry of Supply) and Mike Williams-Thompson.[118] In the late 1960s, Malcom Fraser started working for the Greek Colonels and claimed that he could procure the services of a Labour MP to work for them in Parliament.[119] Founder member Lex Hornsby worked for the East German government, but said, "none of it is political" because "The account was concerned with trade, industry, cultural activities and tourism . . . he had retained two MPs as consultants, because they were experienced in German trade. There was nothing political about their activities."[120]

The anti-Zionist Michael Rice began a lifelong association with Egypt when he accepted a commission from the Egyptian Ministry of Culture and National Guidance to "assist them with their relations with media, parliament and, to a lesser degree, industry." He also cooperated with key figures in the Anglo-Arab community in London "to try to counter the unremitting flow of anti-Arab propaganda, which was being directed at the political arena as much as to the organs of opinion."[121] In the early 1970s, Rice worked for the Arab League "in an attempt to minimise the more arcane statements made about [the Arab States]."[122]

More recently, a number of consultancies have expanded into international work and in the post-Cold War era have lucrative accounts specialising in the privatisation of state-owned enterprises in former Eastern-bloc countries. For example, Dewe Rogerson carried out mass privatisation programmes in Ukraine (1999), Kazakstan (1996–1997), Bulgaria (1996–1997), Slovenia (1996–1997), Georgia (1995–1996), Romania (1992 and 1995–1996), Belarus (1994), and Hungary (1993–1994). Other international economic accounts include Richmond Towers' work for the Ontario Ministry of Agriculture and Food and the U.S. Department of Agriculture, and Gavin Anderson's campaign on behalf of the Ministry of Finance of the Government of Ukraine and I. N. G. Baring to support the restructuring of Ukraine's external debt.[123] Citigate Westminster was appointed by the Polish Treasury to advise on how to manage its state-owned industries, the consultancy JGW worked

---

[118] Kisch, R., pp. 66–67.

[119] IPR 2/2/10 IPR Archive, History of Advertising Trust; Rice, M. (1994). *False inheritance: Israel in Palestine and the search for a solution.* London: Kegan Paul.

[120] IPR 2/2/10 IPR Archive, History of Advertising Trust.

[121] Rice, M., p. 8.

[122] Rice, M., p. 9.

[123] *PR Week.* 26 May 2000.

to avert sanctions to Libya,[124] and Clear Communications organised the visit of eight trainers, sponsored by the UK all-party Westminster Foundation for Democracy, to teach media relations skills to the Social Democratic Party of the Czech Republic.[125] Public relations is now entrenched in international diplomacy and the promotion of capitalism on a grand scale. However, criticism of such developments and work conducted for politically dubious regimes has been relatively muted. In recent times, only Hill and Knowlton's propaganda work for the Kuwaiti Government during the Gulf War attracted any significant outcry.

CONCLUSION

This chapter has illustrated the conflict between public relations and journalism and suggested that the main reasons for this were jurisdictional struggle over which occupation constructed news. In effect, the growth and development of public relations represented an attempt to move the construction of news further up the supply chain to facilitate greater influence by the source. The fact that print and broadcast journalism were contracting as public relations expanded was a bitter pill for journalists to swallow and fueled their hostility. Journalists were the main source of criticism of public relations and, although much of this focused on its impact on the working practices of journalism, the more profound threat posed by public relations in terms of corruption of the channels of political communication was also raised. Much has been revealed about journalists' insecurities concerning their own occupation, self-identity, and perception of themselves as morally responsible truth seekers serving the public. Threatened by the development of the fast-growing occupation of public relations at a time when journalism jobs were in decline, it is not difficult to interpret much of their criticism as self-defence.

[124] *PR Week.* 18 October 1996.
[125] *PR Week.* 2 February 1996.

6

Crime and Punishment: Codes and Regulation, 1948–1998

INTRODUCTION

This chapter presents the story of the IPR's attempts to regulate public relations practice and focuses on some of the minutiae of codes from a philosophical perspective. There has been little direct analysis of codes of ethics in the existing literature on professionalism,[1] however, from the field of business ethics some useful distinctions were made by the philosopher Donaldson between codes of ethics, codes of conduct, and codes of practice, even though they are sometimes referred to as though they were the same and each may include technical, prudential, and ethical requirements.[2] As Donaldson explained, codes of ethics can be distinguished by their brevity, clear ethical principles, and imperative mode; codes of conduct are more specific and practical and may detail particular conditions and exceptions; and codes of practice largely relate to technical standards and the expectations and rights of consumers.

In the Anglo–American business context, the ethical principles that underpin codes of ethics are derived from two of the most important moral theories in Western philosophy, utilitarianism (derived from the

---

[1] Maclagen, P. (1998). *Management and morality*. London: Sage, p. 11.
[2] Donaldson, J. (1989). *Key issues in business ethics*. London: Academic Press, pp. 124, 133.

156

writings of Jeremy Bentham and John Stuart Mill) and deontology (based on the thinking of Immanuel Kant). Moral theories both define *good* and judge right actions. The good of utilitarianism is happiness and a right action is that which is judged to have maximised happiness. Utilitarianism is a type of consequentialism because it makes the rightness of actions solely dependent on their consequences. In contrast to utilitarianism, a deontological approach to ethics entails a judgment that a right act is that which is done out of duty to universal law and not out of inclination. Kant himself thought less highly of kind or good actions done through an impulse of sympathy or generosity and more highly of those motivated strictly out of duty. He attributed the action done out of duty with moral worth because it was the result of rational analysis based on notions of obligation and duty. The moral worth of an act could be evaluated by considering whether one would be willing for that act to become a universal law of behaviour. Of particular importance to the framework was the notion that, where self-interest plays a part in the motivation of an action, then that action is regarded as prudential and cannot be regarded as a morally right action because it has not been carried out with moral as opposed to self-interested intentions.

To apply such moral frameworks to public relations requires the identification of the goods of public relations. A utilitarian might argue optimistically that public relations maximises happiness because it contributes to democracy by assisting the flow of information in society. Such a position assumes that different viewpoints are articulated and that public relations facilitates open discourse. This could be defined as a free-market approach to the economics of information. Identical arguments have in the past been put forward on behalf of journalism.[3] A different approach would be to try to identify those individuals or groups who benefit from the existence of public relations. For a deontologist, this would lead to questions of social justice for equality of access to public relations services and the implications that this might have regarding the distribution of power in society. For a utilitarian, the question about benefits would be crucial to determining utility, but would also demand that public relations practitioners properly evaluate the effects of their work, an aspect of practice that is currently poorly

---

[3]Belsey, A. & Chadwick, R. (1992). Ethics and politics of the media: the quest for quality. In Belsey, A. & Chadwick, R. (eds.). *Ethical issues in journalism and the media*. London: Routledge, pp. 11–13.

developed and generally limited only to media coverage achieved. Because the deontological approach leads to critical questions about the public relations occupation and could lead to a critique of capitalism, we can see that practitioners (and their official bodies) might wish to adopt the free-market, utilitarian view of public relations, even though historically, practitioners have struggled to prove the benefits of the practice.

It is also worth reflecting briefly on the utility of codes themselves. Business ethics literature suggests that codes formulated along the lines of the U.N. Charter for Human Rights are too broad to be useful, whereas codes that are very prescriptive and detailed are never quite adequate for new situations and can additionally foster a "loophole-seeking attitude of mind."[4] Codes are presumed to be for the benefit of society, but can only be so if misdemeanours are punished and sanctions applied to those who transgress the code. If an occupation is unable to enforce its code, or seems reluctant to do so, then the code is no more than window dressing. From a Kantian perspective, the inability to enforce a code would render the code immoral because the failure to observe the duty required by the code would mean that there was no real intention to make the code a universal law.

Public relations practice has often been seen as unethical (in recent times one has only to think of the publicist Max Clifford's boasts about lying and the corruption of Ian Greer and other lobbyists), yet the practice has claimed to be socially responsible and to work in the public interest. The topic of ethics is of importance to a history of the occupation's development for a number of reasons: First, given the present work's focus on professionalisation, the acquisition of a code of ethics is a significant step, according to process theorists; second, the development of a code of ethics by the IPR represents the only attempt to regulate the practice of the occupation; third, a philosophical perspective presents a broader way of thinking about the practice in society, as outlined briefly earlier; fourth, there is the potential to consider relationships with the media; and, finally, a focus on particular problematic cases that reveal heroes and villains can help us to understand the occupational values.

This chapter is structured around a discussion of the key themes arising from the IPR's code of practice (1964) with reference to some of the cases that came before the Institute's Council (prior to 1964) or its pro-

---

[4]Harris, N. (1992). Codes of conduct for journalists. In Belsey, A. & Chadwick, R. (eds.). *Ethical issues in journalism and the media*. London: Routledge, p. 67.

fessional practices and disciplinary committees (after 1964). The discussion focuses on the consistent elements of the various formulations of the IPR code and draws some comparisons between precepts. There is no attempt to trace in detail the subtle changes of wording over half a century, but instead an effort is made to encapsulate the essence of the IPR codes with a view to identifying the key problematics of public relations practice. The cases referred to can be regarded as critical incidents in the Institute's history in terms of exemplifying core values and illustrating areas of concern. They also reveal the Institute's methods of policing practice and of bringing offenders to justice. It should be noted that access to the disciplinary cases was limited to those that took place prior to 1979. Moreover, much of the documentation is incomplete, which made it difficult to reconstruct cases in sufficient detail to be fully comprehensible. The sample is chosen to be representative of the range of cases that occurred. The very first case of expulsion is given most emphasis because it appears to have set the tone for much of what followed and because those who were involved saw it as a major traumatic event.

PREHISTORY: FIRST BRITISH CODE OF ETHICS

The first British code of ethics devised for public relations was developed by Basil Clarke, Editorial Services, in the 1920s in his "Little White Book." The key restrictions on practice were:

> All anonymity or disguise on the part of the PR operator must go. No payment must be accepted from newspapers. No canvassing for accounts. No fraudulent stunts likely to deceive the public—or editors. No promises or threats, about the placing or withholding of advertisements to secure the publication of editorial copy. Payment only by professional fee and not by piece rates or press results.[5]

As will be seen, this code proved to have identified a number of deontological principles that remained dear to the official body and its representatives throughout the 20th century. All of Clarke's ideas were incorporated at one stage or another into the various formulations of

---

[5]Clarke, A. (1969). The life and times of Sir Basil Clarke—PR pioneer. *Public Relations*, 22 (2), p. 10.

the IPR code of ethics. Clarke's code was designed partially to try to separate public relations practice from stunt creation and publicity. He aimed to stop his employees from attempting to influence the operation of news selection by preventing them from using the promise of advertisements to bribe journalists. Clarke was concerned about the standing of public relations practice and was keen to see it operating on a similar basis to established professions in terms of the relationship between practitioners and their clients. Thus, he was opposed to practitioners soliciting potential clients and argued that payment should be for the professional consultation and advice received, not for results achieved. Clarke's interest in the status of public relations was also apparent in the attention he gave to the relationship between public relations and journalism, and in the potential for corruption.

Forty years after Clarke had devised his code, the journalist Richard West critically reviewed its contents in the light of public relations practice in the early 1960s.[6] West pointed out that public relations practitioners commonly concealed themselves as a source, for example, when they ventriloquised a client's views through the medium of "a private person's letter to the editor of a newspaper."[7] Likewise, he argued that the use of apparently impartial bodies or "front organisations" as a source was commonly employed to promote the vested interests of clients. West argued that public relations practitioners often interfered with journalistic practice and by inference distorted societal communications. He gave as an example the apparently frequent practice of public relations practitioners requesting access to proof copy of editorial in order to "check the facts,"[8] because "this makes the journalist reluctant to be critical in his writing."[9] The fact that West could still engage so strongly with Clarke's code so many years later suggests that the issues it addressed were fundamental problems for public relations, journalism, and society.

FIRST STEPS BY THE INSTITUTE

According to Alan Hess, first chairman of the Council of the Institute, the group who inaugurated the Institute in 1947 included among their

---

[6]West, R. (1963). *PR the fifth estate.* London: Mayflower Books.
[7]Ibid. p. 121.
[8]Ibid.
[9]Ibid.

objectives "[t]o encourage and foster observance of high professional standards by its members,"[10] which could imply ethical as well as functional, technical standards. The constitution drafted by founder members in January 1948 included a provision that would allow the Institute to expel its members: "Any member of the Institute may be suspended or expelled from membership, if, in the opinion of the Council, as evidenced by a majority vote of those present and voting, he is guilty of unprofessional conduct or conduct prejudicial to the Institute."[11] This provision was clearly self-interested in its concern with the reputation of the occupation. It also implied a majoritarian approach to definitions of *goodness* and *right acts*, but did not actually define *unprofessional conduct*. It is significant that the Institute's reputation appeared to be of more importance than the impact of public relations on society.

The 1948 Royal Commission on the Press drew attention to the absence of a code of practice, specifically in the area of government information, where it was thought desirable to emphasise the necessity for public relations offices to avoid "boosting their own Departments"[12] and to emphasise "the right of the Press to check official statements by any other sources at their command."[13] Tallents replied that such a code "would be extremely difficult to draw up"[14] but that the newly formed IPR "are considering whether they can get out any sort of code."[15] The AGM of 1948 specified again the need for a code[16] and the need for a termination mechanism.[17] In the same year, John Pringle, PRO of the BMA, pointed out the role that codes had played in making the medical profession respectable: "the BMA has ... laid down standards of professional conduct for doctors and, by doing so, it has contributed enormously to the repute in which the profession is held."[18]

So it seems that at the outset, the motivation behind the creation of a code was more to do with the occupation's reputation than with engaging in serious moral debate about the wider implications of a new and growing occupation. This alone would render a code unethical, if judged

---

[10] Hess, A. (1948). Our aims and objects. *Public Relations, 1* (1), p. 8.
[11] Draft constitution of the IPR (1948, January), IPR Archive.
[12] Royal Commission on the press. *Public Relations, 1* (2) 1948, p. 11.
[13] Ibid.
[14] Ibid.
[15] Ibid.
[16] AGM (1948, 30 September). IPR Archive 2/1/1 12 (a).
[17] AGM (1948, 30 September). IPR Archive 2/1/1 12 (b).
[18] Pringle, J. (1949). Working for 60,000 employers. *Public Relations, 2* (1), p. 14.

by Kantian standards, because the main motivation was self-interest rather than following the categorical imperative of duty.

In 1949, the IPR Council drew up a "Statement of Standards," which included the core belief that "the practice of public relations has an essential contribution to make towards . . . free discussion . . . the widest possible exchange of information and ideas . . . and the cultivation of goodwill."[19] This formulation was broadly utilitarian and thus did not impose any particular duties on individual members or grant specific rights to publics, for, as Belsey and Chadwick pointed out, "the promotion of democracy . . . is not a duty owed to particular individuals."[20] However, the statement did appear to make a direct appeal to human rights in its claim that "The Institute stands for the freedom of every citizen and every interest to offer both facts and opinions; for the reasonable use of all methods of communicating those facts and opinions; and for the right of the public to hear all sides."[21] Thus, through the statement, the Institute acknowledged the rights of the general public to hear all views, but did not lay down specific duties for members beyond the rather vague requirement on members to adopt "the highest standards of integrity," nor was there a method of ensuring transparency.[22] The remaining clauses were largely concerned with reputational issues and the need to "uphold the honour and interests of public relations" and for each member to "do all in his power to maintain and enhance that reputation and the good name of public relations."[23] The final clause specified a variety of broad obligations, but did not perceive that these might conflict with each other: "[i]n addition to his loyalty to his employer and his responsibility to the public and to the organs of public information, a member of the Institute also owes a duty to his fellow members." This appeared to be the only positive duty and required a member to "assist a fellow member in every way open to him," a very vague sentiment rather suggestive of masonry.

A clarion call for a specific code of ethics came from the eminent consultant Fleetwood Pritchard in the context of a talk on persuasion and propaganda at the 1950 IPR conference. At the end of his talk, Pritchard suggested that the IPR "draw up a code for Public Relations Officers [as

---

[19] Statement of standards 1949, IPR Archive History of Advertising Trust.

[20] Belsey, A. & Chadwick, R. (1992). Ethics and politics of the media: the quest for quality, p. 11.

[21] Statement of standards 1949, IPR Archive History of Advertising Trust.

[22] Ibid.

[23] Ibid.

this] would help to guide Public Relations Officers in their activities and would help them secure the recognition and respect they deserve from the public."[24] Pritchard saw a code as a badge of respectability and a sign of professionalism and his proposal was met with enthusiasm so that "the discussion finished on a general note of endorsing the speaker's appeal for the establishment of a Code of Conduct for Public Relations Officers."[25] At the end of 1950, the *Public Relations* editorial noted that there had been "considerable discussion . . . about a definition of Public Relations, and the establishment of a Code of Conduct" at the recent conference and dinner.[26] The issue of ethics was raised separately by the incoming president Alan Hess in 1951 when he said, "I want to emphasise with all the power I may command—more than anything else, true Public Relations depends upon the intrinsic integrity of its practitioners."[27] However, the employment of such a broad and undefined term left morals very much open to the interpretation of the individual practitioner, for no guiding principles or analytical frameworks were laid down. Such loose subjectivism rendered Hess' sentiments meaningless because the purpose of ethics is to provide principles that identify right and wrong behaviour and frameworks of analysis that can facilitate the understanding of complex situations and provide a guide to appropriate choices of action.

These discussions led, in 1951 and 1952, to the development of regulations that owed a debt to Basil Clarke's code. The regulations prohibited payment by results, internal circulars within the membership that advertised particular services, attempting to supplant a fellow member with his employer or client, disclosure of Institute business, and disclosure of confidential employer or client information. Internally rather than externally focused, it is arguable that these regulations actually contributed to a lack of openness and a culture of secrecy. The regulations thus laid bare the fiction that public relations was really concerned with the public interest. There was nothing about duties to publics or their rights. The employer or client came first and the phrasing of the regulations implied that those who purchased public relations services were also buying practitioners' loyalty in perpetuity (a requirement to confidentiality applied to past clients as well as present ones), which

---

[24] Pritchard, F. (1950). Persuasion. *Public Relations*, 2 (4), p. 21.
[25] Discussion. *Public Relations*, 2 (4) 1950, p. 21.
[26] Now for the future. *Public Relations*, 3 (2) 1950, p. 1.
[27] The conference speeches. *Public Relations*, 3 (2) 1950, p. 6.

contradicted notions of open information and the democratic ideals enunciated elsewhere.

Under the influence of his boss, Fleetward Pritchard, Tim Traverse-Healy spoke at the IPR conference at Hastings about the conventions that had, according to him, been adopted by "reputable consultants."[28] These conventions included not taking on work "considered to be contrary to the national or public interest"; not submitting proposals to clients who already retained a consultancy; not taking on competitive accounts; respecting the confidences of clients; being prepared to declare client lists; specifying the source of all material supplied to the media; not evaluating media relations by measuring column inches; neither offering "inducements" to editors nor accepting editorial space in return for the purchase of advertising space; respecting "exclusives" given to individual journalists; and refraining from being paid by results.[29] However, Traverse-Healy's presentation received some mixed reactions. Alan Hess welcomed the suggestion that those who would not subscribe to such a code should be excluded from membership, whereas R. C. Liebman and J. Murray Smith thought the paper "too idealistic" because the "job of the practitioner was to advance the interest of their client in every possible way and too inflexible a code of ethics would act eventually to the detriment of the client."[30] So some were prepared to consider restraints on practice and others were not.

Although there was plenty of discussion and there were fears that "unless we had some rules of the road we'd get into the hands of spivs," ethics was not included in the first IPR educational syllabus in 1956 and there was no substantive development in Britain even though the Public Relations Society of America published a code in 1952, the French in 1954, and the IPRA in 1960.[31] Asked why the British were such laggards, one contemporary attributed this to British culture and suggested that the British were "pragmatic people who disliked being pinned down by regulation."[32] The absence of a code raised problems for the Institute when, for the first time, it wished to expel a member.

---

[28]Traverse-Healy, T. (1953). Public relations consultancy: what it is and how it works. *Public Relations,* 5 (4), p. 62.

[29]Ibid.

[30]General discussion on consultancy. *Public Relations,* 5 (4) 1953, p. 66.

[31]Off the record comment to author 1995; First syllabus. *Public Relations,* 9 (1) 1956, p. 52; The American code of standards for the practice of public relations. *Public Relations,* 4 (3) 1952, p. 6; French code of conduct. *Public Relations,* 6 (4), 1954, p. 22; IPRA draft code of conduct. *Public Relations,* 13 (1) 1960, p. 50.

[32]Interview. 29 March 1999.

THE CASE OF R. C. LIEBMAN, 1957

The British paid for their lack of formality during the presidency of Alan Campbell-Johnson 1956–1957 when the Council wanted to punish R. C. Liebman (recalled by one contemporary as "a sort of prototype Max Clifford . . . and master stunt creator") for what they regarded as unethical activities, but lacked the mechanism to do so.[33]

The Liebman case is of interest not only because it was the first expulsion, but also because available documentation illustrates the internal processes as well as something of the culture of the organisation. The case related to the regulation about advertising services, which stated:

> It shall be deemed a violation of the Constitution for a member by circularisation to other members to advertise the services of his organisation without having first received the consent of the Council. An infringement of this Regulation shall render any member concerned subject to Article 13 of the Constitution, provided that an advertisement in a members' circular or through the Journal shall not be considered as "circularisation."[34]

On 11 November 1957, Liebman was invited to attend a Special Council meeting at which he explained that he had been approached by Assistant Advertisement Manager J. R. Dixon-Payne of *Advertisers' Weekly* in April 1957 to take advertising space in a public relations special issue to be published in May 1957.[35] Liebman claimed he told Dixon-Payne he did not wish to do this because he had been told "by a number of members that it was undignified."[36] According to Liebman, Dixon-Payne had reassured him that many other public relations consultants were taking space, but refused to name them or to disclose any editorial content.[37] Liebman told Dixon-Payne he did not wish to advertise, but then claimed that Dixon-Payne had written to him confirming that he had reserved space for Liebman anyway.[38] According to the minutes of the Council, Liebman was not able to produce that letter. Liebman said he wrote to

---

[33] Off-the-record comment to author. January 1999.
[34] Regulations 1951 IPR Archive, History of Advertising Trust.
[35] Special Council Minutes. 11 November 1957.
[36] Ibid.
[37] Ibid.
[38] Ibid.

reiterate that he did not wish to take the space and then received a telephone call from the editor who wanted to know why Liebman would not be advertising. Liebman claimed to have said that he did not consider the advertising worthwhile, and added that doctors and barristers did not advertise their services in this way. Liebman then received a telephone call from the Institute's general secretary requesting a copy of Liebman's letter to Dixon-Payne saying that he did not wish to take the space. This was followed up by another call from the editor stating that the copy of the letter sent to the Institute had not been the same as that sent to *Advertisers' Weekly*. Liebman admitted this, but later said that he had lost the original letter and had had to reconstruct it from memory. Liebman said that, because the Institute's monthly newsletter had not mentioned the *Advertisers' Weekly* feature, he assumed that the Institute was against it. Liebman thought that this assumption was sufficient grounds for telling Dixon-Payne that he had consulted the general secretary about the matter, even though he had not actually done so. Liebman considered that his own false statement was justified because he thought that Dixon-Payne had also made one.[39]

Allan Ashbourne, Chairman of the Special Council, summed up by declaring that Liebman had made a false statement to *Advertisers' Weekly* and, when asked for a copy of the letter, had deliberately omitted the claim that he had consulted the general secretary. He reminded all those present that the matter was confidential and not to be discussed and Liebman then left the meeting. The Council agreed that Liebman should be expelled.

Ten days later, it was alleged that a member of the Council (Joyce Blow) had told Arthur Cain about the meeting and its decision to expel Liebman and that Cain had phoned Liebman to warn him.[40] Liebman then raised this issue with another member of the Council, Sam Black.[41] Cain (a former special branch policeman whose career included shadowing the British film documentarists)[42] and Blow both denied Liebman's allegations. A unanimous vote in Blow's integrity was passed and "sincere regret [was expressed] that her name had been brought into [the] matter in such a manner."[43] However, Cain alleged that more than one

---

[39] Ibid.

[40] Council Minutes. 23 November 1957.

[41] Ibid.

[42] Hardy, F. (1979). *John Grierson: a documentary biography*. London: Faber & Faber, pp. 85–6.

[43] Council Minutes. 23 November 1957.

Council member had spoken to him about the matter, but he refused to give names. All Council members present declared their innocence. It subsequently emerged that Cain's source had been Liebman himself, but that he had not wished to disclose this for fear of it prejudicing Liebman's appeal for a further hearing (which was initially turned down). Subsequently, a further hearing was granted on the condition that Liebman produce additional written evidence, surrender his membership certificates and card, and cease to present himself as a member of the Institute. Liebman did not return his membership paraphernalia and angrily rejected the notion that he was passing himself off as a member of the Institute by continuing to use the suffix "MIPR," which he claimed stood for Member of the Institute of Psychological Research.[44]

Liebman challenged the Council's actions and argued that their failure to follow Article 12 of the constitution (which specified that a second special meeting could be held at the request of the member) amounted to a breach of contract and that thus he was no longer required to abide by its terms. Liebman's letter concluded:

> Please tell the Council that they really cannot make up new and pointless rules to suit their own convenience as they go merrily along their own self-righteous way. If they could see and hear the vast and continuous flow of messages of sympathy and support I am receiving every day from fellow members of the Institute who are outraged at the disgusting and ham handed way in which I was and continue to be treated by Council. . . . You can assure the Council that although I have plenty of new and relevant facts to give them, I should not dream of submitting them. . . . I am afraid I prefer negotiating with adult people who have adult minds, and who do not comport themselves like the Headmistress of St Trinian's.[45]

Liebman's assessment regarding the reaction of members had some basis in fact. It was reported in the IPR journal *Public Relations* that the degree of secrecy that had surrounded his expulsion caused disquiet with some members at the time because "there was a feeling that the member had been subjected to a secret trial."[46] This expression of discomfort suggests that there was a feeling, at least among some members, that Liebman was being persecuted. There is no documentary evidence to suggest why this should be, other than that he was clearly a

---

[44] Letter to author. 30 December 1957.
[45] Ibid.
[46] Tenth annual general meeting. *Public Relations,* 10 (2) 1958, p. 7.

strong and quite colourful character who spoke his mind and generally did not support some of the idealised notions of what public relations was about.

In March 1959, Liebman wrote to the Council again and the Council agreed that his sentence could be reviewed if he wrote a letter confirming that he wished to be considered for re-admittance to the Institute. On 21 July, the case was discussed again, but "The opinion of the great majority of members present was that there was no reason why the decision taken in November 1957 should be revoked or modified in any way, nor was there any evidence that, by his conduct since his expulsion, Mr Liebman had justified his being re-admitted to the Institute."[47] Arthur Cain expressed the view that Liebman had not been treated fairly by the Council and he and Sam Black proposed that Liebman's application to rejoin be accepted on the condition that he give a binding undertaking regarding his future behaviour.[48] Their proposal was defeated and the Council decided that Liebman should not be re-admitted.

According to the official documentary evidence, it seems that Liebman's transgression was misleading *Advertisers' Weekly* in stating that he had consulted IPR officials about the proposed issue when, in fact, he had not. Although this in itself hardly seems a momentuous offence, it has to be understood in the context of public relations occupational culture, which at this stage claimed truth as a core ideal. Liebman's peccadillo appeared blasphemous. As a senior IPR figure recalled, "We had the guts to get rid of somebody . . . that was very important . . . we were moving towards . . . the Code of conduct and of course the case brought all these things forwards . . . you need a case like that to bite the bullet."[49]

In 1963, Arthur Cain wrote to the Council to ask it to reconsider the termination of membership imposed on Charles Liebman and it was agreed that Liebman should reapply for membership in the usual way. He was re-admitted on 31 July 1963. In 1968, Liebman died,[50] presumably still disgruntled with his fall from grace as a founder member of the IPR. Liebman's case was formative in terms of moving the Institute toward developing a code that would enable them to expel nonconformist members.

---

[47] Council Minutes. 21 July 1959.
[48] Ibid.
[49] Interview. 22 August 1995.
[50] Death of Charles Liebman. *Public Relations*, 21 (8) 1968, p. 12.

A few months after the denouement of the Liebman case, Alan Eden-Green, Chairman of the Council, wrote in *Public Relations:*

> The Institute has scarcely any case law to refer to . . . our constitution is still in the formative stage. . . . It is probably fair to say that the founder members of the IPR were most concerned to protect the profession or craft (What it is hasn't ever been settled!). . . . The Institute has also been increasingly concerned with raising the standards—practical, professional and ethical. . . . Another Constitutional matter was the problem of taking disciplinary action when allegations of "unethical conduct" have to be considered. This is happily a rare thing, but if the Constitution is to help preserve standards it must have some teeth.[51]

The following year, it was again suggested that ethics should be taken more seriously:

> Possibly the time is ripe for a thorough investigation of the ethics of public relations and an examination of the basic principles and professional behaviour. Public relations is not yet above suspicion and there are plenty of people in business who still think of the public relations officer as a man with a genius for "bull" and whitewashing who, by lavishly wining and dining the Press, gets his clients or employers free advertising in the feature and news columns of papers and magazines.[52]

Despite these sentiments, it took until 1963 for a code to be formulated. Perhaps part of the reason for lack of progress was the existence of some fundamental disagreements within membership about the importance of ethics, as suggested by a *Public Relations* editorial in 1961: "There are still too many people in . . . public relations who think that Ethics is a county in the South of England [i.e., Essex—pronounced with a lisp in a rather particular English accent]. And there is an equal number of people so obsessed by the word that in their utterances and writings they invest it with a holiness, when applied to public relations practice, which lays them wide open to those who delight in pricking pompous bubbles."[53]

IPR CODE OF PRACTICE 1963

Despite these painful experiences, it was not until June 1963 that the first code of professional conduct and rules for disciplinary proceedings

---

[51] Account rendered. *Public Relations,* 11 (1) 1958, p. 4.

[52] Wilshire, G. H. (1960). Philosophy or science. *Public Relations,* 12 (3), p. 10.

[53] By their works. Editorial, *Public Relations,* 13 (4) 1961, p. 2.

were adopted by the Council for inclusion in the memorandum and articles. This was done in readiness for the Institute's incorporation and recognition by the Board of Trade in November 1963 as "representing qualified public relations practice."[54] The president, Colin Mann, highlighted the key elements:

> Some of the clauses . . . are for our own benefit and protection as public relations practitioners—we must not attempt to attract business unfairly; we must not seek to supplant another member; we must not accept payment by results, however tempting it may sometimes be to do so. Some are for the protection of employers or clients—we must not disclose confidential information; we must not normally represent conflicting interests. But the most important clauses of all are designed to protect the public, those who are on the receiving end of public relations activities—we must not disseminate false or misleading information; we must not operate "front organizations" whose titles suggest an impartiality which they do not possess, we must disclose the motives behind our actions; we must not corrupt the channels of public communication. All these clauses add up to one basic rule—not to deceive. . . . It is downright forgery to produce pre-fabricated public opinion by writing stooge letters over false names to unsuspecting newspapers. And it is diabolical to lobby Members of Parliament without disclosing who has paid you to do so. These are only examples of sins which may, in the past, have been committed even by Members of this Institute.[55]

The code thus encompassed provisions designed to protect the public interest and those designed to improve professional status. The public interest category included activities that corrupted the channels of information, the dissemination of false or misleading information, and the use of front organisations. An analysis of these clauses helps us to understand how two conceptual models of public relations emerged that remain to the present day: one of public relations as advocacy on behalf of clients and employers, the other of public relations as public information and social responsibility acting in the public interest. The implicit tensions between these two positions has not received the attention it deserves given its wider political implications. Both of these elements were encompassed in the code of practice and remain there to this day. Acting in the public interest was a crucial justification for the existence

---

[54] Annual General Meeting, Special General Meeting. The most important event in the history of the Institute. *Public Relations*, 16 (2) 1964, p. 22.

[55] Mann, C. (1964). Our responsibilities for the future. *Public Relations*, 16 (4), p. 33.

of public relations and an implicit (and sometimes explicit) way for practitioners to distinguish their occupation from propaganda. Cases that related to professionalism were mostly about the supplanting of other members, bringing public relations into disrepute, and client-consultant relations.

DEFINING THE PUBLIC INTEREST

In 1963, the Code of Professional Conduct included a prescription that a member "shall conduct his professional activities with respect for the public interest." But an editorial in the IPR journal mused speculatively:

> Which of us can claim to judge what is or is not in the interest of the public at large? It is, in theory, possible that the Institute might one day have to decide whether public relations action in support of some particular cause was promoting, say, immorality. In so unlikely a case, the Institute would certainly be guided by the climate of public opinion and law in force at the time. . . . It is possible to envisage an unscrupulous practitioner lending himself to the fostering of ill-will between racial communities, or trying to conceal the future ill effects of an industrial process known to cause pollution. Such conduct would be contrary to Clause 1.[56]

The 1999 code also required members to conduct their activities "with proper regard to the public interest," but acknowledged that the "public interest is not easy to define" and thus "calls for a responsible and reasonable attitude to all sections of the public." It would be hard to disagree with such sentiments, but the code does not help in situations where there are genuine conflicts of interests or different interpretations of scientific knowledge, such as over genetically modified food.

High-minded ideals have not solely resided within the clauses of the IPR code in its various iterations. In 1972, Tim Traverse-Healy claimed that public relations practitioners should properly be regarded by society as guardians of the public interest:

> [We are] men and women . . . who are dedicated to the precept that people really do matter and what they think is truly important and that therefore the politics of the concerns we advise or represent must be in the public interest, must in the framing of those policies take into account the opinions of the community and that in the corporate actions that

---

[56]The code of professional conduct. *Public Relations*, 25 (2) 1972, p. 55.

result the rights and dignity of the individual must be fully protected. In the political, economic and social conditions of today it is no easy matter to strike the right balance all the time between what is good for our employers and clients and what is good for the public. . . . The difficulties we encounter and indeed the failures we experience must not, however, be allowed to obscure the fact that in the interests of mankind someone somewhere must keep trying to do just that, and it would appear that Fate has elected that in this modern society we public relations people must carry much of that responsibility.[57]

The preceding quote clearly locates the speaker within the public interest model of public relations. But it omits any notions of accountability to any agency outwith the public relations occupation itself. Both the speech and the IPR code are good examples of ideals so broadly phrased that, although no one could disagree with the sentiments, they could be difficult to apply in practice. Likewise, there were problems over prescriptions against the dissemination of false and misleading information. It is to this aspect that discussion now turns before addressing those activities that are more easily identified: corruption of the channels of information and the use of deception.

FALSE OR MISLEADING INFORMATION

Issues about truth and lies are central to definitions and discussion of the conceptual relationship between public relations and propaganda, but such definitions are contingent on underlying epistemological positions: relativist or universalist. It is the conflation of such opposing fundamentals that can lay public relations practitioners, and their supporters, open to charges of sophistry. In this chapter, discussion is limited to some historical data that illustrates the dilemmas.

It was noted in chapter 3 that a key ideal for practitioners within the Institute was truth telling and this came to the fore in a clause in the IPR code requiring that "[a] member shall not intentionally disseminate false or misleading information and shall use proper care to avoid doing so. He has a positive duty to maintain truth, accuracy and good taste."[58] This was reinforced in Denys Brook-Hart's presidential ad-

---

[57]Traverse-Healy, T. (1972). Tomorrow's world: a challenge for PR. *Public Relations,* 25 (7), p. 162.
[58]IPA Code of professional conduct. 29 November 1963.

dress, in which he declared that a "fundamental discipline for public relations practitioners at every level is the pursuit of truth. . . . Accuracy and attention to detail in the assembly and presentation of facts, figures and information should be a continuous discipline for everyone engaged in public relations practice."[59] Likewise, in 1970, Wilfred Howard, Chairman of the Education Committee and member of Council, urged members:

> Tell the truth. This is not always quite as easy to practise as it is to preach . . . normal commercial and technological security sometimes precludes us from telling the whole truth. Everyone accepts that there are commercial secrets and confidences which must be respected. But it is unpardonable, unethical and in long term damaging to one's reputation ever positively to mislead . . . in the industrial and business context the question "What is Truth?" is not a simple one to answer. The best rule of thumb is that there must be a very compelling reason indeed for withholding information, and that the public comment made by the corporation should never paint a picture that is false to the facts. Tell all the truth if you can, and as much of it as you can if you cannot.[60]

In late 1983, *Public Relations* devoted an editorial to what was now referred to as the "Code of Conduct." The focus of the editorial was the misunderstanding of public relations within society as illustrated by the term *a public relations exercise,* which, according to the editorial, "seems to be based on a damaging and pervasive misunderstanding of what public relations, as practised by the vast majority of those whose jobs fall within its ambit, are all about."[61] The editor, J. Harvey Smith (who formerly worked as PRO to the evangelist Billy Graham and for the Conservative Party),[62] made a clear distinction between "public relations as advocacy or persuasion and public relations as straight communication"[63] and implied that public relations practitioners were not always in a position to influence policy: "The public relations function is often the communications channel only, being neither policy-maker nor fount of truth as seen by an organisation—which itself may have

---

[59]The President suggests seven major disciplines. *Public Relations,* 13 (1) 1963, p. 31.

[60]Howard, W. (1971). Some principles of communication. *Public Relations,* 24 (9), p. 186.

[61]Ibid.

[62]Doing our exercises. Editorial, *Public Relations,* 2 (1) 1983, p. 2; On the move. *Communicator,* September 1979, p. 3.

[63]Doing our exercises. Editorial, *Public Relations,* 2 (1) 1983, p. 2.

neither the ethical constraints nor the conscience of its public relations people."[64]

However, internal disagreements were apparent when Sheelagh Jefferies, Chairman of the Professional Practices Committee,[65] complained that an editorial in *Public Relations* had breached Clause 2 of the code (which required members not to disseminate fake or misleading information and upheld a positive duty to maintain integrity and accuracy) when it stated that "[there are] many times when an organisation wishes to keep quietly to itself, listening, watching; not communicating . . . [there are] times for secrecy, times for silence, times even for distortion, especially when the priorities are survival, morale, gain or power."[66]

Hugh Samson, past Chairman of the Professional Practices Committee, identified difficulties for public relations when he acknowledged that public relations in support of product marketing was "inevitably slanted to the interest of the client . . . and sometimes embod[ies] ambiguities, minor exaggerations and half-truths," but that this was not too serious because editors expected such material to be self-interested. However, such an approach was not acceptable in other areas of society where human interests were at stake (he cited medicine, health and welfare services, education, scientific research, industrial safety, law and order, government, and international relations as key examples) and the use of "minor distortions, half-truths and white lies" have serious social consequences in terms of "morale, well-being, public confidence and the processes of democracy."[67] Samson argued that only in the context of "a just war" (he was using the Falklands as an illustration in the article) could such imperatives be ignored in order to put security first, but that such actions inevitably led to public relations practitioners being "regarded with scepticism by the public and with distrust by the media" and losing credibility. Samson warned against the possibility that practitioners would act prudentially on behalf of their clients or employers:

> [W]hen public relations practitioners begin to extend the areas of justification for media-manipulation on the grounds that commercial success or even economic survival are comparable with human survival, they set the whole profession on a very slippery slope indeed. When our credibility is damaged, trust is diminished and PR sources of information, news

---

[64] Ibid.

[65] What I think. *Public Relations,* 2 (1) 1983, p. 10.

[66] The role of the new journal. *Public Relations,* 1 (1) 1982, p. 2.

[67] Samson, H. (1983). Dissemination of information. *Public Relations,* 2 (1), p. 17.

and comment are brought under suspicion. Indeed, they are already suspected in some quarters. . . . No exceptions should be practised or sanctioned. The code, rooted in morality, should be immutable.[68]

Turning to particular examples, one is struck by the relative pettiness of cases. For example, *Geare* versus *Infoplan* (1967), which focused on truth telling, took place just as Tim Traverse-Healy was about to become President of the Institute.[69] Traverse-Healy was Chairman of Infoplan, which was criticised for claims made in a press release on behalf of *Chambers Encyclopaedia*. The release, which had been checked with the client, claimed that "*Chambers Encyclopaedia* is today the only major world-standard encyclopaedia planned, produced and printed in Britain . . . the most up-to-date in the world."[70] Geare, representing the competitor, *Everyman's Encyclopaedia*, disputed the claims made and provided supporting evidence. Traverse-Healy argued that the terms employed by both parties such as *major* and *world-standard* were a matter of opinion rather than fact and suggested that the correspondence "be referred, via the President of the IPR, to the Professional Practice Committee, as a test case to get them thinking about and discussing this matter." He also suggested that "it would seem to me best if the publishing fraternity itself—or indeed the publishing press including reviewers—could decide what the much used phrases like 'world standard' and 'major work' really meant, as a guide to publicists."[71] However, when he passed the correspondence to the committee's president, Victor Lewis, he did not present the materials as a test case but as a joint decision "to submit the papers on this situation to the Professional Practices committee as a case history for them to study and discuss . . . both of us would like to hear what emerges."[72] This was enough of a steer and Victor Lewis did nothing with the papers until Michael Geare wrote and reminded him about it, by which time Traverse-Healy had been installed as president. In March, the administrative director of the Institute, Peter Bloomfield, wrote to Geare and told him that the Professional Practices Committee had "noted the correspondence with interest but felt that they could take no further action in the belief that you

[68] Ibid.
[69] IPR Archive 3/4/10.
[70] Letter from Traverse-Healy to Geare (1967, 13 October). IPR Archive 3/4/10.
[71] Letter from Traverse-Healy to Geare (1967, 26 October). IPR Archive 3/4/10.
[72] Letter from Traverse-Healy to Victor Lewis (1967, 6 November). IPR Archive 3/4/11.

and Mr Traverse-Healy had taken the matter as far as possible."[73] Geare protested and in different letters asked to know "something of the discussion and of the views that the Committee expressed"[74] and "something of the nature of the consideration in which they have already engaged."[75] The matter was finally resolved by Alan Eden-Green, who telephoned Michael Geare and apologised for Bloomfield's inadequate letters, explaining that the case was a matter for opinion and that "it was not the place of the Committee to make qualitative judgments, provided the code was not contravened."[76]

By the mid-1980s, discussion about ethics had tended to become subsumed into more general discussions about corporate social responsibility, environmentalism, and consumerism arising from the response of corporate elites to social activism of the 1960s and 1970s. The explosion of social responsibility as an issue for business presented an opportunity for public relations to position itself as the "corporate conscience" as part of a wider bid to achieve managerial status in claims such as that made by Tim Traverse Healy: "We have an overriding obligation to the public, a conscience."[77] Likewise, Peter Smith, IPR President in 1985, defined public relations as fundamentally concerned with an organisation's social responsibility because the "dichotomy between the organisation's and the public's interest is at the heart of what we are about as public relations practitioners."[78] Most recently, Pieczka's research showed the enduring nature of this theme:

> [Corporate social responsibility] is defined as "the responsibility of an organisation to its stakeholders beyond its duties to its members . . . [it] . . . involves choices based on ethical and moral principles, not processes of accountability." . . . Thus social responsibility lies in "our contribution to social/societal goals" which is beyond and above the basic duties of profitability and accountability. It is also very clearly allied with the principle of freedom, fundamental to Western culture; and with the Western myth of growth and development . . . there is another, parallel type of alignment . . . if moral principles are evoked, so are pragmatic, business ones—competitiveness and reputation. Indeed, if this pragmatic align-

---

[73] Letter from Bloomfield to Geare (1968, 12 March). IPR Archive 3/4/11.
[74] Letter from Geare to Bloomfield (1968, 18 March). IPR Archive 3/4/11.
[75] Letter from Geare to Bloomfield (1968, 3 April). IPR Archive 3/4/11.
[76] Note from Eden-Green, A. IPR Archive 3/4/11.
[77] Traverse-Healy, T. (1985). Professional ethics. *Public Relations*, 3 (3), p. 14.
[78] Smith, P. (1985). Responsibility. *Public Relations*, 3 (3), p. 11.

ment takes over then responsibility becomes part of the communication expertise claimed by public relations.[79]

Claims to social responsibility and public relations as the corporate conscience were normative and not substantiated with evidence. They were also, from a Kantian perspective, immoral, because they did not arise from a genuine expression of public service or duty, but out of a desire to exploit a current issue for selfish ends.

CORRUPTING THE CHANNELS OF COMMUNICATION

A prohibition against the corruption of societal "channels of communication" had a significant place in the code of practice. It referred to elaborate stunts designed to attract media coverage that were not intrinsically newsworthy. This is an interesting example of journalism "news values" operating within public relations culture. The language employed, though, implies a more serious issue that was not debated: that of the public sphere and its dominance by paid-for interests. Neither were the underlying ethical principles spelt out, either in terms of the utilitarian benefits of open channels of communication and the role of public relations in facilitating that, or in terms of duties to provide factual information to the media and public.

Prior to the existence of the code, there had been, in 1960, a detailed correspondence in *Public Relations* between an overseas member and Alan Eden-Green, Chairman of the Public Relations Committee, about publicity stunts. The correspondence neatly illustrates the difficulties of operationalising such a code and the potential for disagreement arising from personal interpretation. For example, J. L. Rushburn wrote from South Africa that he was "disturbed by the degree to which our profession has been debased" and gave examples including, "putting a group of half-frozen people on top of an electric sign in Times Square, New York, to sing Christmas carols — with the object of publicising the sign and the product or company concerned,"[80] and using a helicopter "to

---

[79]Pieczka, M. (2000). Public relations expertise deconstructed. *The business of organising identities*. Stirling: Stirling Media Research Institute, p. 9.

[80]The stunt menace. Forum, *Public Relations*, 13 (1) 1960, p. 50.

remove wrappings from the roof and door of a new factory in Johannesburg." Although Rushburn acknowledged that the motive was "to make 'news'" his main objection was "'stunts' of this kind reflect the most vulgar showmanship and bad taste," and debased public relations.[81]

Eden-Green explained that the Committee "were wholly sympathetic to the sentiments of your letter but felt it would not be prepared to lay down hard and fast rules about possible stunts of this kind."[82] Furthermore, it became clear that the nature of the judgments made were related not to the effect of the media, but with notions of taste. Eden-Green used an example from his own experience to illustrate an acceptable stunt: "When we wanted to demonstrate the strength of Wedgwood china teacups, we went to considerable trouble to stand a double decker [bus] on six cups. This was a stunt, but it was quite a dignified one."[83] Assessing the examples given by Rushburn, Eden-Green commented:

> The use of the helicopter . . . seems to have been in very poor taste, and unlikely to help the factory in its relations with either the white or the coloured population. . . . To put people on top of an electric sign in Times Square in order to draw attention to the sign is purely a publicity stunt. . . . But to exploit the singing of Christmas carols for publicity purposes is in bad taste and, in my view, therefore bad public relations.[84]

According to this approach, public relations was required to implement vague notions of taste. Exactly how judgments were made and how expertise could be acquired was unclear.

Alan Campbell-Johnson recalled one case of expulsion that infringed both the rule against corruption of the media and the rule against payment contingent on results, as well as illustrating the importance of truth telling as an ideal for public relations:

> He offered a guaranteed sale of his results by saying that he could get stories in [to the press] and that was done by offering products to the newspapers and then when it came to the question of saying what he had done he didn't tell us the truth—a double offence—he had done something contrary to professional ethics and he had lied about it. It was the one thing we were sensitive to which was the selling of services on the

[81] Ibid.
[82] Committee view. *Public Relations*, 13 (1) 1960, p. 50.
[83] Ibid.
[84] Ibid.

guaranteeing of results [which implies] that you trade a reference in the press and that the press is corruptible.[85]

Linked to lying and corruption was the issue of deception, most profoundly illustrated by the employment of front organisations. The Institute was particularly sensitive to the use of front organisations because this was seen very clearly as a propaganda technique. Unfortunately, the documentary sources available do not reveal much detail, but the constant reiteration of the prohibition suggests that, though this was not deemed ethically acceptable, it was perhaps not an uncommon practice.

In contrast to the secrecy that shrouded the Liebman case, there was, by the mid-1960s, much more of a culture of "naming and shaming" those suspended in IPR press releases, thus publicly attempting to prove professional status, as illustrated by the following: "Two members of the Institute have been suspended from membership for a year for unprofessional conduct. They are T. P. Grey, a director of Customer Relations Ltd and a member of the Institute since 1955 and Mark F. Quin, Chairman and Managing Director of Mark Quin and Associates Ltd who has been a member of the Institute for 18 years."[86]

There were also cases of individual deception, for example, in April 1978, Gerald Fitzgerald, Regional PRO for Lothian Regional Council, was accused by the Professional Practice Committee of having infringed the Code of Professional Conduct because he used an assumed name to conceal his identity as an employee of the Council in a Radio Forth phone-in on 23 December 1977.[87] Although the committee "accepted that he had acted without collusion and out of a desire to contribute as an individual to the radio debate on the remuneration of Councillors . . . the method that he chose for resolving the conflict between personal conviction and public duty . . . [showed] poor professional judgement."[88] But this was not an unanimous view and G. L. White from the London Fire Brigade commented sarcastically, "If we are going to make mountains out of molehills, why not go the whole hog and, when the next heinous crime is committed arrange for the perpetrator to be flogged publicly outside 1 Great James Street. What marvellous public-

---

[85] Interview. 22 August 1995.
[86] Suspension. *Public Relations,* 18 (2) 1966, p. 5.
[87] Professionalism. *Communicator,* June 1978, p. 1.
[88] Member violates code. *Communicator,* April 1978, p. 1.

ity that would be for the Institute."[89] The editor defended himself by arguing that the case had caused "enormous damage to public relations and the Institute in Scotland" and that members there had had "a very tough job to do in re-inforcing the professional reputation of PR which the Scottish media sought to destroy."[90]

PROFESSIONAL CONCERNS

Although there are some records of infringements against the public interest, the overwhelming majority of cases submitted to the Professional Practices Committee for consideration for disciplinary action arose from personal complaints by one member about another. This trend reveals much more about the ethics of the occupation and the real importance of the public interest to practitioners than the high-flown phrases in the code. Complaints usually related to commercial interest and individuals who sought "to supplant another member." These included promotional mailings, as in the case *St John Cooper & McNulty* versus *Hornsby* (1965), illustrated a lack of comfort with competition perhaps arising from tension between seeing public relations as a business and seeing it as a profession.

Other complaints were those in which one member thought that another member had brought the occupation or the Institute into disrepute either by action or words. For example, in November 1961, Arthur Cain wrote to the Council to inquire about the case "of a member who had recently been convicted of 'being drunk in charge of a motor vehicle,' and of another member 'convicted of stealing with a previous conviction for stealing recorded against him.'"[91] Neither case was pursued by the Council. Such complaints increasingly suggested an occupational culture of tale telling and self-righteousness.

Brooke-Hart versus *Cain* (1962) is of interest because it illustrates the increasingly litigious nature of members. Both men were accompanied by solicitors and the defendant Cain was also accompanied by his counsel and two pupils.[92] The burden of the case was that Brooke-Hart regarded a letter written by Cain in *World's Press News* as bringing public relations practice, its practitioners, and Brooke-Hart into disre-

---

[89] Public flogging? *Communicator*, July 1978, p. 4.
[90] Ibid.
[91] Council Minutes. 15 November 1961.
[92] Investigating Panel Report 1 June 1962. IPR Archive 2/2/7.

spect. Although the Institute panel did not find in Brooke-Hart's favour, it regretted that Cain had not written "an adequate letter of apology either to Mr Brooke-Hart or to *World's Press News*. Had he done so the panel believes the best interests of all concerned would have been served."[93] Cain's legal team were not impressed and objected to the rider, pointing out that in making such a comment the panel exceeded its jurisdiction as laid out in its rules of conduct and also perpetuated an injustice in being "Thoroughly derogatory of an accused member and liable to do him considerable damage in the eyes of members of Council, while at the same time acquitting him of the complaint made and thus depriving him of any right to answer or controvert the derogatory allegations made in the Report."[94] Nevertheless, the Institute, on the advice of its own solicitors, chose to stand by its report, not wishing to give in to implied threats of further legal action and correctly judging that it would be difficult for Cain to proceed much further.[95]

The implementation of the code of practice seemed likely to infringe members' rights with regard to free speech, as happened in the case of *The Council* versus *Jefkins* (1965). Jefkins, Director of Studies at the time and with experience as Assistant General Secretary of the Advertising Association responsible for operating the Advertising Investigation Department, criticised the Code in an article in *Advertisers' Weekly* on 18 December 1964. In subsequent correspondence with the chairman of the Council, Victor Lewis, Jefkins argued that "[the Code was] an amateurish piece of window dressing coupled with some ambiguous regulations."[96] The Council decided that Jefkins had infringed the Code by failing to cooperate with his fellow members in upholding it and the matter was referred to the Disciplinary Council, where he was criticised for his method in bringing light to bear on any faults in the Code.[97]

By the end of the decade, criticisms about the Institute or the occupation were specifically forbidden in a new, somewhat totalitarian, clause requiring that "[a] member shall not conduct himself in any manner detrimental to the reputation of the Institute or the profession of public relations."[98] The current formulation states that members shall not

---

[93] Ibid.

[94] Ibid.

[95] Letter from Rooper & Whately to Thomas. 20 July 1962.

[96] Jefkins to Lewis. 24 December 1964.

[97] Disciplinary Council Minutes. 23 February 1965.

[98] Revised code of conduct adopted by council. (1970, 8 September). *Public Relations*, 23 (11) 1970, p. 10.

"[p]rofessionally engage in any practice, or be seen to conduct [them-selves] in any manner detrimental to the reputation of the Institute or the reputation and interests of the public relations profession." The supplementary interpretation explains, "This is a 'catch-all' clause. If, for example, a member is seen to be drunk or found to be dishonest, such behaviour may be detrimental to Institute or the public relations profession whether such behaviour is actually in breach of this clause would have to be judged on the particular circumstances."[99] The formu-lation could be utilised to impose conventional manners as Cain at-tempted to do, or to muffle criticism.

Client-consultant relations were also an occasional issue. *Pittard* ver-sus *Kris* (1967) did not come before the Disciplinary Council, but is an interesting example of a client raising issues relating to methodology and evaluation in public relations practice. Pittard asked the Institute whether they were entitled to know which media had been sent editorial information by their consultant so that "one can assess the number of contacts that have to be made to produce such press cuttings."[100] Bloom-field, the administrative director, responded that "my firm opinion is that a client is entitled to know everything that a consultant is doing on his behalf on the basis that the client is paying the bill," but Kris chal-lenged this, arguing, "I am battling with more and more demands for time-wasting reports and proof of the job we are doing . . . a public rela-tions organisation is employed for its knowhow and the result it achieves for its clients. The mechanics of the job should not concern them."[101] Bloomfield responded placatingly that in his view the client had a right to know what publications had been contacted, "but not as to how the consultant goes about it," and his view was subsequently endorsed by the Professional Practices Committee.[102] This case is illustrative of the power struggle between client and consultant over access to knowledge.

CONCLUSION

In the public relations context, codes of ethics soon became, and long remained, a focus of interest and debate. From an instrumental point of

---

[99] IPR Handbook 2000.

[100] Letter from Pittard to the IPR. (1967, 24 July). IPR Archive 3/4/10.

[101] Bloomfield to Pittard (1967, 2 August). IPR Archive 3/4/10; Kris to Pittard (1967, 10 August). IPR Archive 3/4/10.

[102] Bloomfield to Kris (1967, 15 August). IPR Archive 3/4/10.

view, a code of ethics was seen as a way to bestow some respectability on the occupation. Nevertheless, some members have always doubted its value, for example, during a discussion in 1985 where some saw the code as unrealistic or unworkable, for example, "we do not even believe in ourselves as professional people. I think we live, in public relations, in a world of make-believe,"[103] and "ours is a philosophical code rather than a practical code,"[104] or even incomprehensible, "a lot of the code is written in language that is very difficult to understand . . . there is room for simplification."[105]

The construction of a code of ethics by any occupation reveals its values and self-identity. The evidence and testimony presented in the minutes and support documentation points to a culture of tale telling. The cases were generally petty and, quantitatively, were usually concerned with the guarding of individual commercial interests (the part of the code that prohibited "seeking to supplant another member" was used most often). It was rare that serious ethical issues such as the public interest or communication channels arose. The IPR could only reach members and members often resigned before they could be expelled. So although the Institute had, by its very occasional expulsions, shown itself to "have teeth," its professional position was undermined by the fact that it did not monopolise practice. As James Derriman, Managing Director of Charles Barker City and Chairman of the Institute's Professional Practices Committee, commented, "[un]fortunately, in more than one case during my period with the Committee it has not been possible to take effective action because the practitioner responsible had ceased to be in membership."[106] Unfortunately for the public relations occupation, the high-minded ideals of truth telling and working in the public interest have overlapped with the stated goals of journalism and thus provide another example of competition between the two occupations.

To return to points made at the beginning of this chapter, the current IPR code contains elements of codes of ethics, codes of conduct, and codes of practice and clearly attempts to position public relations as a profession. Yet it seems unlikely that this code would reassure public

---

[103] Blackburn, P. (1985). Professional ethics. *Public Relations*, 3 (3), p. 14.

[104] Jefkins, F. (1985). Professional ethics. *Public Relations*, 3 (3), p. 15.

[105] Blackburn, P. (1985). Professional ethics. *Public Relations*, 3 (3), p. 14; Jefkins, F. (1985). Professional ethics. *Public Relations*, 3 (3), p. 15; Smith, P. (1985). Professional ethics. *Public Relations*, 3 (3), p. 14.

[106] Derriman, J. (1970). Professional ethics and the Institute. *Public Relations*, 23 (10), p. 3.

relations' critics: There is little guidance to those working in areas such as government (British or foreign), lobbying, or controversial areas such as tobacco or biotechnology; there is a marked lack of reference to recent public concern over "sleaze"; and there is a lack of detail about relations with the media. Currently, much political public relations is hidden from view and the gradual politicisation of the government information services inevitably raises the spectre of political propaganda. The rise of democratically unaccountable spin doctors and special advisers as key sources that shape media content is not catered for in any of the codes to date. Food scares in the UK have likewise revealed ethical problems in terms of the interpretation and communication of scientific evidence in relation to concepts of the truth. The fundamental ethical issue of the public relations role of stemming negative publicity through the use of crisis communication techniques or withholding information clearly infringes the public interest and makes it obvious that the ethics of public relations are to a large degree governed by its paymasters. Although ethical principles are expressed—as in the current code, which states there is "a positive duty at all times to respect the truth and [not to] disseminate false or misleading information," nothing is said about withholding the truth. Some clauses are not binding and leave action to the individual's discretion, for example, whether "payments, gifts or 'inducements' given to holders of public office" are likely to lead to undue influence on those leaders. The "cash-for-questions" scandal revealed at least some of the corrupt practices engaged in by lobbyists. Spin doctors have received a lot of attention in the political context, but little has been given to those individuals who spin for corporations such as Monsanto and Inchcape.[107]

Nevertheless, much greater efforts have been made recently (2000) by the IPR to raise the level of debate among members regarding the code, its content and application, levels of transparency, and lobbying. Although this is encouraging from the ethical point of view, the impact on the occupation as a whole is necessarily limited by the Institute's ability to control the occupation as a whole.

Historically, the IPR's engagement with ethics failed to address ethical issues that arose from the practice of public relations, specifically those relating to transparency and obligations to publics. In practice it has been left to a presumed adversarial media to test public relations' claims. Curiously, there is no record of the details of the code being pre-

---

[107]McNair, B. (2000). *Journalism and democracy.* London: Routledge.

sented to or discussed with the media. In terms of professionalisation, a code could potentially be used as an exclusionary strategy, but in practice was more often used as a punishment mechanism in an occupational culture that seemed riven with petty vendettas. That so many cases involved senior members and officers of the Institute also suggests that the code was used as an instrument of power internally. All in all, the function of nearly half a century of the IPR's code seems to have been a worthy text to encourage good behaviour, but in reality has proved too general and open to interpretation to be particularly restrictive in practice. Externally, the code has been a symbolic acquisition for use in the public relations campaign for public relations and can be seen thus far as a rather sad attempt to emulate the professions.

7

Educational Developments: 1948–1998

INTRODUCTION

The sociological literature on professionalisation emphasises the significance of education in a number of ways. Those from the trait approach[1] identify intellectual and practical training as an important feature of the professions. The process theorists[2] see establishment of training as the second crucial stage after the emergence of the full-time occupation. Theorists identified with the power approach,[3] who have drawn on Marx and Weber for inspiration, take for granted the importance of education as an instrument in a profession's competitive positioning. Systems theorists focus on the broader societal context, in this case, increasing educational opportunities and government pressure for vocationalisation.[4] Finally, the notion of the professional project focuses

---

[1]Such as Millerson, G. (1964). *The qualifying associations: a study in professionalisation*. London: Routledge & Kegan Paul.

[2]Vollmer, H. M. & Mills, D. L. (eds.). (1966). *Professionalisation*. Englewood Cliffs, New Jersey: Prentice Hall; Caplow, T. (1954). *Sociology of work*. Minneapolis: University of Minneapolis Press; Wilensky, H. L. (1964). The professionalisation of everyone? *American Journal of Sociology, 70*, pp. 137–58.

[3]Friedson, C. (1986). *Professional powers: a study of the institutionalisation of formal knowledge*. Chicago: University of Chicago Press.

[4]Abbott, A. (1988). *The system of professions: an essay on the division of expert labor*. Chicago: University of Chicago Press.

on the translation of scarce resources and specialist knowledge of skills into social and economic rewards: "The structure of the professionalisation process binds together two elements . . . a body of abstract knowledge, susceptible of practical application, and a market—the structure of which is determined by economic and social development, and also by the dominant ideological climate."[5] Thus, the literature of professions leads to the conclusion that "the concept of professional is really unthinkable without the property of educational qualification and licensing."[6] Education has the potential to provide the cognitive core to the occupation and thus define the field of jurisdiction, to develop the body of knowledge via research, to gain elite status, to help legitimate the practice, and to perform a gatekeeping function in terms of entry to the occupation, thus assisting closure. In Bourdieu's terms, education is the way to acquire symbolic capital and thus would distinguish public relations from other communications occupations.

On its establishment, the IPR's aims included that to "consider the institution of examinations or other suitable tests with the object of raising the status of those practising public relations to an agreed professional level."[7] This chapter presents an historical review of British public relations' engagement with education, focusing largely on the activities of the IPR in the context of the professional project. It contributes some understanding of occupational values about education and much of the relevant historical detail for a consideration of public relations' effort to professionalise.

STARTING OUT

A major difficulty for the Institute at its inception was how to define public relations and limit entry. Initially, full membership was to be granted only to those with a wide range of experience. Press agents and publicists were to be excluded from membership, but as those functions were also not clearly defined, the distinction between public relations

---

[5]Larson, M. S. (1977). *The rise of professionalism: a sociological analysis.* Berkeley: University of California Press, p. 40.

[6]Torstendahl, R. (1990). Essential properties, strategic aims and historical development: three approaches to theories of professionalism. In Burrage, M. & Torstendahl, R. *Professions in theory and history: rethinking the study of the professions.* London: Sage, p. 46.

[7]Hess, A. (1948). Our aims and objects. *Public Relations,* 1 (1), p. 8.

and publicity proved hard to draw or defend, as is shown by a report of the first formal meeting of the IPR:

> The rules of the Institute state that any individual who is doing exclusively press agency work cannot become a member. . . . What, the members wanted to know, was the definition of Press Agency work? Could any member of the Council say? None could. Then came the inevitable second question—how can you possibly apply the rule? The answer is that the rule has been applied.[8]

In 1949, Norman Rogers, the assistant secretary of the Institute, argued that full membership should be reserved for those who "unquestionably possess a high all-round standard of technical ability, practical performance and experience in PR practice in his particular field and that he is engaged in putting into effect a bona fide public relations policy of his organisation either as a PR executive, or in a directive or consultative capacity."[9] However, it was not clear how standards or the other criteria were to be judged, nor was it clear who would be in a position to make judgments about others. Rogers pointed to the link between standards, occupational status, and the institution's ability to apply a discriminating rule to applicants for membership:

> The Institute should . . . define the qualifications in training, experience and scope of activity required for eligibility for Full membership . . . *the Institute should boldly state what it considers to be the proper function and scope of the practice* . . . and, with its definitions as yardsticks, admit to Full membership only those who conform to the standards published for all the world to see. . . . The Institute should encourage members to contribute original ideas and views towards *enhancement of the prestige* of Public Relations.[10] (emphasis added)

In his presidential address at the IPR second annual conference (AGM) in 1949, Sir Stephen Tallents suggested that the members' "first function . . . was to educate themselves."[11] Members were invited to submit "any original material on public relations," for which the council might award a diploma or a fellowship if submissions proved to be "of outstanding merit to the literature of public relations."[12] There

---

[8]The first conference. *Public Relations,* 1 (2) 1948, p. 2.
[9]Ibid.
[10]Ibid. pp. 2–3.
[11]Highlights of the conference. *Public Relations,* 2 (2) 1949, p. 3.
[12]Untitled announcement. *Public Relations,* 2 (2) 1949, p. 6.

were no subsequent announcements in the journal of such awards being made to this and similar initiatives, such as the prize sponsored by the LPE "for the best original thesis" of 10,000 words on "the problems associated with the measuring of results" or to the council's offer of "a Diploma to any member of the Institute who makes a contribution of outstanding merit to literature on the thought, practice or methods of Public Relations."[13] In the same year, the IPR council decided that "the institution of some form of examination or test of ability is necessary as a positive step towards establishing the practice of public relations as a recognised profession."[14]

A committee set up to translate proposals into action had to consider the scope of the field, the nature of expertise, the possible curriculum, the level of attainment for qualification, and appropriate educational institution(s).[15] That education was to become a criterion for membership was unchallenged, though, as Norman Rogers pointed out: "We shall be faced with the problems of conducting examinations and assimilating successful examinees into membership alongside old established members who do not possess the qualification."[16]

Rogers suggested that a "more vocational and narrow approach" than a university degree would be preferable, and that the examination should be set at a level comparable with other professional examinations and "be so framed to draw forth from a candidate evidence of (i) a thorough *theoretical knowledge* of the principles of public relations practice; (ii) a sound and adequate *practical experience* gained in one or more of the main fields of work, such as in journalism, advertising, publicity and so on; and (iii) a fitting personality and temperament for public relations practice."[17] The first draft syllabus was drawn up in 1954, but failed to specify the curriculum for "public relations principles and practice." The qualification was part time and was supposed to test theoretical knowledge, evaluate practical experience, and assess personal

---

[13] Still going ahead. Editorial, *Public Relations,* 3 (3) 1951, p. 3.

[14] M. J. Buckmaster, A. Campbell-Johnson, S. Duncan, L. Hardern, A. Hess, L. Hornsby, A. A. McLoughlin, C. J. S. Mumford, R. A. Paget-Cooke, W. Seymour, A. Spoor, F. L. Stevens, Sir Stephen Tallents, and T. F. Usher. The "Officers" in that year were President: R. Wimbush, Vice President: T. Fife-Clark, Honorary Secretary: N. Rogers, Honorary Treasurer: A. K. Vint.

[15] Lex Hornsby, R. A. Paget-Cooke, A. Spoor, N. Rogers, F. L. Stevens, T. Usher, R. Wimbush, and C. W. Birdsall as secretary.

[16] Rogers, N. (1952). Some form of examination. *Public Relations,* 4 (3), p. 7.

[17] Ibid.

suitability. The latter were seen as very important, as illustrated by Lex Hornsby, Chairman of the Council in 1953, who argued, "You have to be concerned not only with qualifications but also with qualities . . . it is necessary to have certain qualities . . . of understanding and sympathy [to] become a public relations man."[18] Likewise, Chairman of the Education Committee F. L. Stevens (publicity officer of the Federation of British Industry) commented, "We all agree that a public relations officer cannot be made from book reading or attending lectures."[19] Emphasis was given to personal qualities and experience in the field rather than expertise and knowledge, as illustrated by the statement that "subjects for the Intermediate examination can be taught but the ability to answer questions in the Final must be based on experience in public relations."[20] It is curious that the ostensibly more advanced examination drew less on theoretical and factual information than the lower level qualification.

That education was not viewed as a requirement for practice is illustrated by Sam Black's comment in 1954: "It is not necessary to have had any specialised training to possess a good public relations outlook. So much depends on natural commonsense and good taste."[21] Similarly, at the annual conference in the same year, J. P. Gaudin seemed to express both hostility to education and a fear of professionalisation and closure when he commented, "Too much attention could be paid to the professional aspect. Public relations . . . was simply communication techniques which anyone of intelligence, imagination and education could learn. There was a danger of [the IPR] developing into a teaching profession with diplomas, degrees and all the concomitants of a closed corporation."[22] Such comments seem linked to the strong emphasis placed by early practitioners on flexibility and even personal destiny. Joyce Blow seemed dubious about the value of education in the public relations context, even though she herself possessed an honours degree from the University of Edinburgh:

> Recognised professional status for public relations practitioners would bring with it obvious advantages, but such "professionalisation" should

---

[18]Eight men in search of an answer. *Public Relations, 6* (1) 1953, p. 18.

[19]Stevens, F. L. (1954). An examination in public relations. *Public Relations, 6* (2), p. 7.

[20]Ibid. p. 8.

[21]The need for mutual understanding. Editorial, *Public Relations, 6* (4) 1954, p. 1.

[22]Riding a hobby horse. Editorial, *Public Relations, 6* (4) 1954, p. 35.

not be allowed to destroy the flexibility essential to the craft. Individuals with widely differing personalities, training and methods are equally successful in public relations, for, more than most careers, it rests on the imponderables of character which cannot be assessed by Gallup poll.[23]

This is a revealing quote because on the one hand it argues that character is important, yet it avoids specifying the type of character or its characteristics. It also shows some suspicion of the quantitative method underpinning market research techniques, which potentially represented a major cognitive base for the occupation and an opportunity to gain professional status.

A rare criticism of the predominant approach to education was made by M. Logan in 1953:

> What have we done towards putting ourselves on an equal footing with the more respected and learned professions? I do not know of one which does not demand a minimum standard of education from entrants. We often hear about the kind of qualities needed in a public relations officer, yet the Institute has not laid down educational standards of any kind. . . . As though to mark its disapproval of such things, the printed membership list does not contain a single reference to the educational or academic qualifications of the members.[24]

British public relations' anti-intellectualism, empiricism, or naiveté was evident in a report in *Public Relations* about a conference hosted by the Italian Public Relations Association at Stresa in 1957, which seems to express the view that intellectual interest in the subject was both a foreign prerogative and eccentricity:

> Delegates were impressed—and sometimes perplexed—by the deeply philosophical nature of most Italian papers read at Stresa. It should be understood that most Italians have a deep love of rhetoric, logic, philosophy . . . the academic aura which enveloped the speeches, pervaded the atmosphere. . . . The conference was divided into three large groups to discuss (i) public relations and democracy; (ii) public relations and society . . . (iii) public relations as a profession.[25]

In early 1955, it was decided that the Institute's first examination would be launched in 1956 and the Council focused its attentions on "the

---

[23] Qualifications for public relations: review of an American survey. *Public Relations*, 7 (1) 1954, p. 10.

[24] Logan, M. (1953). A minimum educational standard. *Public Relations*, 6 (1), p. 25.

[25] 'Observer.' 'Lake side conference.' *Public Relations*, 9 (2) 1957, p. 34.

publication of a really good text book covering the syllabus of the proposed examination," for which an editorial panel was set up.[26]

FIRST BRITISH BOOK

The first British book bearing "public relations" in its title was published in 1949. It remained the only British book until the IPR's own publication appeared nearly 10 years later, in 1958. Bound as a pamphlet, the first book reflected the original connection between the institutes of public administration and public relations, as it was published by the National Council for the Institute of Public Administration. Titled *Public Relations and Publicity*, it was written by J. H. Brebner, whose distinguished career included public relations at the Post Office under Sir Kingsley Wood; membership in the committee that set up the MoI in 1937; Director of the News Division, MoI; special overseas operative (1943–1945), MoI; Director of Press Communications at Supreme Allied Headquarters; and head of PR at the British Transport Commission.[27] The book was enthusiastically received by the Editor of *Public Relations*, Warren Seymour:

> It would be completely inadequate to say that J. H. Brebner's book should be read by everyone who practises the profession of Public Relations.... [it] is packed with sheer common sense, clearly, concisely and forcefully presented. The argument is so closely reasoned it must be read as a whole. It is a book which cannot be reviewed in the usual way, because any attempt to paraphrase would be sheer impudence.[28]

Influenced by management writers Taylor and Barnard, Brebner's argument for the existence and justification of the role of public relations was that public relations was an administrative or managerial tool both to counteract negative results of specialisation within organisations, and to motivate the workforce. Thus, this is the earliest claim in a British context that the role of public relations is to support management: Such an alignment has implications for the internal structure and culture of organisations just as the formalisation of organisational ideology and rhetoric has implications for society. For Brebner, public

---

[26] A year of promise. Editorial, *Public Relations*, 7 (2) 1955, p. 2; The practice of public relations. Editorial, *Public Relations*, 7 (3) 1955, p. 2.

[27] Public relations for British Transport. *Public Relations*, 6 (2) 1954, pp. 35–6.

[28] Brebner's book. Editorial, *Public Relations*, 2 (1) 1949, p. 16.

relations served an integrative and a purifying function, but also had an interventionist and ultimately authoritarian role:

> The great danger of specialisation in any human organisation is that it weakens and undermines the understanding, the interest, and the sympathy that should link the people affected with the sum total of the organisation. Those are the very things that public relations and publicity are designed to protect. . . . The growth of specialisation, which . . . produced a number of unforeseen toxic reactions has yielded an effective anti-toxin by whose aid those reactions may be neutralised.[29]

Brebner defined mass communication as "publicity" and saw the function of public relations as an extension of interpersonal skills arising from "the study of the human factor in industry and to an increasing degree, in government."[30] As an example, he cited:

> The headmaster in his management of tiresome parents and mischievous boys, the politician answering questions from his constituents, the company chairman recommending unpopular measures to a worried board, each of these men is tackling in his own particular walk of life a situation calling for the kind of sensitiveness and skill that we associate with successful public relations and publicity.[31]

When such work was carried out on behalf of an organisation, then, according to Brebner, it became "a professional's job."[32] Brebner argued that the more powerful an organisation, the more it needed public relations and the more complex this task became: "Big animals move slowly, but their movements can be dangerous both to themselves and to others; they have to be very careful where they put their feet. The concentration of power and responsibility may be so great that the cultivation of correct attitudes becomes an absolute condition of survival."[33]

So public relations was seen to be linked to the inculcation of certain beliefs in the interests of the organisation as defined by the managerial class: "The general function of public relations and publicity, being a function of administration, is concerned with the exercise of authority, that is, with giving special kinds of assistance to those in whom is vested

---

[29] Brebner, J. H. (1949). *Public relations and publicity*. London: The Institute of Public Administration, p. 10.
[30] Ibid. p. 7.
[31] Ibid.
[32] Ibid. p. 8.
[33] Ibid.

power of command in all its forms and degrees."[34] The public relations practitioner was "the eyes and ears of the policy maker"[35] and it was "essential that he should have a personal status which enable[d] him to impress authoritatively on the Chairman or the Minister all the facts affecting a particular situation."[36] This was an explicit bid to be part of the elite intersecting both the highest managerial class and the sources of political power: the mandarin civil servants and the politicians.

Brebner emphasised the educative role of public relations in his review of techniques (film, advertising, publications, exhibitions, advisory services) and was particularly excited by what he saw as the potential of film. As had the British advertiser Charles Higham 20 years previously, and the film documentarists in the 1930s, Brebner enthused:

> We are on the threshold of . . . the film as an instrument of education. When the film sets out to explain and to instruct, new and enormous potentialities begin to appear. . . . Already our experience of the educational film is sufficient to show unmistakably the shape of things to come. Perhaps even more significant than our experience of educational films proper is the acknowledged educational influence exercised by films produced for purposes of entertainment.[37]

This raises some important questions about the type of education on offer, especially because Brebner specified schoolchildren as one possible target audience for such films. Was he thinking of the educated citizenry that Grierson idealised, or inculcation into certain beliefs such as the benefits of capitalism? The fact that belief in film as "a national method of education par excellence" was shared by such a renowned propagandist as Goebbels clearly implies conceptual overlaps between the fields.[38] This example further illustrates the point made in chapter 1 that the link between public relations and propaganda lies to a large extent in the concept of education. In terms of the strategic aims, or Hall's *praxis*, it demonstrates the power relationship deemed to be appropriate between the state and citizen.

The IPR book proposal was developed by a committee suggesting topics and possible authors and was divided into five sections: the purpose of public relations, public relations media, assessing public opinion,

---

[34] Ibid. p. 35.
[35] Ibid. p. 16.
[36] Ibid. p. 17.
[37] Ibid. p. 26.
[38] Reuth, R. G. (1993). *Goebbels*. London: Constable, p. 284.

PR and human relations, and public relations practice in special fields.[39] Distinguished practitioners identified as contributors included Sir Stephen Tallents (senior civil servant and former head of the EMB), John Grierson (film documentarist), Kenneth Adam (head of the Light Programme, BBC), J. H. Brebner, Colonel Buckmaster (formerly head of SOE "F" section), E. Rawdon Smith, K. Lockhart Smith (Film Producers Guild), Trevor Powell (Director of Public Relations, Shell Group), Misha Black (one of Britain's greatest industrial designers, referred to in chap. 4), F. L. Stevens (FBI), Graeme Cranch (President, Market Research Association), Louis Moss (Government Social Survey), Tom Fife-Clark (Central Office of Information), and Alan Campbell-Johnson (PRO to Mountbatten during the handover of power in India).[40] The book was edited by Lex Hornsby, Trevor Powell, and F. L. Stevens, and Joyce Blow gave "secretarial assistance . . . [and was] . . . a most helpful collaborator in the work of editing."[41] However, due to the extended negotiations with publishers, it became clear that the book would not be ready in time for the first students.

THE INTERMEDIATE COURSE

In 1956, negotiations were opened with F. A. Heller, Head of the Department of Management Studies at the Regent Street Polytechnic and his deputy, M. D. Callender.[42] There was some debate over the ownership of the qualification, but it was eventually agreed that "the courses in public relations should be run not by the Institute itself but by the Polytechnic in connection with the Institute and supplemented if necessary by Institute evening study sessions."[43]

Teaching contact hours on the diploma were calculated at 72 hours in total.[44] The fee was 5 guineas.[45] Candidates for the intermediate exam had to be "at least 20 years old and . . . hold a General Certificate of Education . . . [but] need not be engaged in public relations prac-

---

[39] IPR Minutes of the Education Committee. (1954, 10 August). IPR 3/7/1.

[40] Ibid.

[41] *A guide to the practice of public relations.* (1958). The Institute of Public Relations. London: Newman Neame.

[42] Editorial, *Public Relations*, 9 (1) 1956, p. 2.

[43] IPR Minutes of the Education Committee. (1956, 10 May). IPR Archive 3/7/2.

[44] IPR Minutes of the Education Committee. (1956, 5 July). IPR 3/7/1.

[45] £5-5s-0d (£5-25p).

tice."[46] Candidates for the final exam must be "at least 21 years of age, must have passed the Intermediate Examination and must have spent at least three years in public relations practice."[47] The proposed "lecturers" were all practitioners and the British education system was criticised for lack of interest: "Educationists in America have made generous contributions with lectures, courses and degrees for new and established workers in this field. It is a little disappointing that the British universities have not yet awakened to this challenge."[48]

It is significant that the aspiration was to university-level work (advanced education) rather than further education or technical college level (some of which might be classed as training). The choice of higher education signals the ambition to professional status because the establishment of university-level qualifications should indicate an occupation has "arrived," at least in terms of social cachet, given that higher education includes abstract knowledge and a profession's jurisdictions are "Maintained, extended and redefined on the basis of a knowledge system governed by abstraction [because only abstraction] can redefine [the system's] problems and tasks, defend them from interlopers and seize new problems."[49]

By the late 1950s, it was acknowledged that communications was becoming a major focus for academic research and that this might be a useful source of theory:

> The impending appointment of a Professor of Communication at the University of North Staffordshire, Keele [in fact no one was appointed]. . . . The occupier of the Granada Research Chair in Communication [eventually located at Leeds University] will pursue research in one or more of such fields as linguistics, cybernetics, information theory, the sociological and psychological aspects of communication &c. In short—public relations theory?[50]

However, there is little evidence in *Public Relations* that practitioners attempted to engage with such ideas. The committee decided that the final examination should consist of exam papers "to test a candidate's general public relations knowledge and experience" and "give the can-

---

[46] Examination in public relations. *Public Relations,* 9 (3) 1957, p. 11.

[47] Ibid.

[48] Editorial, *Public Relations,* 9 (1) 1956, p. 2.

[49] Abbott, A. (1988). *The system of the professions: an essay on the division of expert labor.* Chicago: University of Chicago Press, p. 9.

[50] As the editor sees it. *Public Relations,* 12 (3) 1960, p. 5.

didate the opportunity of disclosing his knowledge and experience of public relations in a specialised field." It should also include "a compulsory viva voce to enable the Board of Examiners to assess a candidate's personality and to enable a candidate to think and express himself clearly on a specific public relations problem."[51] This reemphasises the importance of the "personality requirement" for practitioners and a dependence by the Institute on cultural capital as conceived by Bourdieu as a method of exclusion.[52]

The first intermediate course ran in 1956 and 1957, although the Institute's book was not published until 1958. Unsurprisingly, one student recalled that one of the problems with the first course was that there were no textbooks.[53] Other teething problems were experienced and practitioners involved in teaching complained that the "range of intelligence [sic] of the students was too wide and that for future courses it might be advisable to have a thorough screening to ensure that all were approximately at the same intelligence level" or even to "stream" the groups. They suggested that there should be an entrance examination "to ensure the suitability of students both for Public Relations as a career and for the course itself," which yet again implies an interest in selecting certain types of persons or personalities.[54] In response to this feedback the Education Committee noted that "arrangements had been made with Mr Heller for the 'screening' of students," but there is no remaining record of how this was done.

One practitioner commented on "the very very poor quality of teaching that was available because there were very few active good practitioners who could give up their time to teach."[55] Concern over teachers was shared by the Education Committee, and on 18 February 1958, they discussed "Training Teachers in Public Relations." Interestingly, their biggest difficulty was in finding people to teach "Principles and Practice of Public Relations" and, even more extraordinary, "Press Relations."[56] A fundamental problem was that no such principles were articulated. As late as 1964, the final examination paper included the following compulsory question: "1) What do you consider to be the

---

[51] Ibid.

[52] Wacquant, L. D. (1989). Towards a reflexive sociology: a workshop with Pierre Bourdieu. *Sociological Theory, 7*, p. 50.

[53] Interview. 18 August 1995.

[54] IPR Minutes of the Education Committee. (1957, 10 May).

[55] Interview. 12 April 1997.

[56] IPR Minutes of the Education Committee. (1958, 18 February).

most important principles involved in the practice of public relations? Illustrate your answer with examples taken from your own experience (which will be treated in strict confidence) or from your own imagination."[57] This suggests that theory was supposed to evolve out of practice either intuitively or from specific critical incidents in practice.

The first intermediate examination results were announced in November 1958. Out of 37 candidates, 13 passed both papers and 10 passed the first paper only.[58] The Chairman of the Examiners, Lex Hornsby, reported that students "Were repeating almost parrot-wise without any deep understanding. . . . The examinees generally seemed to be weakest on the subject of the principles of public relations. It may be that the Institute's guide book will help correct this in future years."[59] Norman Rogers, who examined the "Public Relations Principles and Practice" element, commented in even stronger terms that the students "seem to have underestimated what was likely to be required of them. Their approach was woefully inadequate . . . surprising since . . . this was almost certainly to be the most exacting, calling for the clearest evidence of some serious attempt to master what is admittedly a still vague and largely uncharted and undocumented territory."[60] In short, it seems that those setting the exams expected the students to do something that none of the lecturers (apart from Brebner) had attempted to do.

BRITISH TEXTBOOK PUBLISHED

In 1958, the Institute's book *A Guide to the Practice of Public Relations* was finally published at the cost of 30 shillings. The publication was reviewed in the lead editorial of *Public Relations* by Arthur Cain, whose comments illustrate the absence of systematic thinking and a knowledge base appropriate for a profession:

> This book is so essentially English. It has no check lists, and it does not
> include any case histories. Some of the writing is outstanding and some
> is dull for the editors decided to let each contributor paddle his
> noe in his own style; and this contributes a variety that adds to

ination. 9 April 1964.

elations, 9 (2) 1957, p. 2.

of Examiners to the Education Committee. (1958, 11 March).

the whole book. The editors themselves write that they asked the contributors to address themselves to beginners. That is a calculated understatement. *Perhaps we are all beginners,* for there are few people engaged in public relations in any part of the world who cannot learn something positive from this work.[61] (emphasis added)

A former president, Alan Hess, described it as "Europe's first authoritative guide to these age-old yet ever-new techniques in the propagation of prestige."[62] Optimistically, he perceived that there was "a growing awareness . . . all over the world, of the important part played by conscientious Public Relations in promoting higher standards of taste and behaviour." Here we can see public relations used as an agent of the class system presuming that taste (the term here implies high culture as opposed to low culture) is appropriately defined by the elite. So public relations gives us an example of Bourdieu's interest in how tastes are mobilised in struggles for social recognition or status.[63] For Hess, public relations was "such a personal activity that a generalised compendium on the subject is beyond human contriving," but the role was fundamentally evangelical, as illustrated by his reference to "the gospel one is spreading."[64] According to him, the book led to the "inescapable implication that the practice of Public Relations is . . . 70% applied common sense and 30% specialised and expert knowledge." He concluded, "Public Relations is a vast subject . . . (contrary to popular misconception) . . . by no means a job for any Tom, Dick or Harry. It demands a certain flair, a very great deal of application, an illimitable degree of tact and above all, an essential personal integrity."[65]

A further review by a journalist who shared the notion that the book "won't make him [the reader] a PRO"[66] offered criticism of the book's style and perceived some gaps between ideals and practice:

The book lacks life. . . . The going is too often unnecessarily heavy. . . . PR must get away from this jargon-like talk. . . . I find little excuse for such . . . grandiloquence as "Think of it [public relations] . . . as helping to lighten the darkness which envelops men's minds, getting rid of igno-

---

[61] The guide. *Public Relations,* 10 (3) 1958, p. 1.
[62] Hess, A. (1958). A second opinion. *Public Relations,* 10 (4), p. 40.
[63] Jenkins, R. (1992). *Pierre Bourdieu.* London: Routledge, p. 129.
[64] Hess, A., p. 41.
[65] Ibid. pp. 41–2.
[66] England, F. E. (1958). A Fleet Street opinion. *Public Relations,* 10 (4), p. 44.

rance, misunderstanding, bias, and fears which have been born in him for centuries." No PRO, I feel sure, has ever found that in his brief![67]

The book was structured around four sections: "What is Public Relations?," "The Public," "The Media," and "Organisation of Public Relations Practice," but did not contain any material that specifically dealt with public relations principles, although Lex Hornsby's chapter included a section on "Putting Principles into Practice." The latter consisted of a multistage procedure to be adopted, starting with "you must have, and you must insist on, a good brief," followed by a critical review of questions that should be asked, such as "Can the job be done by public relations methods? Could it be done by some other and less expensive means? Is the product or service right? . . . Might anything you are asked to put to the public stimulate a bad reaction from them?," followed by the opaquely described "message formulation," and finally "the follow-up stage, to assess the results you have obtained and see what other action may be necessary."[68]

Public relations was regarded as a vocation—there was reference to "entrants to the calling"[69]—with a broad remit: "public relations . . . is virtually without limit, because it is an attitude of mind, an aspect of management and inseparable from the problems of coexistence,"[70] performing an educative role in society ("our job in public relations is essentially to educate")[71] in which "you must cultivate an interest in people and a liking for people . . . believe in what you are doing . . . have pride in the organisation for which you are working."[72] The public relations practitioner was not "an authority on everything . . . [but] the interpreter of the specialist."[73] The early chapters gave a few examples of occasions when public relations might have a particular role to play, but the bulk of the book concentrated on descriptions of the media industries and their operation.

---

[67] Ibid.

[68] Hornsby, L. (1958). Its purpose and functions. In Institute of Public Relations, *A guide to the practice of public relations.* London: Newman Neame, pp. 13–14.

[69] Tallents, Sir S. (1958). By way of introduction. In Institute of Public Relations, *A guide to the practice of public relations.* London: Newman Neame, p. 3.

[70] Paget-Cooke, R. A. (1958). Recognising the problems. In Institute of Public Relations, *A guide to the practice of public relations.* London: Newman Neame, p. 19.

[71] Hornsby, L., p. 9.

[72] Ibid. p. 11.

[73] Tallents, Sir S., p. 3; Paget-Cooke, R. A., p. 19; Hornsby, L., p. 9.

Public relations was seen as an extension of interpersonal relations. The practitioner's time was apparently taken up with, "innumerable informal, off-the-record and social exchanges that take up so much of a PRO's time and nervous energy."[74] This evidently had implications for selection because it was thought that "unless a PRO has the necessary 'gift of the gab' he will not get far. He must be an extrovert, and that entails a liking for talk at all times and to all comers."[75] This approach extended to media relations: "Start with the idea that you are helping the journalist to do his job.... Trust the journalist. If for any reason you cannot answer a question then tell the journalist why you cannot. He is a human being and will understand and probably help you."[76]

EDUCATION AND MEMBERSHIP CRITERIA

In December 1958 the first final examination was taken and six candidates passed. They were awarded their certificates at a lunch in March 1959 and it was declared that "It is the Institute's aim, eventually, to admit as Full Members of the Institute only those who have passed our examinations—thus putting the Institute on a par with other professional organisations."[77] At the end of 1961, the council decided to "work towards the principle of new full Membership to be by examination only, with effect from 1965."[78] The importance of this for professionalisation and for the public relations of public relations was also noted: "In a world in which examinations are so much regarded as an index to a man's ability to practise this or that, public relations should fall in line. Our public face needs to have immediately recognizable features."[79]

In 1962 the difficulties of recruitment and selection were raised. It is rather curious that this should emerge as an issue after the time when books were beginning to be published and courses made available and, presumably, applicants were rather better informed than they could have been a few years previously. James Derriman (future IPR president 1973–1974) argued that the exponential growth of public relations

---

[74] Reilly, P. (1958). The spoken word. In Institute of Public Relations, *A guide to the practice of public relations.* London: Newman Neame, p. 207.

[75] Ibid.

[76] Hornsby, L., p. 15.

[77] Editorial, *Public Relations,* 11 (3) 1959, p. 2.

[78] Towards 1965. Editorial, *Public Relations,* 13 (2) 1961, p. 1.

[79] Ibid.

represented a problem in terms of standards. The prewar practitioner Hereward Phillips blamed the postwar intake from the services as responsible for the poor reputation of the practice:

> Hundreds of people coming out of the Services without knowledge of newspapers or other media, and only a smattering of an idea of what it was all about, decided they were God's gift to public relations or that public relations was an easy way of earning money. Many of these people were engaged to handle public relations and, failing to achieve anything, the whole practice came under a cloud.[80]

Likewise, Richard Williams-Thompson, Chief Information Officer of the Ministry of Supply (1946–1949), commented:

> The rapid growth of PR in the last ten years—due of course largely to the war—has not been a happy one. Wasters, unqualified people, friends of people in power have often been appointed to PR jobs for which they had no qualification whatsoever. . . . Or, equally bad, ex-journalists who just could not make the grade in journalism—all these have tended to give the PR system as a whole a bad name.[81]

Derriman saw a degree as an asset in terms of "maturity and breadth of mind," added to which the aspirant should have specific personal attributes and a certain type of personality:

> Imagination, curiosity . . . a clear mind . . . ability to express oneself . . . a cool head . . . a businesslike approach, initiative and persistence . . . integrity and responsibility [and] a personality acceptable to management on the one hand (not too brash; well-groomed and well-spoken; deferent, but knowing his or her own mind) and to the general run of employees, journalists and the public (hence no dictatorial or superior manner).[82]

In short, this was a list of qualities that would be beneficial in most working environments and functions of the era. At the same time, others were trying to persuade educational institutions of the importance of public relations education. Alan Eden-Green (IPR President 1960–1961) reported at the end of his presidential year: "We are still a long

---

[80]Phillips, H. (1961). Then (1935) . . . now (1961) . . . tomorrow (1986). *Public Relations, 13* (3), p. 12.

[81]Williams-Thompson, R. (1951). *Was I really necessary?* London: World's Press News, p. 3.

[82]Derriman, J. (1962). People for public relations: the problem of recruiting and selection. *Public Relations, 14* (2), pp. 5–7.

way from convincing the authorities responsible for advanced education that there is an urgent need for full-time comprehensive training in public relations—probably at the post-graduate level."[83] The IPR's Fourteen Point Plan of 1962 specified the intention to clarify categories of membership so that the level of qualification between them was clearly defined, and also to establish admission into the IPR solely by examination by 1964.[84] However, that ambition became modified and, later in the year, Eden-Green wrote, "The Council hopes that this principle can be enforced within the next few years, probably less than five."[85]

The 1962 conference focused specifically on education and its role in the process of professionalisation. During the conference and subsequently through the letters page and columns of *Public Relations*, there was discussion of entry criteria to the Institute as well as criticism of the qualifications of some of those previously admitted to full membership. However, as Alan Hess pointed out, "In the early days the Institute needed members and entry was easier."[86] Denis Inchbald (a future IPR president, 1969–1970) suggested that members should encourage their colleagues and staff to take the exams. But concern was expressed by Director of Studies Roger Wimbush that successful examinees might create a divide within the Institute and, in a statement that would appear to contradict the goal of professional status, claimed:

> It is unfortunate . . . that there has been a tendency for a few people who have been successful in the final examination and who have subsequently been elected to membership to be described as "MIPR (by exam)." . . . This is untrue in that to pass this examination cannot of itself make anybody automatically eligible for membership, but it unwittingly reflects on the vast majority of the members, who have never had this opportunity, and whose experience and ability is unquestioned. . . . I am sure that it cannot be the intention of anyone who has been fortunate enough to pass this examination to create either a foolish or a fictitious élite![87]

This suggests that not all members were pursuing professionalisation, perhaps because they were made to feel insecure. It seemed that there

---

[83]The world is waiting for a gigantic public relations job to be done. Editorial, *Public Relations*, 14 (2) 1962, p. 23.

[84]This is the fourteen point plan. *Public Relations*, 14 (2) 1962, p. 24.

[85]San José and Regent Street. *Public Relations*, 15 (1) 1962, p. 7.

[86]Closed session discussed 'The plan.' *Public Relations*, 14 (4) 1962, p. 30.

[87]MIPR (by exam). *Public Relations*, 14 (4) 1962, p. 52.

was greater discomfort in dealing with the rather more objective criteria of exams than fuzzier elements such as personality and calibre. It also suggests that exams were seen as a threat to the existing class system of membership and thus to the earlier members who were trying to maintain personal control over admission decisions.

Turning to the issue of professionalisation, Herbert Lloyd (future IPR President, 1968–1969) clearly recognised the symbolic power of education and argued at the conference, "We must establish a Chair . . . at the London School of Economics. You must have public relations taught at the university level. Once you've done that you've gone a long way towards increasing its status."[88] Tim Traverse-Healy (IPR President, 1967–1968) disagreed with Herbert Lloyd: "In taking on people, degrees don't matter a damn. What does matter is to have critical ability, to be able to assess a situation and the factors affecting it. You must have maturity. This is the sort of man who will go to the top."[89] These opposing views reflect the tension intrinsic to public relations' engagement with education. On the one hand there was the view that university-level education would contribute to the status of the occupation, on the other, that education was irrelevant and that age and experience led to the ability to make good judgments about a given situation. It is clear from Traverse-Healy's quote that there was a complete lack of understanding that a university degree might actually develop critical and analytical skills.

In his 1963 presidential address, Denys Brooke-Hart moderated the principle of entry by exam:

> I'm sure it will not be possible to limit admission to the Institute to people who have passed the examinations as soon as 1964, as was at one time envisaged. But as each year more and more people are passing the examinations, the time is not so very far ahead when there will be more members who have, in fact, passed the examinations than members who have not. That will be the time when those who have passed the examinations will exert the majority influence within the membership of the Institute. . . . This will be an admirable thing.[90]

In November 1963, members were given the opportunity to approve resolutions regarding revisions of the Institute's categories for mem-

---

[88]The future of public relations as a profession. *Public Relations*, 14 (4) 1962, p. 35.
[89]Ibid. p. 34.
[90]The President suggests seven major disciplines. *Public Relations*, 15 (4) 1963, p. 35.

bership and the creation of a code of conduct.[91] It was agreed that, from July 1965, entry to the Institute would be by examination only.[92] The editorial announcing that the Rubicon had, indeed been crossed, noted that there were still a proportion of "experienced and distinguished practitioners" who had not joined the Institute.[93] Just a hint of concern could be detected about future recruitment in the statement that, "before the ranks were closed, so to speak, a considerable recruiting effort was made, and much success achieved."[94]

The Institute widened its interest in education and began to look for opportunities to expand public relations education beyond its own examinations, particularly in the context of business and management education. It established a working party "to start an investigation into ways and means of encouraging leading management and business training establishments to give a (rightful) place to public relations (as a managerial function) in their courses."[95] There was discussion about the possibility of "a British Harvard" (once again indicating the importance of status to the occupation) and a front runner was considered to be the Glasgow School of Management Studies; it was also reported that there were "stirrings in the long moribund Department of Business Administration at the London School of Economics."[96] Finally, after several years of complaints, evening courses were set up in Birmingham, Bristol, and Glasgow. By the mid-1960s, the IPR had cooperated with International Correspondence Schools (ICS) to develop a home-study course designed to prepare students for the IPR intermediate examination.[97] In June 1965, the first government information officers course was organised by the Training and Education Division of the Treasury and similar courses were planned for all new entrants to the information officer class of the Whitehall-based departments.[98] Education was now on the IPR agenda in a major way, even though at this time only 19% of IPR members had a university degree.[99] In his presidential address Colin

---

[91]D (for development) day. Editorial, *Public Relations, 16* (1) 1963, p. 3.

[92]As the editor sees it. Editorial, *Public Relations, 17* (3) 1965, p. 2.

[93]Ibid.

[94]Ibid.

[95]As the editor sees it. Editorial, *Public Relations, 16* (1) 1963, p. 4.

[96]Ibid.

[97]Advertisement placed in *Public Relations, 18* (2) 1966, p. 23.

[98]O'Ballance, E. (1966). First government information officers' courses. *Public Relations, 18* (1), pp. 42–3.

[99]A survey [supplement]. *Public Relations, 16* (2) 1964, p. ix.

Mann shared a vision that "The public relations man of the future . . . is going to approximate closely to the ideas of Professor Edward Robinson, of Boston University, who describes him as 'an applied social scientist.'"[100]

FIRST COMPANY TRAINING SCHEME

Joyce Blow suggested in 1962 that companies should be encouraged to set up training schemes in public relations in order to reposition it as a career for graduates.[101] The first company training scheme was planned in 1963 by Michael Higgins, Director of PRP Group of Companies, who thought that the lack of training meant that "we were in danger of producing a profession (if we consider ourselves to be a profession) of semi-trained, partially skilled young men and women . . . these young people would project the worst possible image."[102]

Higgins' scheme was 3 years long. A formal contract that stipulated responsibilities on both sides required the trainee to take the Institute's examinations and to undergo external training such as a 3-month placement in a newspaper, another placement at a print works, and in the final year a business management course.[103] But only one person would benefit every 3 years and, reflecting the overt gender discrimination of the era, "It was decided we should take a young man, rather than a woman, because of the field of work in which the company at that time specialised."[104]

The scheme was advertised in *The Times* and, from the 11 applicants, "we chose a young man of 21 with a BA in history from one of the Oxford colleges."[105] The "young man" was Colin Trusler, who later became Managing Director of Shandwick, so his case is of interest given that he has held an influential position in the field. As far as the training scheme was concerned, Trusler offered a rather cautious assessment: "Training in public relations cannot, as in some subjects, turn out a fully moulded end-product, even after the longest course. Public relations is a complex compendium of skills, embracing not only involved technical

---

[100] Our responsibilities for the future. *Public Relations, 16* (4) 1964, p. 34.

[101] Closed session discussed 'The plan.' *Public Relations, 14* (4) 1962, p. 30.

[102] Higgins, M. (1966). A pioneer training scheme. *Public Relations, 18* (2), p. 18.

[103] Ibid. pp. 18–19.

[104] Ibid. p. 18.

[105] Ibid.

skills that can be learnt, but also much that is intangible and instinctive and which can only be acquired slowly."[106]

Although he welcomed the course in business management in the final year, which he thought was "a very important part of the overall training" for the reason "that public relations is an essential function of management," he also felt that "academic study had to be closely married to practice in actual projects . . . there are few things as useless as theories unrelated to the facts of daily administration."[107] Trusler thought that the 3-month newspaper attachment was "probably excessive" and that the most useful aspect was "an understanding of the way in which press and public relations can mutually supply each other's needs."[108]

In the course of his traineeship, Trusler won the Institute's President's Award for an essay on the use of films as a medium in public relations.[109] Perhaps rather curiously for one with a degree in history, Trusler's prize-winning essay made no reference to the Griersonian influence on public relations, even though he adopted some of its precepts: "If we believe that public relations means education by communication, the influencing of public attitudes by the dissemination of information, then film offers an impressive medium for establishing a dramatic and articulate bridge between an organization and its public."[110]

SOCIAL CLOSURE: RECRUITMENT AND FINANCIAL CHALLENGES

The notion of social closure, or "formal or informal, overt or covert rules governing the practices of monopolisation and exclusion,"[111] was borrowed from Weber's ideas about the powerfulness of paradigms.[112]

---

[106]Trusler, C. (1966). And from the trainee's point of view. *Public Relations, 18* (2), p. 20.

[107]Ibid.

[108]Ibid.

[109]Prizewinner. *Public Relations, 17* (4) 1965, pp. 40–7 (July 1965—note that both this issue and the following issue October 1965 were printed with identical volume numbering).

[110]Ibid. p. 40.

[111]Murphy, R. (1988). *Social closure: the theory of monopolisation and exclusion.* Oxford: Oxford University Press, p. 1.

[112]Gerth, H. H. & Wright Mills, C. (eds.). (1946). *Max Weber: essays in sociology.* New York: Oxford University Press, cited in Murphy, R. (1988). *Social closure: the theory of monopolisation and exclusion.* Oxford: Oxford University Press, p. 1.

Sociologists such as Larson showed that the concept of the professional project had as its aim the exclusion of "ineligibles" via complete social closure.[113]

The late 1960s was a period of rapid change in which entry criteria to the Institute were first tightened and then relaxed following a sharp fall in recruitment. This section charts the ambitious move to social closure and the failure to achieve it due to the inability to win over nonmembers and ineligibles to the professional project. Professional status was not abandoned as a goal, but modified in that practical experience remained a criterion for membership at the same time that the Institute's own qualification was aligned with national standards set and monitored by government.

In 1966, the new president, Leslie Hardern, gave emphasis to education, declaring, "We must embark on a radical review of the whole of our educational structure."[114] He envisaged:

> The public relations officer of tomorrow as a man or woman with the broadest basis of education, leading up to a high degree of specialisation in public relations and communications. . . . Council has agreed . . . to a more general type of examination, which would embrace a knowledge of basic management subjects—economics, law, psychology, finance, marketing, research, labour relations and international relations.[115]

Educational initiatives included discussions with the Department of Education and Science about how public relations might be integrated into national certificates in business studies and with universities about the possibility of including the subject in their curricula.

Despite the optimism and ambition expressed for the occupation by Leslie Hardern, there was also a cautionary note that proved prophetic. It had become clear that the restriction of membership to those who passed the Institute's examinations was already having some impact on recruitment: "We are faced with a declining membership, and, as a corollary, declining revenue."[116] Practitioners outside the Institute rejected the need for educational qualifications and "voted with their feet." Many joined before the new rule was applied and numbers dropped

---

[113]Murphy, R., p. 1; Gerth, H. H. & Wright Mills, C.; Larson, M. S. (1977). *The rise of professionalism: a sociological analysis*. Berkeley: University of California Press; Macdonald, K. (1995). *The sociology of the professions*. London: Sage, p. 188.

[114]The presidential address. *Public Relations, 18* (3) 1966, p. 17.

[115]Ibid.

[116]Ibid. p. 18.

back radically thereafter. Thus, the ambition to establish educational standards made it difficult to establish control over the field, which in turn reduced the power of the Institute: a conundrum yet to be resolved.

By 1967, the Institute was, according to the president-elect Tim Traverse-Healy, "in danger of insolvency."[117] Neatly illustrating the systems perspective that much later evolved within the sociology of the professions, he suggested that the Institute's examination:

> Be reconstructed so that it is related to current academic standards in other fields and means something. I believe a fair comparison should be possible with the examinations of the Institute of Personnel Administration, the Institute of Marketing, the Institute of Public Administration, the Institute of Practitioners in Advertising and the like. All these have achieved recognition in varying degrees in the academic world. After 12 years' efforts our examination has not.[118]

Traverse-Healy proposed that the standards of the qualifications be raised, but that eligibility for membership be made much more flexible: balancing experience against qualifications and providing three alternative routes to membership, including a category for those with 10 years of experience that would entail "a special examination for the older and experienced practitioner."[119]

Since the Institute's incorporation in 1963, entry criteria to the Institute had to be approved by the Board of Trade. Traverse-Healy sounded them out about his new proposals, specifically in relation to those with experience and no qualifications: "Talks that have been held with the Board of Trade on this last point lead me to state that a form of examination can be evolved that, far from offending the dignity of the experienced man, would lend distinction to his success and highlight his contribution to the profession."[120] Traverse-Healy had ambitions for the status of membership and fellowship reminiscent of the great aspirations held by the senior members of the Institute in the late 1940s and early 1950s: "As for Fellowship—I would only award it to the individual who had served five years as a member and had taken the time and trouble to contribute to the thinking of his craft by the submission of a thesis. To me, membership of the Institute would be the

---

[117]Traverse-Healy, T. (1967). Blueprint for change. *Public Relations, 19* (2), p. 8.
[118]Ibid. p. 15.
[119]Ibid.
[120]Ibid.

equivalent of a Bachelor's degree and Fellowship the Masters."[121] Such ambitions were never realised and seem to have been more to do with morale building within the IPR, and the public relations of public relations outside.

Herbert Lloyd, president-elect, confirmed to an extraordinary general meeting that changes to membership entry had been approved by the Board of Trade. These raised the age requirement (life experience) for all categories of membership.

The Board of Trade were prepared to allow some entry to the Institute without examination, provided that the Institute undertook to raise the level of its diploma to "a very high level," according to the editor of *Public Relations*, who added, "the underlying suggestion being that the Diploma level should be raised to Degree level within five years."[122] However, such ambitions were rather meaningless, as examinations were dropped as an essential qualification for membership. The Institute opted for an "all-out bid to bring every qualified PR practitioner under the Institute umbrella so that it may become, truly and permanently the recognised body representing the interests of all who practise."[123] Traverse-Healy's energy and enthusiasm were dampened by the lack of recruitment, and on 5 April 1968, he wrote in a letter to members: "Fundamentally, there is only one problem facing the Institute of Public Relations—it no longer represents the majority of experienced practitioners in the field. . . . My view is that the 'entry by examination only' policy, desirable as it may be in the long term, has proved disastrous to the health and strength of the Institute in the short-term."[124]

Consequently, the IPR retained a variety of entry routes while still pursuing the professional goal. At the end of January 1968, the IPR council adopted the HNC in Business Studies as part of the Institute's educational structure, which allowed those with the qualification to bypass Part I of a new IPR diploma.[125] Exemptions to Part I would be granted to those with HNDs, diplomas in business studies, graduates, "holders of appropriate professional qualifications," and "mature candi-

[121] Ibid.

[122] Future courses and examinations. *Public Relations*, 21 (8) 1968, p. 12; Overwhelming support for entry without examination. *Public Relations*, 20 (5) 1968, p. 11.

[123] The amber light. Editorial, *Public Relations*, 21 (8) 1968, p. 1.

[124] IPR archive [unreferenced, untitled letter from Traverse-Healy to members].

[125] Bloomfield, P. (1968). The future of PR education. *Public Relations*, 20 (2), pp. 11–13.

dates who can prove a good background of executive work."[126] After 2 years of negotiations with the Department of Education and Science, public relations was introduced as an optional subject on both HNC and HND business studies syllabuses.[127] The new diploma was based on the definition of public relations articulated by the American academic John Marston (based at the Michigan State University): "the management function which evaluates public attitudes, identifies the policies and procedures of an organisation with the public interest, and executes a programme of action and communication to earn public understanding and acceptance."[128] A list of topics was generated "from the history and literature of PR through the PR process, including fact finding, persuasion, techniques and media of communication, to identification of, and types of public, research and evaluation and a thorough review of all the types of PR practice."[129] Educational objectives were formulated that would help meet future management objectives by producing graduates capable of adaptation to environmental change. Part II of the diploma (which would take 1 year) would be restricted to problem analysis and public relations strategy in relation to organisational goals.[130] Assessment included case study examination and a "dissertation" of 5,000 words.[131] Acknowledged by the Institute as "the main architect" in formulating the new structure, Peter Bloomfield then left the Institute and was not replaced, thus allowing the Institute "to consolidate its financial position."[132]

From 1970, there were three study options: a certificate (which had been set up and run by Arthur Cain since 1966) for those with school-leaving qualifications, the HNC in Business Studies, and the new Diploma in Public Relations. However, "work experience and professional backgrounds" were still taken into account as the Institute granted exemptions on an ad hoc basis.[133]

---

[126] Big educational changes. *Public Relations,* 20 (2) 1968, p. 18.

[127] Ibid.

[128] Bloomfield, P. (1968). Toward a diploma in public relations. *Public Relations,* 20 (3), p. 14, quoting from Marston, J. (1963). *The nature of public relations.* New York: McGraw-Hill.

[129] Bloomfield, P. Toward a diploma in public relations, p. 14.

[130] Ibid. p. 15.

[131] Ibid.

[132] Director leaves: no replacement for time being. *Public Relations,* 20 (3) 1968, p. 21.

[133] Education for public relations in the seventies. *Public Relations,* 22 (11) 1969, p. 13.

THE COMMUNICATION, ADVERTISING, AND MARKETING EDUCATION FOUNDATION (CAM)

In the late 1960s, the Institute relinquished some control over the educational process for the first time. Courses and examinations for Part I were devolved to a new organisation of which the Institute was a cofounder: The Communication, Advertising and Marketing Education Foundation (CAM), a registered charity (educational trust).[134] Cofounders with the IPR were: the Advertising Association, the Incorporated Society of British Advertisers, the Incorporated Advertising Managers' Association, and the Institute of Practitioners in Advertising. The Institute of Marketing was represented on the board of governors.[135] CAM was founded to "promote . . . the general advancement of communication, advertising and marketing education at all levels . . . to provide educational facilities . . . to assist in the improvement of educational and training standards."[136]

The Director of CAM, John Dodge, had previously been Director of the National Council for the Training of Journalists, on the editorial board of the Thompson Foundation, and on the Board of the UNESCO Mass Communications Centre at Strasbourg.[137] An important founder governor of CAM was Amanda Barry, Chairman of the IPR Education Committee, who:

> Undertook the onerous task of revising the Institute's education structure and played a major part in the design and production of a completely new curriculum [and later] devoted her remarkable energies to integrating the IPR's new curriculum with CAM's development programme, work for which she was later rewarded by being only the second woman to be elected a Fellow (and she was also appointed a Fellow of the Institute of Practitioners in Advertising).[138]

The first public relations person entitled to use the suffix "Dip.Cam" was prominent public relations author Frank Jefkins, in 1971.[139]

---

[134] Ibid. p. 14.

[135] Ibid.

[136] Ibid.

[137] Ibid.

[138] Amanda Barry elected FIPR. *Public Relations,* 24 (7) 1971, p. 146.

[139] Amanda Barry elected FIPR. *Public Relations,* 24 (7) 1971, p. 146; Amanda Barry makes it a double. *Public Relations,* 25 (3), 1972, p. 45; Frank Jefkins is our first Dip.CAM. *Public Relations,* 25 (3) 1972, p. 74.

The diploma was effectively split into two stages: Part I would lead to the award of the CAM certificate (a more broadly based qualification) and Part II the Diploma in Public Relations.[140] In 1973, exemptions were introduced for the CAM certificate for those who held a "senior position" in public relations, who had spent at least 10 years in communications, advertising, and marketing, who were already members of the IPR, or who successfully passed a viva.[141] First to register to sit for the diploma under the new arrangements were James Derriman, the new president, and Colin Mann (a past president, 1963–1964), Wilfred Howard (a future president, 1974–1975), Margaret Nally (a future president, 1975–1976).[142] Derriman declared, "The CAM Diploma is recognized by the Department of Education and Science as . . . equivalent to the exams of the bankers or chartered secretaries. . . . Everyone entering public relations under the age of 30 should study for his (or her) CAM certificate and Diploma at the very beginning of his career. . . . Qualification by exam cannot much longer remain optional."[143]

EDUCATION IN THE 1970s

In the 1970s, the public relations industry began to think more ambitiously about education. This was in part due to a loss of faith in CAM and an awareness of the opportunities that increased vocationalism within education could offer.

In 1974, a new chairman of the Education Committee, John Cole-Morgan (whose career included a stint at the British Council from 1982 to 1985) thought that it was no use having a "well-based education and examination system unless steps were taken to ensure that its standard of excellence was appreciated by the outside world."[144] Cole-Morgan worked for many years at the Agricultural Research Council and was influenced in his thinking by his work experience with scientists and the scientific media. He considered that a fellowship should be attained by thesis and that this step would be the first move "towards establishing a far more academic approach to public relations" as well as "stimulating research activity to ensure that public relations activity was based on sound evidence rather than hunches, which might be

[140]Education for public relations in the seventies. *Public Relations*, 22 (11) 1969, p. 14.
[141]CAM's new scheme for diploma exam. *Public Relations*, 26 (7) 1973, p. 129.
[142]New route to CAM diploma for senior PR people. *Public Relations*, 27 (1) 1974, p. 1.
[143]The way ahead. *Public Relations*, 26 (12) 1973, p. 215.
[144]The need for learning. *Public Relations*, 27 (10) 1974, p. 190.

acquired by experience but could not be taught."[145] He also thought that the Institute's journal should become more academic and that articles should be subjected to blind review.[146] Cole-Morgan's clarion call for more intellectual rigour fell on stony ground: He remembered that there was simply "no reaction"[147] and he attributed the "lack of fundamental interest in communication" to the tendency "to see it [public relations] as a business rather than as a profession."[148] He explained this distinction in terms of consultancy practice as "only doing those things the client will register as being in his interests—they are afraid of tackling the subject in a more academic way because they think the client wouldn't understand it."[149]

The IPR's education trust laid out new objectives in 1976, which included the "establishment of a Chair of Communication at a University; international professional exchange of personnel; initiation of research programmes; initiation of the production of case histories."[150] These aims illustrate a more outward-looking set of ambitions. The emphasis given to case histories can be explained by the astonishing dearth of such material despite the vain pleas of several editors. The poverty of material is best illustrated by the fact that one case study was published in 1974, 16 years after the events had taken place.[151] Presumably, trustees thought that academics would be more likely to gain access. The trust's new aims also revealed something about what was expected of academics in the field. The chair emphasised, "The establishment of a University Chair offers the opportunity for a donor's name to be perpetuated. Apart from being a most valuable contribution to the future of our profession, this objective has the potential of an excellent public relations exercise."[152]

UNIVERSITY QUALIFICATIONS

Between 1971 and 1998, around 2,000 students were awarded the CAM Diploma in Public Relations.[153] Between the early 1960s and the mid-

---

[145] Ibid.
[146] Ibid.
[147] Interview. 25 October 1998.
[148] Ibid.
[149] Ibid.
[150] Ibid.
[151] Galitzine, Prince Y. (1974). A cut above the others. *Public Relations,* 27 (2), p. 24.
[152] Education trust revival. *Communicator* April 1977, p. 1.
[153] Fax from CAM to author, 20 October 1998.

1970s, the opportunities for higher education in Britain had expanded enormously. Increased access was threatened by the economic downturn, followed by the oil crisis of 1973 and by the government imposing a series of funding cuts on higher education. By 1984, the British government was continuing to cut budgets and grants to the sector and emphasising the country's need for skilled personnel and vocational education. The university sector responded by developing a portfolio of applied degrees such as the MBA and new subjects such as organisational behaviour and psychology, which could help provide much needed funds.[154] These developments coincided with calls from the public relations industry for university-level education, such as the 1981 report "Education for Business Communicators" produced by the Business Graduate Association, which recommended the establishment of two postgraduate degrees in communications within university business schools.[155]

The first postgraduate degree in public relations in the UK was established at the University of Stirling in 1988. It was the brainchild of Professor John Horden, an expert in bibliographical systems, who had set up innovative publishing studies degrees at the Universities of Stirling and Leeds. Shortly after moving to the English Department at Stirling from Leeds in 1982, Horden began to draft a possible public relations syllabus. In 1984 a mutual acquaintance introduced him to Sam Black, who gradually developed the informal role of broker between the university and the professional bodies. The connection was valuable to the university and, on 30 January 1988, a resolution was passed by the IPRA board of directors at its meeting in Geneva: "The International Public Relations Association notes with approval the introduction of the Master's (M.Sc.) Degree Programme in Public Relations at the University as it is based closely on the IPRA Gold Paper No.4 and recommends it to those wishing to study public relations at the postgraduate level."[156]

In terms of professionalisation, it is also of interest to note the remarks made by the then Vice Chancellor of Stirling (and businessman), Sir Monty Finniston, in *PR Week* that "Thirty years ago PR was a dirty phrase, linked with a form of brainwashing that certainly is not the case today."[157] It seems that the university sector itself needed

---

[154] For example, degrees of this nature were established by Birkbeck College, University of London in the early 1980s.

[155] Mastering educational needs. *Public Relations*, 1 (3) 1983, p. 2.

[156] Letter from S. Black to Prof J. Horden in Professor Horden's personal archive 1987.

[157] Stirling University to hold the first MSc course in PR. *PR Week* 25/2–2/3/1987. [From Professor Horden's personal archive—page number unclear on photocopy.]

to legitimise the subject of public relations as a field of vocational study. To do this, it had to take an explicitly functional rather than critical view of the topic. Undergraduate degrees were subsequently established at Leeds Polytechnic, the Dorset Institute, and the College of St. Mark and St. John (under the aegis of Exeter University) in 1989.

Practitioners retained a strong stake in higher education developments. Even the original idea of an academic network came from a practitioner, Tim Traverse-Healy. He hosted a lunch at his London club, The Athenaeum, which was attended by Professor Tim Wheeler (Bournemouth), Dr. Jon White (Cranfield), Sam Black (Honorary Professor, Stirling), Danny Moss (the first M.Sc. course director at Stirling, later Director of the M.A. at Manchester Metropolitan), and Betty Dean (course director for the postgraduate Diploma at Watford College), to establish the Public Relations Educators' Forum (PREF). Early meetings of PREF consisted largely of debates about jurisdictional issues in relation to the focus and content of the ideal curriculum. It was not until 1998 that PREF hosted a fully refereed conference.

The desire to control the curriculum and also to exert influence over those who taught public relations became apparent in 1991 when the IPR introduced a system of "recognition" of courses. Initially, the evidence required was scanty, but by 1996 a detailed document was required, similar to that of the government's Teaching Quality Assessments. An important requirement was that a "senior" member of staff should produce "evidence of professional experience and up-to-date knowledge about public relations practice."[158]

Although public relations courses within the UK found themselves in a variety of academic homes, it was clear that the IPR preferred the topic to be located in business and management, and in 1996 the Education and Training Committee saw its role as:

> Protecting and promoting the standing of public relations as a strategic and vigorous *management* discipline. . . . The Committee's responsibility to aspiring members of the profession is chiefly to act as the guardian of the professional relevance of education and training in the programmes recognised by the Institute and to monitor and encourage excellence in teaching and research in the subject. (emphasis in original)

Respectability was as hard for academics as it was for practitioners, but for academics it was a war on two fronts because they had to win

---

[158]Criteria and procedures for IPR recognition of public relations programmes. (1996). *Institute of Public Relations,* unpaginated.

respect from practitioners and from academics from established disciplines. Although public relations academics enjoyed many cooperative and productive relationships with the practice (and the vast majority had themselves been practitioners), some tensions did arise, often focused on curriculum content. At least one academic, Bill Mallinson, was opposed to academic notions of the subject, and wrote in 1996:

> Who, then, is best qualified to teach public relations? The answer must be the practitioner, since he or she is less likely to be biased by an academic hobby-horse. In the case of a full-time public relations teacher, he or she must have practised beforehand, or receive adequate training. According to Doug Smith, a former President of the ... IPR ... education is killing public relations—when it is taught by academics.[159]

In the same year, Sir Derek Roberts, Provost of University College London, was quoted as saying in relation to developments in higher education standards, "We are talking about intellectually challenging subjects ... some vocational subjects come into this category, but public relations and media studies certainly do not."[160] Undergraduate degrees in particular have continued to attract criticism from the industry newspaper *PR Week* (not an IPR publication) and a number of practitioners have articulated their preference for new recruits to the industry to possess degrees in more established subjects such as history, politics, and even sociology. Thus, public relations shares similar problems of credibility with media studies in relation to the media industry, which, like that of public relations, values the "university of life."

In 1998, there was a new educational development: The IPR introduced its own new diploma (taught at selected educational establishments) to form the basis for entry to membership of the IPR. The motivation behind this development was to achieve "Chartered Status," for which the Institute had to demonstrate that 50% of its members held an approved qualification. This initiative finally bound the professional body and universities together in a joint enterprise that can only benefit the practice. The diploma is a demanding qualification encompassing both theoretical and practical aspects of PR. Necessarily, it is more restricted in scope than any of the university degrees, but it makes appropriate demands of its students in terms of intellectual ability with

---

[159]Mallinson, B. (1996). *Public lies and private truths: an anatomy of public relations.* London: Cassell, p. 82.

[160]*The Observer.* 22 December 1996.

its specialised vocational focus. It has proved popular and a number of centres have been set up. Another key development has been the establishment of Continuous Professional Development (CPD). This may include the acquisition of formal qualifications, contribution to IPR groups, in-house training, and leading strategic discussions on policy. Launched as "Developing Excellence," IPR members have the opportunity to commit themselves to future development and training to enhance their knowledge, professionalism, and PR skills. Only history will tell whether sufficient numbers will take up the variety of educational opportunities available at the beginning of the 21st century to allow the IPR to achieve chartered status and the enhanced professional position this represents.

CONCLUSION

Successive attempts to impose a rigorous system of entry by qualification failed in the sense that experience remained a tradable commodity. Expertise was evidently a combination of interpersonal and writing skills, common sense, good manners and "clubbability," and that elusive quality, "calibre." The emphasis on personal qualities made it impossible for the Institute to monopolise practice. Even in the era when public relations was defined as an extension of personal relations, there appears to have been little engagement with communications theory or psychology (particularly from the mid-1960s onward) judging from the Institute's journals.

From the outset, the Institute had a rather ambivalent relationship with education. Education had the potential to increase the respectability and status that practitioners desired, and to provide theoretical knowledge to underpin a specific expertise. But education quickly became synonymous with training (processes, procedures, and routines) and practitioners' interest in education was purely instrumental. For example, between 1952 and 1954, the proposed academic content of the Institute's examination was reduced, leaving a largely technical and factual body of knowledge with the exception of "public opinion" and the unidentified "public relations principles." Qualifications were seen as a way of improving the image of public relations, but compliance was constantly deferred and delegated to the next generation. The reliance on practitioners for teaching implies something of an apprenticeship culture and possibly hints at the belief that academia did not have much to offer, at least until the mid-1960s, when business and management education began to expand. Jumping on the management bandwagon was a political move to achieve higher status rather than an intellectual decision. It perhaps also marks the moment when public relations began to move away from one jurisdictional competitor—journalism—only to discover another—marketing.

This chapter has shown that the public relations occupation has seen education as an instrument to achieve professional status both in terms of gaining social approval (or licence and mandate, to use the terminology from the sociology of the professions) and in terms of achieving social closure and being able to exclude nonapproved practitioners. This facilitated the formation of part of the public relations occupation into an interest group, and was thus vital to the development of its identity and sense of self. Nevertheless, the history of public relations' engagement with education to date suggests that it is unlikely to achieve full professional status, at least in the foreseeable future.

8

Implications
and Conclusions

PROFESSIONALISATION

This book has addressed a significant gap in the literature by providing a first narrative account of the emergence of British public relations in the political, social, and economic context of the 20th century. It has focused on the development of public relations as a discrete occupational group and analysed how that group sought to win professional status. It therefore goes some way toward explaining the emergence of the public relations phenomenon and additionally gives an in-depth account of its key features.

In this book, I aimed to answer the following questions: How did public relations in Britain emerge and why? How did public relations develop as a discrete occupation and in what form? The central story that emerges is that of the failure of the public relations occupation to professionalise, despite its rapid growth and contribution to the development of promotional culture. This apparent paradox can be explained by the inability of the professional body to establish control over the practice in the face of rapid postwar change. The lack of a coherent definition that explained the purpose of public relations rather than its ideals or techniques made it difficult to establish a clear jurisdiction. This failure can be explained by a lack of intellectual rigor in the field and also by practitioners' desire to separate their practice from propaganda. These characteristics have remained features of the public relations landscape.

In some ways, the establishment of professional bodies came too late and reflected the prewar social order of old-boy networks, pubs, and clubs, rather than the values of professionalism to which they aspired. In particular, the reluctance to enforce educational standards and regulatory frameworks meant that it was impossible to distinguish between members and nonmembers in terms of the quality of service on offer. This problem escalated dramatically with the growth of the occupation in the second half of the 20th century, as evidenced by the fact that only around 6,000 of the estimated 45,000 to 60,000 public relations practitioners in the UK currently belong to the IPR. In the current political and economic climate, the vast demand for public relations services means that practitioners do not actually need full-blown professional status. Professional status has therefore become the loudly articulated aim of a small subgroup of practitioners. Historically, such practitioners have often not been the leading lights of the business, many of whom have remained outside the Institute. Some of the IPR activists have been inward looking, more concerned with achieving position within the Institute than engaging seriously with issues of knowledge, expertise, and education. Fundamentally, the professional project was an effort to legitimate public relations in relation to its main competitor and critic—the media—whose response was largely to discredit the practice. The efforts of the IPR to define the field, its boundaries, and its jurisdictional scope have so far failed. The ultimately hopeless power plays have reduced many of the Institute's efforts to rhetorical exercises—the public relations of public relations. That this remains the case today demonstrates that the historical faults of the occupation have so far not been corrected.

The history of the professionalisation of public relations reveals an occupational group pursuing its own interests in relation to the state and social elites as the source of cultural and ideological power. Professional status has been sought to establish social legitimacy. Social respectability was the aim of many within the IPR, and proving the occupation's value to society and democracy in general was a strategy drawn from the local government public service ethos. Thus, the route taken to legitimate the practice was that of the public interest, which, though appropriate in the public service context, was rather more difficult to sustain in a profit-making enterprise. The effort put into idealistic discourse has generally not been seen as credible by much of the media and the wider society, and public relations practice has proved very slow to take up the rational or scientific discourse that might appease some of its critics. The IPR's changing definition of public relations practice in the 1990s from one encompassing "mutual understanding" to a more pragmatic definition focused on the notion of reputation, and that body's efforts to proselytise the importance of research and evaluation, marks a shift in that direction.

The progressivist accounts of public relations practice that dominate American histories have been used rhetorically as part of the strategy to gain professional status. But this book has shown that the history of British public relations has featured a number of interwoven strands of influence arising from the particular culture and its history, some recurring problematics, some aporia, and some oscillation between various approaches to practice that coexisted over the years. To exemplify this, one can point to the importance given to environmental scanning and strategic approaches (though of course these terms were not employed at the time) to public relations in the 1920s and 1930s by those in local and central government, which contrasted with the importance placed on interpersonal relations in the pre–Second World War colonial context, or the advertising and publicity approach that became more apparent in the consumer public relations of the 1960s when the British economy began to recover from the impact of the Second World War. This pattern of development appears to contrast with the distinct phases of development and improvement that have been claimed for American practice.

The implications of the different historical trajectory do have some theoretical implications for the public relations discipline. Much emphasis to date has been placed on the phases of American development that apparently illustrate defined types of practice and this typology has been used as a theoretical framework to organise much quantitative research in the field in the United States and elsewhere. One of the implications of this book is that it throws into question the universal applicability of that model and the assumptions that lie behind it. Although in a globalised society we may now assume constants of public relations practice within the huge communications conglomerates, it is perhaps unwise to attribute these to some natural path of evolution defined by American practice. In any case, it is clear that intercultural communication presents particular challenges to large companies and organisations and that public relations practice varies tremendously between Singapore, Kenya, and Malta. Rather than holding up the American model as an ideal, perhaps it would be better to learn and understand more fully how communications practice and public relations developed in different cultures from the political and socioeconomic histories of those countries and the particular models that evolve from those cultures, not least because we can all learn from the experience of others. Sadly, at present, little is known about the origins of public relations in many countries, so that much of the rich diversity of the history of public relations remains uncovered and many lessons unlearned. It is clear that, within Britain at least, we can reject in part the notion that public relations was invented by the Americans and exported to the UK, because it was clear that much that was important emerged as a consequence of specifically British history, politics, economics, culture, ideology, technology, and the creative industries.

HISTORICAL EVOLUTION

Turning to the overall development and growth of the occupation in Britain, it can be seen that one of the most significant features of British developments, especially in the first half of the 20th century, was the large role played by local and central governments and the relatively small contribution of the private sector. During both world wars, the British government made substantial propaganda efforts both at home and overseas using a range of media. The postwar era threw up new challenges for the state, notably in its relationships with other countries, and the growth of public relations beyond Britain was in some cases stimulated by the process of decolonisation, which affected not only the British government, but also companies operating in the colonies. In terms of domestic politics, the major policy shift was that of nationalisation, whereby government took ownership of core industries away from the private sector. The threat of nationalisation roused a response from private enterprises in the form of organisations that could lobby on their behalf. Subsequent governments engaged in both nationalisation and privatisation and these policies necessitated substantial rhetorical communication. The stimuli for the development and growth of public relations can be seen as arising from the political, economic, cultural, and technological spheres and the relative influence of these is now considered.

The Political Environment

The political domain was of crucial importance in stimulating the growth of public relations in Britain during a turbulent period of European history. Although the concepts of public relations and propaganda have for the most part remained entangled, it is evident that the motivation behind some public relations efforts was to improve democracy. Fundamental contributions to its development were made by local government officials and the establishment of the Institute of Public Administration and its journal were key factors. Central government's efforts were, to a large extent, focused on propaganda during the two world wars and the Cold War. This period of history shows the difficulties in drawing clear distinctions between the practice of propaganda, public relations, information management, intelligence, persuasion, and psychological warfare. The fact that a number of individuals had careers that overlapped these fields and that they were regarded admiringly, if not romantically, by their peers suggests that the apparent ethical boundaries between the concepts were ignored in practice.

After the Second World War, the scope of diplomacy and public relations became broader as technology facilitated increasing communications across national boundaries and created more opportunities for governments to target the domestic publics of other nations on a range of issues, including those of the country targeted. Such changes in the international arena provided opportunities for individual consultants, as well as governments, and a number of practitioners in the 1950s and 1960s took advantage of the commercial opportunities offered by decolonisation and other political events to work for foreign governments, sometimes controversially. Decolonisation entailed information, propaganda, intelligence, and in some cases psychological warfare. Public relations was involved in aspects of this work as well as in assisting new independent governments to develop information structures (sometimes replicating the British model) and new national identities (achieved through publicity to support tourism and new national airlines). The political domain proved a fertile breeding ground for public relations activities and this book suggests that, within this sphere, distinguishing between public relations and propaganda is not a straightforward matter. The British government did not restrict its discourse work solely to wartime propaganda, but was also active in the economic and cultural spheres and it is to these developments that I now turn.

The Economic Environment

There were a variety of government interventions in the economy throughout the 20th century. The creation of the EMB proved highly significant in public relations' history because, even though it was dissolved after a couple of years, it provided a forum for Sir Stephen Tallents to develop his ideas and facilitated the opportunity for his partnership with John Grierson. Tallents' ideas had a long-term impact in the cultural and economic propaganda of the British Council. Other state-inspired and crucial stimuli to the development and growth of the public relations industry after the Second World War were the policies of nationalisation and privatisation, and the debates and campaigns that these programmes provoked. As pointed out by Gandy[1] and, in the UK, Miller and Dinan,[2] orchestrating the sales of privatised industries in the Thatcher period required a massive communication effort by the GIS and, furthermore, the establishment of competitive companies required a considerable public relations effort to establish corporate identities, promote services, and maintain customer, shareholder, and employee loyalty. It can therefore be seen that political interventions in the economic sphere, and change within it, resulted in growth for the public relations sector in the postwar era.

The Cultural Environment

The British government was also a key sponsor of activities in the cultural field, particularly in the first half of the 20th century. Technological developments in communications facilitated the growth of the film industry. The significance of the British Documentary Movement was crucial to much of the ideology of the public relations industry in relation to its public service role in upholding democracy.[3] On the entertainment side, the popularisation of film as a leisure activity alongside traditional showbiz also created opportunities for publicists and press agents.[4] After the Second World War, the phenomenal growth of the popular music industry, coinciding with the development of new marketing techniques, increased affluence, and the creation of teenage and

---

[1]Gandy, O. (1992). Public relations and public policy: the structuration of dominance in the information age. In Toth, E. & Heath, R. (eds.). *Rhetorical and critical approaches to public relations.* Hillsdale, New Jersey: Lawrence Erlbaum Associates, p. 148.

[2]Miller, D. & Dinan, W. (2000). The rise of the PR industry in Britain 1979–98. *European Journal of Communication,* 15 (1), pp. 5–35.

[3]L'Etang, J. (1998). State propaganda and bureaucratic intelligence: the creation of public relations in twentieth century Britain. *Public Relations Review,* 24 (4), pp. 413–41; L'Etang, J. (1999). John Grierson and the public relations industry in Britain. In *Screening the Past: An International Electronic Journal of Visual Media and History.*

[4]Interview. 30 October 1996.

youth markets, also yielded new opportunities. More recently, the development of sport as a business suggests yet further potential for public relations growth.

This book also points to the significance of the rise of the British design industry (partially sponsored by government) to developments in public relations. The development of the design industry is part of the story of growth of what has been described as "promotional culture."[5] Wernick explored the notion that promotional messages have become totally embedded in our culture in a taken-for-granted fashion. He argued that rhetoricised culture has become a dominant feature that commodifies our daily existence. This book elucidates some of that process within Britain. One aspect of promotional culture is what has been termed "the rise of professional society."[6] This is the context for public relations' struggle for a better status. Professionalisation requires promotional efforts and the aspiration for professional status is both a function and a symptom of promotional culture.

Professionalisation is a part of the development of promotional culture and, in the case of public relations (and other service occupations), requires positioning in a market and the possession of a clear jurisdiction separate from advertising, marketing, and journalism. The trappings of professional status symbolise power. Public relations' professional project is about achieving elite status. A profession is a promotional product. Professionalisation is a device to transform a service into income, hence the importance of the notion of cultural capital identified by Bourdieu.[7]

The Technological Environment

Postwar technological change, often stimulated by wartime research and development, facilitated the growth of new industries, products, and markets, such as pharmaceuticals, cars, television, white goods, and hi-tech industries, which needed to be marketed to business customers and individual consumers, thus contributing to the expansion of pro-

---

[5]Wernick, A. (1991). *Promotional culture: advertising, ideology and symbolic expression*. London: Sage.

[6]Perkin, H. (1989). *The rise of professional society: England since 1880*. London: Routledge.

[7]Bourdieu, P. (1989). *Distinction: a social critique of the judgement of taste*. London: Routledge.

motional culture. One of the major new industries was international air travel, which, quite apart from its impact on communications, business, and leisure, opened up a new area for the development of both corporate and national identities: a major goal for many of the decolonised countries was to establish their own airlines.

Of substantial importance was the impact of technological developments on the media. The explosion of broadcast media, the end of hot-metal print production, the death of Fleet Street, and the vast developments in communications technology changed the way that journalists worked and put them under time pressures that encouraged increasing dependence on public relations services.

An intellectual technical development that directly affected the role of public relations was the commercial take-up of sampling capability in the 1930s. The issue of technical expertise naturally takes us back to issues of professionalisation, a major focus of this book. The formation of the IPR in 1948 was a crucial development in the occupation's history that gave the occupation an institutional voice and a focus for professionalisation. Within the IPR, work began on the professional project and continues to the present day when ambitions are focused on achieving chartered status. Historically, the IPR sought to gain entry to the elite strata of society alongside other occupations in an increasingly professionalised society. That it has struggled to achieve this to date is the consequence of a failure to establish clearer jurisdiction, a cognitive base, or social legitimacy, at least in the eyes of the media. More importantly, it has self-evidently thrived in its unprofessional state and continues to attract budgets from the elite and powerful institutions. In the face of this, one wonders if the professional project will be sustained in the future or quietly abandoned.

In Summary

This book argues that a range of crucial structural developments facilitated the development of public relations in Britain. It can be seen that, although some individuals were particularly important in terms of their ability to articulate the scope of the field (e.g., Stephen Tallents and John Grierson), on the whole, growth was not particularly attributable to such enterprising individuals. Indeed, rank opportunism, combined with inexperience and overindulgence in the expense account culture of many of those who entered public relations in the postwar period, can be seen to have adversely affected the reputation of public relations as an occupation in the UK.[8] Neither was it the case that public relations was imported directly from the United States. British public relations developed its own unique characteristics that arose from Britain's political, economic, technological, and cultural changes throughout the 20th century. Thus, the history of public relations cannot be separated from the structural aspects of a specific society: Public relations is quite properly an area of interest for sociologists.

This book demonstrates the overwhelming influence of the political sphere and the presence of public relations at the heart of international conflicts and national power struggles over policy, as well as its being intrinsic to widening participation in democracy. Such positioning necessarily raises questions of accountability, transparency, and access. As I point out, in recent times this has posed ethical problems for public relations at the heart of government. Historically, public relations had an ambiguous role in changes in the public sphere. Although it has clearly been involved in limiting access, it has also been used to facilitate democratic practice.

Public relations in Britain has had a rhetorical role in both the private and public sectors and has acted opportunistically for its paymasters. Its association with propaganda is clear from the historical evidence and its continuing activities for and on behalf of a variety of governments means that this connection cannot be consigned to the history books. The occupation of public relations has not been a purely technical communication skill and certainly not a neutral one. It can be seen that public relations plays a crucial role both in government (where it helps to communicate the rules of the game in the political, economic, and cultural spheres) and in the free market (which exists by courtesy of the state). Public relations in Britain has arisen largely from the intersection between the political and economic spheres and has played a crucial role in the rhetoric of the free market. Its embeddedness in British culture and its contribution to the development of a promotional culture means that public relations helps shape reality for citizens at a phenomenological level.

Public relations' historical roots in documentary film, its continual merging into government propaganda, its links to design, advertising,

---

[8]L'Etang, J. Organising public relations' identity: an historical review of the discourse work conducted within and on behalf of the Institute of Public Relations in the UK. Conference paper presented to *The business of organising identities*, Stirling Media Research Institute, June 2000.

and marketing industries, and its emphasis on education position the occupation as an important, though not always visible, aspect of 20th-century Britain. Present at the crux of society, its central communication role appears to be as an agent of forces focused on contemporary issues and problems and engaged in intellectual and cultural production.[9]

In conclusion, this book provides an overview of the development of public relations in 20th-century Britain. Its focus on professionalisation and access to many of the key players provides insight into the critical period when public relations became established as a discrete occupation, if not a profession.

---

[9]Bourdieu, P. (1971). Intellectual field and creative project. In Young, M. F. D. (ed.). *Knowledge and control: new directions in the sociology of education.* London: Collier-Macmillan, p. 161.

References

A   Archival sources
   A1   IPR journals
   A2   IPRA publications
   A3   Books written by practitioners
   A4   Newspaper reports and articles
   A5   IPR's archive documents
   A6   Grierson archive (University of Stirling)
   A7   CBI archive (University of Warwick)
   A8   Miscellaneous
B   Academic journal articles
C   Academic books and book chapters

A1   PR journals (presented in chronological order)

The first conference. Editorial, *Public Relations*, 1 (1) 1948, pp. 1–2.
Firms and organisations represented. *Public Relations*, 1 (1) 1948, pp. 16–17.
Hess, A. Our aims and objects. *Public Relations*, 1 (1) 1948, p. 8.
McLoughlin, A. Edward Kingsley Holmes: an appreciation. *Public Relations*, 1 (1) 1948, p. 3.
Seymour, W. J. S. An invitation to the critics. *Public Relations*, 1 (1) 1948, p. 1.
Who are these people? *Public Relations*, 1 (1) 1948, p. 14.
Wimbush, R. The birth of an institute. *Public Relations*, 1 (1) 1948, p. 2.
Items of news. *Public Relations*, 1 (2) 1948, p. 12.
Royal Commission on the press. *Public Relations*, 1 (2) 1948, pp. 10–11.

Tallents, Sir S. Speeches at the luncheon. *Public Relations,* 1 (2) 1948, p. 5.

The first conference. Editorial, *Public Relations,* 1 (2) 1948, p. 2.

Groom, F. S. Factory visits. *Public Relations,* 1 (3) 1949, p. 14.

Hardern, L. Work under monopoly conditions. *Public Relations,* 1 (3) 1949, p. 11.

Murray Milne, F. Public relations in a wholesale way. *Public Relations,* 1 (3) 1949, pp. 4–6.

Our first discussion: members seek definition of public relations. *Public Relations,* 1 (3) 1949, p. 4.

A member hits out. *Public Relations,* 2 (1) 1949, p. 1.

Brebner's book. Editorial, *Public Relations,* 2 (1) 1949, p. 16.

Highlights of the conference. *Public Relations,* 2 (2) 1949, pp. 3, 6.

Public relations and advertising. *Public Relations,* 2 (2) 1949, pp. 7–11.

Untitled announcement, *Public Relations,* 2 (2) 1949, p. 6.

Pringle, J. Working for 60,000 employers. *Public Relations,* 2 (1) 1949, pp. 12–15.

Seeing themselves from another angle. *Public Relations,* 2 (3) 1950, p. 8.

So a public relations officer was appointed. *Public Relations,* 2 (3) 1950, p. 1.

Some things they said. *Public Relations,* 2 (3) 1950, p. 5.

Discussion. *Public Relations,* 2 (4) 1950, p. 21.

Hornsby, L. The qualities of a public relations officer. *Public Relations,* 2 (4) 1950, p. 4.

Pritchard, F. Persuasion. *Public Relations,* 2 (4) 1950, pp. 20–21.

Public relations in Holland. *Public Relations,* 2 (4) 1950, p.26.

The qualities of a PRO. Discussion. *Public Relations,* 2 (4) 1950, p. 15.

What they said. *Public Relations,* 2 (4) 1950.

Grierson, J. The scope of film in public relations. *Public Relations,* 3 (1) 1950, p. 13.

Paget-Cooke, R. The press and public relations officers. *Public Relations,* 3 (1) 1950, p. 10.

Hess, A. The conference speeches. *Public Relations,* 3 (2) 1950, pp. 5–7.

Now for the future. *Public Relations,* 3 (2) 1950, p. 1.

The conference speeches. *Public Relations,* 3 (2) 1950, p. 6.

What they said at dinner. *Public Relations,* 3 (2) 1950, p. 11.

Planning a home publicity campaign. Address given by T. Fife-Clark, Controller Home COI. *Public Relations,* 3 (3) 1951, p. 6.

Paget-Cooke, R. A. Good business. *Public Relations,* 3 (3) 1951, pp. 9–10.

Still going ahead. Editorial, *Public Relations,* 3 (3) 1951, p. 3.

Public relations and the arts. *Public Relations,* 3 (4) 1951, p. 7.

Medboe, O. Developments in Norway. *Public Relations,* 4 (1) 1951, p. 25.

Dodson-Wells, G. Bulwark of freedom. *Public Relations,* 4 (1) 1951, pp. 6–7.

Johnson, B. You cannot get such men. *Public Relations,* 4 (1) 1951, p. 9.

Telling the tale. *Public Relations,* 4 (1) 1951, p. 18.

Those who were there. *Public Relations,* 4 (1) 1951, p. 2.

Usher, T. The personal approach. *Public Relations,* 4 (2) 1952, pp. 8–9.

Rogers, N. Some form of examination. *Public Relations,* 4 (3) 1952, p. 7.

The American code of standards for the practice of public relations. *Public Relations,* 4 (3) 1952, p. 6.

Fife-Clark, T. Towards an international public relations association. *Public Relations,* 4 (3), 1952, p. 11.

White, H. Information and the law. *Public Relations,* 4 (3) 1952, p. 22.

Another successful conference. *Public Relations,* 4 (4) 1952, p. 1.

Adam, General Sir R., Bt. GCB, DSO, OBE. Public relations in industry. *Public Relations,* 4 (4) 1952, p. 2.

Curran, C. What I think of PROs and why. *Public Relations,* 4 (4) 1952, p. 5.

Black, M. The influence of the South Bank and Battersea on public taste. *Public Relations* 4 (4) 1952, pp. 9–14.

Morgan, D. You make me feel at home. *Public Relations,* 4 (4) 1952, p. 16.

AGM. *Public Relations,* 5 (2) 1953, p. 9.

Talking of food and wine. *Public Relations,* 5 (2) 1953, p. 28.

Wimbush, R. The presidential address. *Public Relations,* 5 (2) 1953, p. 11.

General discussion on consultancy. *Public Relations,* 5 (4) 1953, p. 66.

Lipscombe, E. Let's get lost: seventh session of the conference. *Public Relations,* 5 (4) 1953, p. 1.

Powell, T. Public relations in industry. *Public Relations,* 5 (4) 1953, pp. 42–3.

Traverse-Healy, T. Public relations consultancy: what it is and how it works. *Public Relations,* 5 (4) 1953, pp. 57–67.

Eight men in search of an answer. *Public Relations,* 6 (1) 1953, p. 18.

Logan, M. A minimum educational standard. *Public Relations,* 6 (1) 1953, p. 25.

The printed word. *Public Relations,* 6 (1) 1953, p. 9.

One man's week: a PRO in industry. *Public Relations,* 6 (1) 1953, p. 8.

New members. *Public Relations,* 6 (2) 1954, p. 45.

Public relations for British Transport. *Public Relations,* 6 (2) 1954, pp. 35–6.

Stevens, F. L. An examination in public relations. *Public Relations,* 6 (2) 1954, pp. 7–8.

Elvin, R. Public relations consultancy. *Public Relations,* 6 (3) 1954, p. 23.

Black, S. The need for mutual understanding. *Public Relations,* 6 (4) 1954, p. 2.

French code of conduct. *Public Relations,* 6 (4) 1954, p. 22.

Riding a hobby horse. Editorial, *Public Relations,* 6 (4) 1954, pp. 4–6, 35–6.

Simpson, A. Taking army public relations across the world! *Public Relations* 6 (4) 1954, p. 25.

The need for mutual understanding. Editorial, *Public Relations,* 6 (4) 1954, p. 1.

Qualifications for public relations: review of an American survey. *Public Relations,* 7 (1) 1954, p. 10.

A year of promise. Editorial, *Public Relations,* 7 (2) 1955, p. 2.

McLoughlin, A. A. The presidential address. *Public Relations,* 7 (2) 1955, p. 18.

Phillips, H. Public relations for an emperor. *Public Relations,* 7 (2) 1955, p. 25.

New Institute members. *Public Relations,* 7 (3) 1955, p. 37.

Reilly, P. Ten years of public relations for good design. *Public Relations,* 7 (3) 1955, p. 3.

The practice of public relations. Editorial, *Public Relations,* 7 (3) 1955, p. 2.

White, H. Bringing radio and television to the East Africans. *Public Relations,* 7 (4) 1955, p. 35.

Grégoire, M. R. Public relations—key to international co-operation. *Public Relations,* 7 (4) 1955, pp. 15–18.

Vogels, R. J. International public relations. *Public Relations,* 7 (4) 1955, p. 20.

The development of the industry. *Public Relations,* 8 (1) 1955, p. 2.

Nationalism and public relations. *Public Relations,* 8 (1) 1955, p. 29.

Editorial. *Public Relations,* 8 (2) 1956, p. 1.

The history and aims of IPRA: address by Tom Fife-Clark. *Public Relations,* 8 (2) 1956, p. 10.

Public relations convention in Brussels. *Public Relations, 8* (3) 1956, p. 11.

Deedes, F. W. Government and public relations. *Public Relations, 8* (4) 1956, p. 5.

Elliott, Sir J. Why should we mind what the public think? *Public Relations, 8* (4) 1956, p. 25.

Dunn, S. Hospitality in PR. *Public Relations, 8* (4) 1956, p. 28.

Public relations debate in the House of Commons. *Public Relations, 8* (4) 1956, p. 50.

Sinker, Sir P. Some aspects of British public relations overseas. *Public Relations, 8* (4) 1956, pp. 35–8.

Black, S. Belgium at home to the world. *Public Relations, 9* (1) 1956, pp. 21–4.

Blow, J. Promoting the Design Centre: a case history. *Public Relations, 9* (1) 1956, pp. 5–19.

Editorial, *Public Relations, 9* (1) 1956, p. 2.

First syllabus. *Public Relations, 9* (1) 1956, p. 52.

Mark Abrams: a profile. *Public Relations, 9* (1) 1957, pp. 43–4.

Bickerton, F. D. So that the people shall know. *Public Relations, 9* (2) 1957, pp. 48–52.

Cain, A. Editorial. *Public Relations, 9* (2) 1957, p. 1.

Fife-Clark, T. The administrator and the PRO. *Public Relations, 9* (2) 1957, pp. 7–17.

'Observer,' 'Lake side conference.' *Public Relations, 9* (2) 1957, p. 2.

Examination in public relations. *Public Relations, 9* (3) 1957, p. 11.

Blow, J. PR through the press cuttings. *Public Relations, 9* (3) 1957, p. 24.

Editorial, *Public Relations, 9* (3) 1957, pp. 1–2.

Jacob, Sir I. The BBC—a national and international force. *Public Relations, 9* (3) 1957, p. 15.

Butler, Rt. Hon. R. A. CH MP. The government and the public. *Public Relations, 9* (3) 1957, p. 15.

Alan Hess and Richard Dimbleby join forces in a public relations organisation. *Public Relations, 10* (1) 1957, p. 56.

IPR meeting with Newspaper Society. *Public Relations, 10* (2) 1958, p. 5.

Harvey, I. MP. Information—instrument of policy. *Public Relations, 10* (2) 1958, p. 58.

Presidential address. *Public Relations, 10* (2) 1958, p. 5.

Public relations day. *Public Relations, 10* (2) 1958, p. 15.

Rogers, N. Birth of the Institute. *Public Relations, 10* (2) 1958, pp. 9–10.

Tenth annual general meeting. *Public Relations, 10* (2) 1958, p. 7.

The guide. *Public Relations, 10* (3) 1958, p. 1.

Morrison, H. World understanding—can we achieve it? *Public Relations, 10* (3) 1958, pp. 14–15.

England, F. E. A Fleet Street opinion. *Public Relations, 10* (4) 1958, p. 44.

Hess, A. A second opinion. *Public Relations, 10* (4) 1958, pp. 40–1.

Account rendered. *Public Relations, 11* (1) 1958, p. 4.

Public relations for public relations. *Public Relations, 11* (2) 1959, p. 1.

Editorial. *Public Relations, 11* (3) 1959, p. 2.

The institute is growing up. *Public Relations, 12* (1) 1959, pp. 1–2.

Black, S. London needs a new exhibition centre. *Public Relations, 12* (1) 1959, pp. 21–4.

Vegrin, Dr. E. V. Letters. *Public Relations, 12* (2) 1960.

As the editor sees it. *Public Relations, 12* (3) 1960, p. 5.

Wilshire, G. H. Philosophy or science. *Public Relations, 12* (3) 1960, p. 10.

McCrory, P. Protecting, maintaining and developing a good reputation. *Public Relations, 12* (3) 1960, pp. 20–4.

Consultancy in America. *Public Relations, 12* (4) 1960, p. 14.

Presidential address. *Public Relations, 12* (4) 1960, p. 23.

Earley, E. Telling the world about British industry. *Public Relations, 12* (4) 1960, p. 47.

Galitzine, Prince Y. Philosophy of public relations. *Public Relations, 12* (4) 1960, p. 51.

As the editor sees it. *Public Relations, 13* (1) 1960, pp. 2–5.

Committee view. *Public Relations, 13* (1) 1960, p. 50.

IPRA draft code of conduct. *Public Relations, 13* (1) 1960, p. 50.

Miller, H. A private view of public relations. *Public Relations, 13* (1) 1960, p. 37.

The stunt menace. *Public Relations, 13* (1) 1960, p. 50.

By their works. *Public Relations, 13* (2) 1961, pp. 2–5.

Still a vast job of explanation to be done. *Public Relations, 13* (2) 1961, p. 5.

The problems of budgeting and costing. Conference supplement. *Public Relations, 13* (2) 1961, pp. xii–xiv.

Towards 1965. Editorial. *Public Relations, 13* (2) 1961, p. 1.

Phillips, H. Then (1935) . . . now (1961) . . . tomorrow (1986). *Public Relations, 13* (3) 1961, p. 12.

Eden-Green, A. The presidential address: responsibility to society. *Public Relations, 13* (4) 1961, pp. 29–33.

Simmons, C. Parliament and public relations. *Public Relations, 13* (4) 1961, p. 41.

Derriman, J. People for public relations: the problem of recruiting and selection. *Public Relations, 14* (2) 1962, pp. 5–7.

The world is waiting for a gigantic public relations job to be done. Editorial. *Public Relations, 14* (2) 1962, p. 23.

This is the fourteen point plan. *Public Relations, 14* (2) 1962, p. 24.

Waller, I. I do not condemn public relations—BUT. *Public Relations, 14* (2) 1962, pp. 27–9.

Wilson, Rt. Hon. H. MP. Public relations and parliament. *Public Relations, 14* (3) 1962, p. 5.

Closed session discussed 'The Plan.' *Public Relations, 14* (4) 1962, p. 30.

MIPR (by exam). *Public Relations, 14* (4) 1962, p. 52.

The future of public relations as a profession. *Public Relations, 14* (4) 1962, pp. 34–5.

Boyle, Sir E. MP. Politics, public opinion and public relations. *Public Relations, 14* (4) 1962, pp. 23–4.

San José and Regent Street. *Public Relations, 15* (1) 1962, p. 7.

As the editor sees it. *Public Relations, 15* (3) 1963, pp. 2–7.

The unhidden dissuaders. *Public Relations, 15* (3) 1963, p. 10.

Fawcett, J. I'm no Levin lover but . . . *Public Relations, 15* (3) 1963, p. 46.

Independents' complaint. *Public Relations, 15* (3) 1963, p. 46.

The President suggests seven major disciplines. *Public Relations, 15* (4) 1963, p. 31–3.

As the editor sees it. *Public Relations, 16* (1) 1963, p. 4.

D (for development) day. *Public Relations, 16* (1) 1963, p. 3.

Eden-Green, A. Profile of Colin Mann: president elect. *Public Relations, 16* (1) 1963, p. 28.

The most important event in the history of the Institute. *Public Relations, 16* (2) 1964, p. 22.

A survey. [Supplement] *Public Relations, 16* (2) 1964, p. ix.

Lyons, D. A costing system for public relations. *Public Relations, 16* (3) 1964, pp. 9–13.

Mann, C. Our responsibilities for the future. *Public Relations*, 16 (4) 1964, p. 33.

Our responsibilities for the future. *Public Relations*, 16 (4) 1964, p. 34.

Runge, P. Industry's obsession with secrecy. *Public Relations*, 16 (4) 1964, p. 46.

Crisford, J. Author versus 'blurb.' *Public Relations*, 17 (1) 1964, p. 49.

Ellis, N. The institution and the union. *Public Relations*, 17 (1) 1964, pp. 34–5.

Eden-Green, A. Account control. *Public Relations*, 17 (2) 1965, p. 13.

Liebman, R. C. Shooting a 'mighty line.' *Public Relations*, 17 (2) 1965, pp. 28–31.

Murray, M. The importance of reporting to clients. *Public Relations*, 17 (2) 1965, p. 22.

Sad practitioner. That 'line shoot.' *Public Relations*, 17 (3) 1965, p. 38.

As the editor sees it. Editorial, *Public Relations*, 17 (3) 1965, pp. 2–3.

Liebman, R. C. In answer to 'Sad practitioner.' *Public Relations*, 17 (4) 1965, p. 52.

Martin-Bates, J. P. The public acceptance of new techniques in management education. *Public Relations*, 17 (4) 1965, p. 27.

Prizewinner. *Public Relations*, 17 (4) 1965, pp. 40–7 (July 1965—note that both this issue and the following issue October 1965 were printed with identical volume numbering).

O'Ballance, E. First government information officers' courses. *Public Relations*, 18 (1) 1966, pp. 42–3.

Advertisement placed in *Public Relations*, 18 (2) 1966, p. 23.

Higgins, M. A pioneer training scheme. *Public Relations*, 18 (2) 1966, pp. 18–19.

Suspension. *Public Relations*, 18 (2) 1966, p. 5.

Trusler, C. And from the trainee's point of view. *Public Relations*, 18 (2) 1966, p. 20.

Hardern, L. Report from Dublin. *Public Relations*, 18 (3) 1966, p. 19.

The presidential address. *Public Relations*, 18 (3) 1966, pp. 17–18.

The big reappraisal starts. *Public Relations*, 18 (4) 1967, p. 28.

Traverse-Healy, T. Blueprint for change. *Public Relations*, 19 (2) 1967, pp. 8–15.

Big educational changes. *Public Relations*, 20 (2) 1968, p. 18.

Bloomfield, P. The future of PR education. *Public Relations*, 20 (2) 1968, pp. 11–13.

Bloomfield, P. Toward a diploma in public relations. *Public Relations*, 20 (3) 1968, p. 14.

Director leaves: no replacement for time being. *Public Relations*, 20 (3) 1968, p. 21.

Lovell, T. The jungle days of PR. *Public Relations*, 20 (3) 1968, p. 33.

Professor Roland Smith educational adviser to the institute. *Public Relations*, 20 (3) 1968, p. 23.

Gray, M. Planning the corporate image. *Public Relations*, 20 (4) 1968, pp. 2–4.

Overwhelming support for entry without examination. *Public Relations*, 20 (5) 1968, p. 11.

Death of Charles Liebman. *Public Relations*, 21 (8) 1968, p. 12.

Future courses and examinations. *Public Relations*, 21 (8) 1968, p. 12.

The amber light. *Public Relations*, 21 (8) 1968, p. 18.

Lovell, T. The jungle days of PR—methods used to get new business. *Public Relations*, 21 (9) 1968, p. 22.

Men with tin voices. *Public Relations*, 21 (10) 1968, p. 2.

The Institute and the BBC. *Public Relations*, 22 (1) 1969, p. 20.

Clarke, A. The life and times of Sir Basil Clarke—PR pioneer. *Public Relations*, 22 (2) 1969, pp. 9–10.

The life and times of Sir Basil Clarke—a pioneer. *Public Relations*, 22 (2) 1969, p. 8.

Don't be late for summer school. *Public Relations*, 22 (4) 1969, p. 8.

Political PR discussed on television and radio. *Public Relations,* 22 (4) 1969, p. 10.

PR and parliament: the official (IPR) view. *Public Relations,* 22 (4) 1969, p. 8.

Is journalism experience necessary? Letter page. *Public Relations,* 22 (5) 1969, p. 25.

Fellowship for man who started Board of Trade PR. *Public Relations,* 22 (7) 1969, p. 12.

The PR scene. *Public Relations,* 22 (7) 1969, p. 19.

Education for public relations in the seventies. *Public Relations,* 22 (11) 1969, pp. 13–14.

John Greenall gets Open University post. *Public Relations,* 22 (11) 1969, p. 15.

Four elected to fellowship. *Public Relations,* 23 (1) 1970, p. 15.

Wadham, G. Increasing importance of outside specialist services. *Public Relations,* 23 (3) 1970, p. 4.

IPR recommended reading. *Public Relations,* 23 (7) 1970, p. 2.

Derriman, J. Professional ethics and the institute. *Public Relations,* 23 (10) 1970, p. 3.

Revised code of conduct adopted by council. (1970, 8 September). *Public Relations,* 23 (11) 1970, p. 10.

Amanda Barry elected FIPR. *Public Relations,* 24 (7) 1971, p. 146.

Howard, W. Some principles of communication. *Public Relations,* 24 (9) 1971, p. 186.

The code of professional conduct. *Public Relations,* 25 (2) 1972, p. 55.

Amanda Barry makes it a double. *Public Relations,* 25 (3) 1972, p. 45.

Frank Jefkins is our first Dip.CAM. *Public Relations,* 25 (3) 1972, p. 74.

Traverse-Healy, T. Tomorrow's world: a challenge for PR. *Public Relations,* 25 (7) 1972, p. 162.

CAMS new scheme for diploma exam. *Public Relations,* 26 (7) 1973, p. 129.

The way ahead. *Public Relations,* 26 (12) 1973, p. 215.

New route to CAM diploma for senior PR people. *Public Relations,* 27 (1) 1974, p. 1.

Galitzine, Prince Y. A cut above the others. *Public Relations,* 27 (2) 1974, p. 24.

The need for learning. *Public Relations,* 27 (10) 1974, p. 190.

Educational trust revival. *Communicator,* April 1977, p. 1.

Ethical v. practical. *Communicator,* February 1978, p. 1.

Member violates code. *Communicator,* April 1978, p. 1.

Professionalism. *Communicator,* June 1978, p. 1.

Public flogging. *Communicator,* July 1978, p. 4.

Letters. *Communicator,* 1979, p. 4.

On the move. *Communicator,* 1979, p. 3.

Pick up their pens. *Communicator,* 1979, p. 3.

The role of the new journal. *Public Relations,* 1 (1) 1982, p. 2.

Mastering educational needs. *Public Relations,* 1 (3) 1983, p. 2.

Doing our exercises. *Public Relations,* 2 (1) 1983, p. 2.

Samson, H. Dissemination of information. *Public Relations,* 2 (1) 1983, p. 17.

What I think. *Public Relations,* 2 (1) 1983, p. 10.

Blackburn, P. Professional ethics. *Public Relations,* 3 (3) 1985, p. 14.

Jefkins, F. Professional ethics. *Public Relations,* 3 (3) 1985, p. 15.

Smith, P. 'Responsibility', *Public Relations,* 3 (3) 1985, pp. 11–15.

Traverse-Healy, T. Professional ethics. *Public Relations,* 3 (3) 1985, p. 14.

Having the same thoughts as everyone else. *Public Relations Association,* 12 (4) 1993, p. 5.

Criteria and procedures for IPR recognition of public relations programmes. *Institute of Public Relations,* 1996.

A2   IPRA publications

Gillman, F. C. (1978). Public relations in the United Kingdom prior to 1948. *International Public Relations Review,* pp. 43–4, 46, 50.

Traverse-Healy, T. (1988). Public relations and propaganda: values compared. [Gold Paper]. *International Public Relations Association.* Bournemouth: Roman Press.

Black, S. & Murdoch, T. (eds.). (1995). A commitment to excellence: the first forty years. *International Public Relations Association.* Sweden: GormanGruppen.

IPRA Newsletter, 41 (2) 1997, p. 2.

International Public Relations Membership directory and service guide 1997–8, p. 250.

International Public Relations Membership directory and service guide 1998–9, p. 221.

A3   Books written by practitioners

The Institute of Public Relations (1958). *A guide to the practice of public relations.* London: Newman Neame.

Bernays, E. (1947, March). Engineering of consent. *Annals of the American academy of political and social science,* No. 250, pp. 113–20.

Black, S. (1962, 1976). *Practical public relations.* London: Pitman.

Blake, A. (1984). *Misha Black.* London: The Design Council.

Brebner, J. H. (1949). *Public relations and publicity.* London: The Institute of Public Administration.

Delmer, S. (1962). *Black boomerang.* London: Secker & Warburg.

Greer, I. (1985). *Right to be heard.* London: Ian Greer Associates.

Hargrave, J. (1940). *Propaganda the mightiest weapon of all words win wars.* London: Well, Gardner, Darton & Co.

Harrison, S. (1995). *Public relations: an introduction.* London: Routledge.

Higham, Sir C. (1925). *Advertising: its use and abuse.* London: Williams & Norgate.

Higham, Sir C. (1920). *Looking forward: mass education through publicity.* London: Nisbet & Co. Ltd.

Hill, J. W. (1993). *The making of a public relations man.* Chicago: NTC Business Books.

Hornsby, L. (1958). Its purpose and functions. In Institute of Public Relations. *A guide to the practice of public relations.* London: Newman Neame, pp. 13–14.

Huxley, G. (1970). *Both hands: an autobiography.* London: Chatto & Windus.

Kelley, S. Jr. (1956). *Professional public relations and political power.* Baltimore: John Hopkins Press.

Kisch, R. (1964). *The private life of public relations.* London: McGibbon & Kee.

Lloyd, H. (1963, 1970, 1980). *Teach yourself public relations.* Sevenoaks, Kent: Hodder & Stoughton.

Paget-Cooke, R. A. (1958). Recognising the problems. In Institute of Public Relations. *A guide to the practice of public relations.* London: Newman Neame, p. 19.

Paterson, W. (1968). *Industrial publicity management.* London: Business Books Ltd.

Phillips, H. (1958). Consultancy. In Institute of Public Relations. *A guide to the practice of public relations.* London: Newman Neame.

Plant, A. (ed.). (1937). *Some modern business problems.* London: Longman, pp. 123–52.

Reilly, P. (1958). The spoken word. In Institute of Public Relations. *A guide to the practice of public relations.* London: Newman Neame, p. 207.

Rotha, P. (1973). *Documentary diary: an informal history of the British documentary film 1928–1939.* London: Secker & Warburg.

Sampson, A. (1969). *The anatomy of Britain.* London: Book Club Associates.

Spoor, A. (1967). *White-collar union.* London: Heinemann.

Tallents, Sir S. R. (1932, 1955). *The projection of England.* London: Olen Press.

Tallents, Sir S. (1958). By the way of introduction. In Institute of Public Relations. *A guide to the practice of public relations.* London: Newman Neame, p. 3.

West, R. (1963). *PR the fifth estate.* London: Mayflower Books.

White, A. J. S. (1965). *The British Council: the first 25 years 1934–1959.* London: The British Council.

Williams-Thompson, R. (1951). *Was I really necessary?* London: World's Press News.

Wilson, P. A. (1937). Public relations departments. In Plant, A. (ed.). *Some modern business problems.* London: Longman, pp. 123–52.

A4 Newspaper reports and articles (presented in chronological order)

Bringing facts to light: role of public relations. Letter to the editor. *The Times,* 23 June 1961.

Persuasion. Letter to the editor. *The Times,* 27 June 1961.

Coren, A. (1976, 17 July). A matter of trust or tricks. *The Times,* p. 23.

Jobey, L. (1982, 24 January). Promotion and the art of puffery. *The Observer,* p. 42.

Toynbee, P. (1984, 5 November). Information officer often means disinformation officer, or even downright liar. *The Guardian,* p. 12.

Irwin, A. (1994, 30 September). Science's social standing. *The Times Higher,* p. 17.

Atkins, P. (1994, 30 September). For against: no science is not a social construct because it is independent of society. *The Times,* p. 18.

Collins, H. (1994, 30 September). For against: yes, science is a social construct. *The Times Higher,* p. 18.

Dawkins, R. (1994, 30 September). The moon is *not* a calabash. *The Times Higher,* p. 17.

Hollis, R. (1997, 6 October). Milner Gray: the grandest old man of British design. *The Guardian.*

McCartney, J. (1998, 10 January). *The Spectator,* p. 8.

A5 IPR's archive documents

Memorandum on industrial propaganda and publicity. (1940, 15 August). CBI Archive MSS.200/F/3/I/1/1.

Draft constitution of the IPR. January 1948. IPR Archive.

AGM. (1948, 30 September). IPR Archive 2/1/1 12 (a).

AGM. (1948, 30 September). IPR Archive 2/1/1 12 (b).

Statement of standards. (1949). History of Advertising Trust. IPR Archive.

Regulations. (1951). History of Advertising Trust. IPR Archive.

Planning a home publicity campaign. Address given by Fife-Clark, T. COI 3 (3) 1951, p. 6.

IPR Minutes of the Education Committee. (1954, 10 August). IPR Archive 3/7/1.

IPR Minutes of the Education Committee. (1954, 12 August). IPR Archive 3/7/1.
IPR Minutes of the Education Committee. (1956, 10 May). IPR Archive 3/7/2.
IPR Minutes of the Education Committee. (1956, 5 July). IPR Archive 3/7/1.
IPR Minutes of the Education Committee. (1957, 4 March). IPR Archive 3/7/2.
Minutes of Council Meeting. (1957, 4 May). IPR Archive 2/2/4, p. 3.
Minutes of the Education Committee. (1957, 10 May). IPR Archive.
Special Council Minutes. (1957, 11 November).
Council Minutes. (1957, 23 November).
IPR Minutes of the Education Committee. (1958, 18 February).
Report of the Board of Examiners to the Education Committee. (1958, 11 March). IPR
    Archive 3/7/2.
IPR Archive. (1958, 18 March).
Council Minutes. (1958, 8 May). A list of public relations consultants. Both IPR Archive
    3/5/2.
Council Minutes. (1959, 19 March).
Council Minutes. (1959, 21 July).
Public relations consultants and the IPR. (1960). Notes by Cain, A. IPR Archive 3/5/3.
Notes sent to the IPR Consultancy Committee. (1960, 6 May). IPR Archive 6/5/60.
Minutes of the Joint Committee set up by Council. (1960, 19 May). IPR Archive 3/5/1.
Minutes of the Consultancy Committee. (1960, 2 December). IPR Archive 3/5/2.
Minutes of the Consultancy Committee. (1961, 17 January). IPR Archive 3/5/2.
Minutes of the Consultancy Committee. (1961, 11 April). IPR Archive 3/5/2.
Minutes of the Consultancy Committee. (1961, 19 July). IPR Archive 3/5/2.
Council Minutes. (1961, 15 November).
Investigating Panel Report. (1962, 1 June). IPR Archive 2/2/7.
Minutes of the Consultancy Committee. (1962, 27 June). IPR Archive 3/5/7.
Letter from Rooper & Whately to Thomas. (1962, 20 July).
IPR code of professional conduct. (1963, 29 November).
Final examination. (1964, 9 April).
Letter to Lex Hornsby & Partners Ltd. (1964, 2 December).
Jefkins to Lewis. (1964, 24 December).
Council Minutes. (1965, 22 February). IPR Archive 2/2/8.
Disciplinary Council Minutes. (1965, 23 February).
Disciplinary Committee Hearing. (1965, 18 March). IPR Archive 3/4/1.
Council Minutes. (1965, 11 May).
Council Minutes. (1966, 27 September). IPR Archive 2/2/9.
Letter from Francis Butters & Nigel Ellis. (1966, 9 December).
Letter from Pittard to the IPR. (1967, 24 July). IPR Archive 3/4/10.
Bloomfield to Pittard. (1967, 2 August). IPR Archive 3/4/10.
Kris to Pittard. (1967, 10 August). IPR Archive 3/4/10.
Bloomfield to Kris. (1967, 15 August). IPR Archive 3/4/10.
Council Minutes. (1967, 27 September). IPR Archive 2/2/9.
Letter from Traverse-Healy to Geare. (1967, 13 October). IPR Archive 3/4/10.
Letter from Traverse-Healy to Geare. (1967, 26 October). IPR Archive 3/4/10.
Letter from Traverse-Healy to Victor Lewis. (1967, 6 November). IPR Archive 3/4/11.
Letter from Bloomfield to Geare. (1968, 12 March). IPR Archive 3/4/11.
Letter from Geare to Bloomfield. (1968, 18 March). IPR Archive 3/4/11.

Letter from Geare to Bloomfield. (1968, 3 April). IPR Archive 3/4/11.
Note from Eden-Green, A. IPR Archive 3/4/11.
IPR Archive/1.
IPR Archive 2/1/1.
History of Advertising Trust. IPR Archive 2/2/10.
IPR Archive 3/4/10.
IPR Archive 8/1/a.
IPR Archive [unreferenced, untitled letter from Traverse-Healy to members].
Interview. (1996, 14 August).

A6   Grierson archive (University of Stirling)

Grierson, J. Propaganda: a problem for educational theory and for cinema. *Sight and Sound,* Winter 1933–34. G3A: 5: 1.
Grierson, J. A review of reviews: notes on a pre-war chapter in British propaganda. *Grierson Archive* G6: 33: 14.
Leslie, S. C. The formation of public opinion. (15 October 1938). *Grierson Archive* G3: 16: 4.
Critic. (1950, 16 March). John Grierson gave us something to think about. *World's Press News.* G5A: 1: 3.

A7   CBI archive (University of Warwick)

Crookham, A., Wilcox, M., Woodland, C., & Storey, R. (1997). *The Confederation of British Industry and Predecessor Archives.* Coventry: University of Warwick Occasional Publications No. 26, MSS.200/F/3/I.
Memorandum on industrial propaganda and publicity. (1940, 15 August). CBI Archive, MSS.200/F/3/I/1/1.
Letter from Oppenheim, Sir D., Chair COID to Drogheda, Lord. (1963, 2 September). University of Warwick CBI Archive MSS. 200/F/3/02/5/39.

A8   Miscellaneous

Publications (in chronological order)

Editorial. *The Hospital and Social Service Journal* (Vol. LVIII, No. 2940) 1948, p. 5.
Editorial. *Director,* July 1951, p. 50.
The Institute of Public Relations 1948–1973. The first twenty-five years. *The Institute of Public Relations.* Bedford: The Sidney Press, 1973.
Firsts in the history of the institute. *The Institute of Public Relations 1948–1973.* Bedford: The Sidney Press, 1973, p. 14.
McLoughlin, A. A. (1973). See how it ran. *The Institute of Public Relations 1948–1973.* Bedford: The Sidney Press, p. 42.
Rogers, R. M. (1973). The architects. *The Institute of Public Relations 1948–1973.* Bedford: The Sidney Press, p. 11.

Press and Public Relations Branch: the first 21 years. Pamphlet published by the NUJ, 1978, p. 2.

Aims of industry. 40th anniversary publication [undated, presumed 1982].

Wring, D. (1995). From mass propaganda to political marketing: the transformation of the Labour party election campaigning. *British Election Party Yearbook.*

PR Week. 2 February 1996.

PR Week. 18 October 1996.

Royal Institute of Public Administration report (1998), p. 10.

IPR Handbook 2000.

PR Week. 26 May 2000.

Archive

BMA Archive, Tavistock House, London [unnumbered, undated material].

Letter from S. Black to Prof J. Horden in Professor Horden's personal archive 1987.

Stirling University to hold the first MSc course in PR. PR Week 25/2–2/3/1987. [From Professor Horden's personal archive—page number unclear on photocopy.]

Correspondence

Fax from Ivy Lee, Jr. 15 July 1998.

Fax from CAM. 20 October 1998.

E-mail from P. Standish, Senior Lecturer in Education, University of Dundee. 19 October 1999.

B   Academic journal articles

Anderson, A. (1991). Source strategies and the communication of environmental affairs. *Media, Culture and Society, 13* (4), pp. 459–76.

Bonnell, V. (1980). The use of theory, concepts and comparison in historical sociology. *Comparative Studies in Society and History, 22* (2), pp. 156–73.

Calhoun, C. (1987). History and sociology in Britain, a review article. *Comparative Studies in Society and History, 27* (3), pp. 615–25.

Corner, H. G. (1923). The aims of the Institute of Public Administration. *Public Administration, 1,* p. 50.

Corner, J. & Schlesinger, P. (eds.). (1993). Public relations and media strategies. *Media, Culture and Society , 15* (3).

Cowell, F. R. (1931). The uses and dangers of publicity in the work of government. *Public Administration, 13,* p. 292.

Davis, A. (2000). Public relations, news production and changing patterns of source access in the British national media. *Media, Culture and Society, 22* (1), pp. 39–59.

Finer, H. (1931). Officials and the public. *Public Administration, 9,* p. 30.

Foot, M. R. D. (1981). Was SOE any good? *Journal of Contemporary History, 16* (1), pp. 170–1.

Grunig, J. (2000). Collectivism, collaboration and societal corporatism as core professional values in public relations. *Journal of Public Relations Research , 12* (1), pp. 24, 57–8.

Hall, J. R. (1992). Where history and sociology meet. *Sociological Theory.* pp. 164–93.

Hall, S. (1969, December). The technics of persuasion. *New Society,* pp. 948–9.

Herbst, S. (1993). The meaning of public opinion: citizens' constructions of political reality. *Media, Culture and Society,* 15 (3), pp. 437–54.

Hill, L. (1937). Advertising local government. *Public Opinion Quarterly,* Vol. 1 (April), p. 64.

L'Etang, J. (1997). Public relations and the rhetorical dilemma: legitimate 'perspectives,' persuasion or pandering? *Australian Journal of Communication,* 24 (2), pp. 33–54.

L'Etang, J. (1998). State propaganda and bureaucratic intelligence: the creation of public relations in twentieth-century Britain. *Public Relations Review,* 24 (4), pp. 413–41.

L'Etang, J. (1999). Public relations education in Britain: an historical review in the context of professionalisation. *Public Relations Review,* 25 (3), pp. 413–41.

Lee, J. M. (1972). The dissolution of the EMB. *The Journal of Imperial and Commonwealth History,* 1 (1), p. 51.

Magarey, S. (1987). That hoary old chestnut, free will and determinism: culture v structure, or history v theory in Britain. *Comparative Studies in Society and History,* 29 (3), pp. 626–39.

Megill, A. (1989). Recounting the past: 'description,' explanation and narrative in historiography. *American Historical Review,* 94 (3), pp. 627–53.

Miller, D. (1993). Official sources and 'primary definition': the case of Northern Ireland. *Media, Culture and Society,* 15 (3), pp. 385–406.

Miller, D. & Dinan, W. (2000). The rise of the PR industry in Britain 1979–98. *European Journal of Communication,* 15 (1), pp. 5–35.

Pieczka, M. (2002). Public relations expertise deconstructed. *Media, Culture and Society,* 24 (3), pp. 301–23.

Pronay, N. (1989). John Grierson and the documentary. *Historical Journal of Film, Radio and Television,* 9 (3), p. 231.

Rogow, A. A. (1952, Summer). The public relations program of the Labor Government and British industry. *Public Opinion Quarterly,* pp. 202–3, 218, 221.

Schuyler, H. Jr. (1939). The official propaganda of Great Britain. *Public Opinion Quarterly,* 3, pp. 263–5, 268.

Signitzer, B. & Coombs, T. (1992). Public relations and public diplomacy: conceptual convergences. *Public Relations Review,* 18 (2), pp. 137–47.

Simey, T. S. (1923). A public relations policy for local authorities. *Public Administration, (13),* p. 243.

Sussman, L. (1948, Winter). The personnel and ideology of public relations. *Public Opinion Quarterly,* pp. 697–708.

Tallents, Sir S. R. (1933). Salesmanship in the public service: scope and technique. *Public Administration, (11),* p. 265.

Taylor, P. (1981). If war should come: preparing the fifth arm for total war 1935–39. *Journal of Contemporary History,* 16 (1), p. 31.

Tulloch, J. (1993). Policing the public sphere: the British machinery of news management. *Media, Culture and Society,* 15 (3), pp. 363–85.

Wacquant, L. D. (1989). Towards a reflexive sociology: a workshop with Pierre Bourdieu. *Sociological Theory,* 7, p. 50.

Walicki, A. (1987). Hegel's historical context. *Comparative Studies in Society and History,* 27 (3), pp. 608–14.

Whitehead, H. (1933). Salesmanship in the public service. *Public Administration, 11,* p. 272.

Wilensky, H. L. (1964). The professionalisation of everyone? *American Journal of Sociology, 70,* pp. 137–58.

Willcox, T. (1983). Projection or publicity? Rival concepts in the pre-war planning of the British Ministry of Information. *Journal of Contemporary History, 18,* p. 98.

Wilson, H. H. (1951). Techniques of pressure—anti-nationalization propaganda in Britain. *Public Opinion Quarterly, 15,* p. 232.

Wood, S. H. (1936). Intelligence and public relations. *Public Administration, 14,* p. 43.

Wring, D. (1996). Political marketing and party development in Britain: a 'secret' history. *European Journal of Marketing, 30* (10/11).

Wylie, F. W. (1995). Book review. *Public Relations Review, 21* (2), pp. 161–75.

C   Academic books and book chapters

Abbott, A. (1988). *The system of professions: an essay on the division of expert labor.* Chicago: University of Chicago Press.

Aitkin, I. (1993). *Film and reform: John Grierson and the documentary film movement.* London: Routledge.

Altschull, J. H. (1995). *Agents of power: the media and public policy.* New York: Longman.

Anderson, A. (1993). Source–media relations: the production of the environmental agenda. In Hansen, A. (ed.). *The mass media and environmental issues.* Leicester: Leicester University Press, pp. 51–68.

Ashworth, W. (1991). *The state in business: 1945 to the mid-1960s.* London: Macmillan.

Auckland, R. G. (1977) *British black propaganda to Germany 1941–1945.* Blatter Catalogue No. 13. First published by Psywar Society, January 1977.

Ayer, A. J. (1982). *Philosophy in the twentieth century.* London: Unwin.

Balfour, M. (1979). *Propaganda in war 1939–1945.* London: Routledge & Kegan Paul.

Barrow, R. & Woods, R. (1988). *An introduction to philosophy of education.* London: Routledge.

Becker, H. S. et al. (1961). *Boys in white.* Chicago: University of Chicago Press.

Belsey, A. & Chadwick, R. (1992). Ethics and politics of the media: the quest for quality.

Belsey, A. & Chadwick, R. (eds.). (1992). *Ethical issues in journalism and the media.* London: Routledge.

Berlin, Sir I. (1974). The objectivity of history. In Gardiner, P. (ed.). *The philosophy of history.* Oxford: Oxford University Press.

Bernays, E. (1928). *Propaganda.* New York: Boni & Liveright.

Bernays, E. (1961). *Crystalling public opinion.* New York: Boni & Liveright.

Bloch, M. (1954). *The historian's craft.* Manchester: Manchester University Press.

Botan, C. H. & Hazleton, V. (eds.). (1989). *Public relations theory.* Hillsdale, New Jersey: Lawrence Erlbaum Associates.

Bourdieu, P. (1989). *Distinction: a social critique of the judgement of taste.* London: Routledge.

Bourdieu, P. (1971). Intellectual field and creative projects. In Young, M. D. F. (ed.). *Knowledge and control: new directions in the sociology of education.* London: Collier-Macmillan.

Bryman, A. & Burgess, R. (1994). *Analyzing qualitative professions.* London: Sage.

Burke, P. (1980). *Sociology and history.* London: George Allen & Unwin.

Burn, A. R. (1954, 1981). Introduction. In *Herodotus: the histories.* London: Penguin.

Burrage, M. & Torstendahl, R. (eds.). (1990). *Professions in theory and history: rethinking the study of the professions.* London: Sage.

Calder, A. (1969, 1990). *The people's war 1939–1945.* London: Pimlico.

Calvocoressi, P. (1978). *The British experience 1945–1975.* London: The Bodley Head.

Caplow, T. (1954). *Sociology of work.* Minneapolis: University of Minneapolis Press.

Carruthers, S. L. (1995). *Winning hearts and minds.* Leicester: Leicester University Press.

Chomsky, N. (1989, 1993). *Necessary illusions: thought control in democratic societies.* London: Pluto Press.

Chomsky, N. (1998). Propaganda and control of the public mind. In McChesney, R. W., Wood, E. M., & Foster, J. B. (eds.). *Capitalism and the information age: the political economy of the global communication revolution.* New York: Monthly Review Press.

Cole, R. (1990). *Britain and the war of words in neutral Europe 1939–1945.* London: Macmillan.

Collingwood, R. G. (1974). Human nature and human history. In Gardiner, P. (ed.). *The philosophy of history.* Oxford: Oxford University Press.

Culbertson, H. M. & Chen, N. (eds.). (1996). *International public relations: a comparative analysis.* Mahwah, New Jersey: Lawrence Erlbaum Associates.

Cull, N. (1995). *Selling war: the British propaganda campaign against American 'neutrality' in World War II.* Oxford: Oxford University Press.

Curran, C. & Seaton, J. (1988). *Power without responsibility: the press and broadcasting in Britain.* London: Routledge.

Cutlip, S. M. (1994). *The unseen power: public relations. A history.* Hillsdale, New Jersey: Lawrence Erlbaum Associates.

Cutlip, S. M., Center, A. H., & Broom, G. M. (1994). *Effective public relations.* Englewood Cliffs, New Jersey: Prentice Hall.

D'Amico, R. (1989). *Historicism and knowledge.* London: Routledge.

Degenhardt, M. A. B. (1976). Indoctrination. In Lloyd, D. L (ed.). *Philosophy and the teacher.* London: Routledge & Kegan Paul.

Delmer, S. (1962). *Black boomerang.* London: Secker & Warburg.

Denzin, N. K. & Lincoln, Y. S. (eds.). (1994). *Handbook of qualitative research.* London: Sage.

De Selincourt, A. (1954). *Herodotus: the histories.* London: Penguin.

Donaldson, J. (1989). *Key issues in business ethics.* London: Academic Press.

Dozier, D. M. & Grunig, L. (1992). The organisation of the public relations function. In Grunig, J. E. (ed.). *Excellence in public relations and communication management.* Hillsdale, New Jersey: Lawrence Erlbaum Associates.

Dray, W. (1974). The historical explanation of actions reconsidered. In Gardiner, P. (ed.). *The philosophy of history.* Oxford: Oxford University Press.

Elliott, P. (1972). *The sociology of the professions.* New York: Herder & Herder.

Ellul, J. (1965). *Propaganda.* New York: Alfred Knopf Inc.

Ewen, S. (1996). *PR! A social history of spin.* New York: Basic Books.

Ferguson, M. (ed.). (1990). *Public communication: the new imperatives: future directions for research.* London: Sage.

Friedson, E. (1986). *Professional powers: a study of the institutionalisation of formal knowledge.* Chicago: University of Chicago Press.

Friedson, E. (1994). *Professionalism reborn: theory, prophecy and policy.* Cambridge: Polity Press.

Gandy, O. (1982). *Beyond agenda setting: information subsidies and public policy.* Norwood, NJ: Ablex.

Gandy, O. (1992). Public relations and public policy: the structuration of dominance in the information age. In Toth, E. & Heath, R. (eds.). *Rhetorical and critical approaches to public relations.* Hillsdale, New Jersey: Lawrence Erlbaum Associates, pp. 131–63.

Gardiner, P. (ed.). (1974). *The philosophy of history.* Oxford: Oxford University Press.

Gerth, H. H. & Wright Mills, C. (eds.). (1946, 1958). *Max Weber: essays in sociology.* New York: Oxford University Press.

Geertz, C. (1973). *The interpretation of cultures: selected essays.* New York: Basic Books.

Goldman, E. F. (1948). *Two-way street, the emergence of the public relations counsel.* Boston: Bellman Publishing Co.

Gourvish, T. (1991). The rise (and fall?) of state-owned enterprise. In Gourvish, T. & O'Day, A. (eds.). *Britain since 1945.* London: Macmillan.

Grant, M. (1994). *Propaganda and the role of the state in inter-war Britain.* Oxford: Clarendon Press.

Grierson, J. & Hardy, F. (eds.). (1946, 1979). *Grierson on documentary.* London: Faber & Faber.

Grunig, J. E. (1989). Symmetrical presuppositions as a framework for public relations theory. In Botan, C. H. & Hazleton, V. (Jr.). *Public relations theory.* Hillsdale, New Jersey: Lawrence Erlbaum Associates, pp. 17–44.

Grunig, J. E. (2001). Two-way symmetrical public relations: past, present, and future. In Heath, R. L. (ed.). *Handbook of public relations.* Thousand Oaks: Sage, pp. 11–30.

Grunig, J. E. (ed.). (1992). *Excellence in public relations and communication management.* Hillsdale, New Jersey: Lawrence Erlbaum Associates.

Grunig, J. E. & Grunig, L. (1992). Models of public relations and communication. In Grunig, J. E. (ed.). *Excellence in public relations and communication management.* Hillsdale, New Jersey: Lawrence Erlbaum Associates.

Grunig, J. E. & Hunt, T. (1984). *Managing public relations.* New York: Rinehart & Winston.

Grunig, L. (1992). Toward the philosophy of public relations. In Toth, E. L. & Heath, R. L. (eds.). *Rhetorical and critical approaches to public relations.* Hillsdale, New Jersey: Lawrence Erlbaum Associates.

Habermas, J. (1989). *The structural transformation of the public sphere: an inquiry into a category of bourgeois society.* Cambridge: Polity Press.

Habermas, J. (1991). *The theory of communicative action: reason and rationalization of society.* Cambridge: Polity Press.

Hall, S. et al. (1978). *Policing the crisis: mugging, the state and law and order.* London: Macmillan.

Halsey, A. H., Heath, A. F. & Ridge, J. M. (1991). Origins and destinations. In Worsley, P. (ed.). *The new modern sociology readings.* London: Penguin, pp. 196–201.

Hammersley, M. (1992). *What's wrong with ethnography?* London: Routledge.

Hansen, A. (1994). *The mass media and environmental issues.* Leicester: Leicester University Press.

Hardy, F. (1979). *Grierson on documentary.* London: Faber & Faber.

Hardy, F. (1979). *John Grierson: a documentary biography.* London: Faber & Faber.

Harkner, R. (1990). Bourdieu: education and reproduction. In Harkner, R., Makar, C., & Wilkes, C. *An introduction to the work of Pierre Bourdieu: the practice of theory.* London: Macmillan.

Harkner, R., Makar, C., & Wilkes, C. (1990). *An introduction to the work of Pierre Bourdieu: the practice of theory.* London: Macmillan.

Harris, N. (1992). *Codes of conduct for journalists.* In Belsey, A. & Chadwick, R. (eds.). *Ethical issues in journalism and the media.* London: Routledge.

Harrisson, T. (1982). Films and the home front—the evaluation of their effectiveness by 'mass observation.' In Pronay, N. (ed.). *Propaganda, politics and film 1918–1945.* London: Macmillan.

Heath, R. (1992). Vision of critical studies in public relations. In Toth, E. & Heath, R. (eds.). *Rhetorical and critical approaches to public relations.* Hillsdale, New Jersey: Lawrence Erlbaum Associates, pp. 317–8.

Heath, R. L. (ed.). (2001). *Handbook of public relations.* London: Sage.

Hempel, C. G. (1994). The function of general laws in history. In Martin, M. & McIntyre, L. C. (eds.). *Readings in the philosophy of social science.* Cambridge, Massachusetts: MIT Press.

Herman, E. S. & Chomsky, N. (1988). *Manufacturing consent: the political economy of the mass media.* New York: Pantheon Books.

Hertz, R. & Imber, J. (eds.). (1995). *Studying elites using qualitative methods.* London: Sage.

Hill, M. R. (1993). *Archival strategies and techniques.* Newbury Park, California: Sage.

Hodder, I. (1994). The interpretation of documents and material culture. In Denzin, N. K. & Lincoln, Y. S. (eds.). *Handbook of qualitative research.* London: Sage.

Hodgson, G. (1963). The steel debates. In Sissons, M. & French, P. (eds.). *Age of austerity.* London: Hodder & Stoughton.

Holstein, J. A. & Gubrium, J. K. (1995). *The active interview.* London: Sage.

Hughes, E. C. (1958). *Men and their work.* New York: The Free Press.

Hughes, J. (1990). *The philosophy of social research.* Harlow: Longman.

Hume, D. (1980). *A treatise of human nature.* Oxford: Oxford University Press.

Izod, J. & Kilborn, R. with Hibberd, M. (eds.). (2000). *From Grierson to the docu-soap: breaking the boundaries.* Luton: University of Luton Press.

Jarausch, K. H. & Hardy, K. A. (1991). *Quantitative methods for historians.* Chapel Hill: University of North Carolina Press.

Jenkins, R. (1963). Bevan's fight with the BMA. In Sissons, M. & French, P. *Age of austerity.* London: Hodder & Stoughton, pp. 246–425.

Jenkins, R. (1992). *Pierre Bourdieu.* London: Routledge.

Johnson, T. (1972). *The professions and power.* London: Macmillan.

Jowett, G. S. & O'Donnell, V. (1986). *Propaganda and persuasion.* London: Sage.

Keith-Lucas, B. & Richards, P. G. (1978). *A history of local government in the twentieth century.* London: George Allen & Unwin.

Lacey, A. R. (1990). *A dictionary of philosophy.* London: Routledge.

Larson, M. S. (1977). *The rise of professionalism: a sociological analysis.* Berkeley: University of California Press.

Lasswell, H. D., Casey, R. D., & Smith, B. L. (1996). Propaganda and promotional activities: an annotated bibliography. In Ewen, S. *PR! A social history of spin.* New York: Basic Books, p. 174

L'Etang, J. (1996). Public relations and rhetoric. In L'Etang, J. & Pieczka, M. (eds.). *Critical perspectives in public relations.* London: International Thompson Business Press, pp. 106–23.

L'Etang, J. (1996). Public relations as diplomacy. In L'Etang, J. & Pieczka, M. (eds.). *Critical perspectives in public relations.* London: International Thompson Business Press, pp. 14–35.

L'Etang, J. (2000). Grierson and the public relations industry in Britain. In Izod, J. & Kilborn, R. with Hibberd, M. (eds.). *From Grierson to the docu-soap: breaking the boundaries.* Luton: University of Luton Press, pp. 83–94.

L'Etang, J. & Muruli, G. (2004). Public relations, decolonisation and democracy: the case of Kenya. In Tilson, D. J. (ed.). *Toward the common good: perspectives in international public relations.* Allyn & Bacon.

L'Etang, J. & Pieczka, M. (eds.). (1996). *Critical perspectives in public relations.* London: International Thompson Business Press.

Lindlof, T. (1992). *Qualitative communication research methods.* London: Sage.

Lippman, W. (1998). *Public opinion.* London: Transaction Publishers.

Locke, J. (1979). *An essay concerning human understanding.* Nidditch, P. H. (ed.). Oxford: Oxford Clarendon Press.

Macdonald, K. (1995). *The sociology of the professions.* London: Sage.

Mackenzie, J. (1985). *Propaganda and empire: the manipulation of British public opinion 1880–1960.* Manchester: Manchester University Press.

Maclagen, P. (1998). *Management and morality.* London: Sage.

MacLaine, I. (1979). *Ministry of morale.* London: Allen & Unwin.

Mallinson, B. (1996). *Public lies and private truths: an anatomy of public relations.* London: Cassell.

Mandelbaum, M. (1974). The problem of 'covering laws.' In Gardiner, P. (ed.). *The philosophy of history.* Oxford: Oxford University Press.

Marston, J. (1963). *The nature of public relations.* New York: McGraw-Hill.

Martin, M. & McIntyre, L. C. (eds.). (1994). *Readings in the philosophy of social science.* Cambridge, Massachusetts: MIT Press.

McChesney, R. W., Wood, E. M., & Foster, J. B. (eds.). (1998). *Capitalism and the information age: the political economy of the global communication revolution.* New York: Monthly Review Press.

McCracken, G. (1988). *The long interview.* London: Sage.

McLaine, I. (1979). *Ministry of morale.* London: Allen & Unwin, p. 18.

McNair, B. (1994). *News and journalism in the UK.* London: Routledge.

McNair, B. (1996). Performance in politics and the politics of performance: public relations, the public sphere and democracy. In L'Etang, J. & Pieczka, M. (eds.). *Critical perspectives in public relations.* London: ITBP.

McNair, B. (2000). *Journalism and democracy.* London: Routledge.

Miles, M. B. & Huberman, A. M. (1994). *An expanded sourcebook: qualitative data analysis.* London: Sage.

Miller, D. (1998). Public relations and journalism: promotional strategies and media power. In Briggs, A. & Cobley, P. (eds.). *The media: an introduction.* London: Longman, pp. 65–80.

Miller, D., Kitzinger, J., Williams, K., & Beharrell, P. (1998). *The circuit of mass communication: media strategies, representation and audience reception in the AIDS crisis.* London: Sage.

Miller, K. (1999). *The voice of business: Hill & Knowlton and postwar public relations.* Chapel Hill: University of North Carolina Press.

Millerson, G. (1964). *The qualifying associations: a study in professionalisation.* London: Routledge & Kegan Paul.

Mink, L. O. (1994). The autonomy of historical understanding. In Martin, M. & MacIntyre, L. C. (eds.). *Readings in the philosophy of social science.* Cambridge, Massachusetts: MIT Press.

Moloney, K. (1996). *Lobbyists for hire.* Aldershot: Dartmouth Publishing Company.

Morse, J. (ed.). (1994). *Critical issues in qualitative research methods.* London: Sage.

Murphree, V. (1991). Public relations, 1900–1950: tool for profit or social reform? In Sloan, W. M. (ed.). *Perspectives on mass communications history.* Hillsdale, New Jersey: Lawrence Erlbaum Associates.

Murphy, R. (1988). *Social closure: the theory of monopolisation and exclusion.* Oxford: Oxford University Press.

Nagel, E. (1974). Determinism in history. In Gardiner, P. (ed.). *The philosophy of history.* Oxford: Oxford University Press.

Nevett, T. R. (1982). *Advertising in Britain: a history.* London: Heinemann.

O'Gandy, O. (1982). *Beyond agenda setting: information subsidies and public policy.* Norwood, NJ: Ablex.

O'Gandy, O. (1992). Public relations and public policy: the structuration of dominance in the information age. In Toth, E. & Heath, R. (eds.). *Rhetorical and critical approaches to public relations.* Hillsdale, New Jersey: Laurence Erlbaum Associates, pp. 131–63.

Olasky, M. N. (1987). *Corporate public relations: a new historical perspective.* Hillsdale, New Jersey: Lawrence Erlbaum Associates.

Parenti, M. (1993). *Inventing the politics of the news media reality.* New York: St Martin's Press.

Passmore, J. (1966). *A hundred years of philosophy.* London: Penguin.

Passmore, J. (1974). The objectivity of history. In Gardiner, P. (ed.). *The philosophy of history.* Oxford: Oxford University Press.

Pearson, R. (1992). Business ethics as communication ethics: public relations practice and the idea of dialogue. In Botan, C. H. & Hazleton, V. (eds.). *Public relations theory.* Hillsdale, New Jersey: Lawrence Erlbaum Associates.

Pearson, R. (1992). Perspectives on public relations history. In Toth, E. L. & Heath, R. L. (eds.). *Rhetorical and critical approaches to public relations.* Hillsdale, New Jersey: Lawrence Erlbaum Associates.

Perkin, H. (1989). *The rise of professional society: England since 1880.* London: Routledge.

Perkin, H. (1996). *The third revolution: professional elites in the modern world.* London: Routledge.

Pieczka, M. & L'Etang, J. (2001). Public relations and the question of professionalism. In Heath, R. (ed.). *Handbook of public relations.* London: Sage, pp. 223–36.

Piette, A. (1995). *Imagination at war: British fiction and poetry 1939–1945.* London: Papermac.

Pimlott, J. A. R. (1951). *Public relations and American democracy*. Princeton, New Jersey: Princeton University Press.

Popper, K. (1961). *The poverty of historicism*. London: Routledge.

Popper, K. (1962). *The open society and its enemies*. London: Routledge.

Pringle, H. W. (1933). General introduction. In *The library of advertising*. London: Butterworth & Co.

Pronay, N. (ed.). (1982). *Propaganda, politics and film 1918–1945*. London: Macmillan.

Pronay, N. (1982). The news media at war. In Pronay, N. (ed.). *Propaganda, politics and film 1918–1945*. London: Macmillan, p. 174.

Psathas, G. (1995). *Conversation analysis*. London: Sage.

Reuth, R. G. (1993). *Goebbels*. London: Constable.

Rice, M. (1994). *False inheritance: Israel in Palestine and the search for a solution*. London: Kegan Paul.

Roberts, D. D. (1987). *Benedetto Croce and the uses of historicism*. Berkeley: University of California Press.

Roth, P. A. (1994). Narrative explanations: the case of history. In Martin, M. & McIntyre, L. C. (eds.). *Readings in the philosophy of social science*. Cambridge, Massachusetts: MIT Press.

Rousseau, J. J. (1968). *The social contract*. Harmondsworth: Penguin.

Rowell, A. (1996). *Green backlash: global subversion of the environment movement*. London: Routledge.

Rubin, H. J. & Rubin, I. S. (1995). *Qualitative interviewing the art of hearing data*. London: Sage.

Scannell, P. & Cardiff, D. (1991). *A social history of British broadcasting*, Vol. 1. Oxford: Basil Blackwell.

Schlesinger, P. (1990). Rethinking the sociology of journalism: the source strategies and the limits of media centrism. In Ferguson, M. (ed.). *Public communication: the new imperatives: future directions for research*. London: Sage.

Scruton, R. (1984). *A short history of modern philosophy*. London: Routledge.

Silverman, D. (1993). *Interpreting qualitative data*. London: Sage.

Sissons, M. & French, P. (eds.). (1963). *Age of austerity*. London: Hodder & Stoughton.

Sklar, R. (1993). *Film: an international history of the medium*. London: Thames & Hudson.

Skocpol, T. (ed.). (1984). *Vision and method in historical sociology*. Cambridge: Cambridge University Press.

Sloan, W. M. (1991). *Perspectives on mass communication history*. Hillsdale, New Jersey: Lawrence Erlbaum Associates.

Smith, D. (1991). *The rise of historical sociology*. Cambridge: Polity Press.

Smith, L. M. (1994). Biographical method. In Denzin, N. K. & Lincoln, Y. S. (eds.). *Handbook of qualitative research*. London: Sage.

Smith, T. III. (1989). *Propaganda*. New York: Praeger.

Spoor, A. (1967). *White-collar union: sixty years of NALGO*. London: Heinemann.

Sproule, J. M. (1989). Social responses to twentieth century propaganda. In Smith, T. III. *Propaganda*. New York: Praeger.

Startt, J. D. & Sloan, W. D. (1989). *Historical methods in mass communication*. Hillsdale, New Jersey: Lawrence Erlbaum Associates.

Strauss, A. & Corbin, J. (1990). *Basics of qualitative research: grounded theory procedures and techniques*. London: Sage.

Swann, P. (1989). *The British documentary movement 1926–1946*. Cambridge: Cambridge University Press.

Taylor, P. (1981). *The projection of Britain 1919–1939*. Cambridge: Cambridge University Press.

Taylor, P. (1990). *Munitions of the mind*. Glasgow: William Collins.

Tedlow, R. S. (1979). *Keeping the corporate image: public relations and business 1900–1950*. Greenwich, Connecticut: JAI Press.

Tilson, D. (ed.). (2003). *Toward the common good: perspectives in international public relations*. Boston: Pearson.

Torstendahl, R. (1990). Essential properties, strategic aims and historical development: three approaches to theories of professionalisms. In Burrage, M. & Torstendahl, R. (eds.). *Professions in theory and history: rethinking the study of the profession*. London: Sage.

Torstendahl, R. & Burrage, M. (1990). *The formation of professions*. London: Sage.

Toth, E. L. & Heath, R. L. (eds.). (1992). *Rhetorical and critical approaches to public relations*. Hillsdale, New Jersey: Lawrence Erlbaum Associates.

Trompf, G. W. (1979). *The idea of historical recurrence in western thought*. Berkeley: University of California Press.

Tuchman, J. (1993). Historical social science: methodologies, methods and meanings. In Denzin, N. K. & Lincoln, Y. S. (eds.). *Handbook of qualitative research*. London: Sage.

Tunstall, J. (1964). *The advertising man in London advertising agencies*. London: Chapman & Hall.

Tunstall, J. (1983). *The media in Britain*. London: Constable.

Van Leuven, J. K. (1996). Public relations in South East Asia: from nation building campaigns to regional interdependence. In Culbertson, H. M. and Chen, N. (eds.). *International public relations: a comparative analysis*. Mahwah, New Jersey: Lawrence Erlbaum Associates, p. 209.

Van Leuven, J. K. & Pratt, C. B. (1996). 'Public relations' role: realities in Asia and in Africa south of the Sahara. In Culbertson, H. M. & Chen, N. (eds.). *International public relations: a comparative analysis*. Mahwah, New Jersey: Lawrence Erlbaum Associates, pp. 95–7.

Vidich, A. J. & Lyman, S. M. (1994). Qualitative methods: their history in sociology and anthropology. In Denzin, N. K. & Lincoln, Y. S. (eds.). *Handbook of qualitative research*. London: Sage.

Vollmer, H. M. & Mills, D. L. (eds.). (1966). *Professionalisation*. Englewood Cliffs, New Jersey: Prentice Hall.

Walsh, W. H. (1974). Colligatory concepts in history. In Gardiner, P. (ed.) *The philosophy of history*. Oxford: Oxford University Press.

Ward, K. (1989). *Mass communication and the modern world*. Basingstoke: Macmillan.

Watkins, J. W. N. (1994). Historical explanation in the social science. In Martin, M. & McIntyre, L. C. (eds.). *Readings in the philosophy of social science*. Cambridge, Massachusetts: MIT Press.

Wernick, A. (1991). *Promotional culture: advertising, ideology and symbolic expression*. London: Sage.

Wilkinson, P. & Bright Astley J. (1993, 1997). *Gubbins & SOE*. London: Leo Cooper.

Williams, K. (1998). *Get me a murder a day! A history of mass communication in Britain*. London: Arnold.

Winch, P. (1974). *Concepts and action*. In Gardiner, P. (ed.). *The philosophy of history*. Oxford: Oxford University Press.

Winston, B. (1995). *Claiming the real: the documentary film revisited*. London: British Film Institute.

Wolcott, H. F. (1990). *Writing up qualitative research*. London: Sage.

Worsley, P. (ed.) (1991). *The new modern sociology readings*. London: Penguin.

Young, M. D. F. (ed.). (1971). *Knowledge and control: new directions in the sociology of education*. London: Collier-Macmillan.

Yow, V. R. (1994). *Recording oral history*. California: Sage.

Researching the History of British Public Relations: An Account of Methods Employed

INTRODUCTION

This appendix seeks to describe, explain, and justify the basic research question, the research paradigm, and data collection and analysis techniques employed in the research.

THE RESEARCH QUESTION

Given the absence of published literature on the topic, a broad, exploratory research question was generated: How and why did public relations develop in Britain?

The question implied a strong narrative or historical structure defining key events, organisations, and people, drawn together to offer a convincing explanation for the development and expansion of the public relations occupation after the Second World War. At the same time, however, other questions arose that implied a sociological approach, such as: What was the relationship between the development of this occupation and social, economic, and technological advancements?

What transformations in society facilitated the growth of the field? What role was public relations performing in society? How did the occupation relate to concepts of professionalism and processes of professionalisation?

THE RESEARCH FOCUS

As initial empirical research progressed, a supplementary research question was posed: How and in what form did public relations develop as an occupation? This secondary question was chosen because, after the Second World War, the occupation began to formalise and to set up professional bodies and an understanding of that process seemed crucial to gaining insight into the overall development of the occupation.

The scope of the research was limited to the 20th century, with a particular concentration on the postwar era. Because of the richness of archive material, the focus was on themes that related to professionalisation and, within that, on key historical moments that could also be subjected to sociological analysis.

THE RESEARCH PARADIGM

The rhetorical and diplomatic aspects of public relations suggest a strong connection with the sources and processes of institutional and social change brought about through communication. Consequently, the research fell between the boundaries of history and sociology and could be defined as historical sociology: work that uses historical data to support sociological interpretation and analysis.

Debates about the nature of historical methodology and the underpinning epistemology have focused on two aspects: the degree to which historians can claim to be objective and to make impartial historical judgements, and the balance between recreating past events and theorising about underlying causes for those events. Increasingly, the role of the trained historian has been seen as going beyond the mere chronicling of events to include interpretation and contextualisation, going beyond the source where necessary.[1] The acknowledgement of histori-

---

[1]Collingwood, R. G. (1974). Human nature and human history. In Gardiner, P. (ed.). *The philosophy of history.* Oxford: Oxford University Press, p. 37; Ayer, A. J. (1982). *Philosophy in the twentieth century.* London: Unwin, p. 208.

ans' sensitivity and the development of the role of the historian in establishing themes beyond factual data clearly bring the historian closer to the orientation of the qualitative researcher, and history itself closer to interpretations of interpretations (of key witnesses and sources). Many historians see themselves in the field of social sciences rather than the arts. The overlap between history and social science and their shared methodological problems becomes more explicit when considering the ambition of historians who have aimed at complete description,[2] an approach surely comparable to the ethnographer's thick description[3] of events, rituals, and customs that guide understanding of a particular research setting. Constructing the researcher as *bricoleur*, and research as *bricolage*, facilitates a multidimensional interpretive historical process. The boundaries between history and sociology have become blurred as social science moves closer to the traditional humanities.[4] Furthermore, although historical technique has been traditionally hermeneutic, emphasising the scholarly values of *quellenkritik*, historians since Herodotus[5] have always used other techniques, such as qualitative interviews with key witnesses and field trips to sites of important events.

The research on which this book is based aimed to facilitate interplay between specific historical data and broader level sociology. Abbott, a sociologist who has published extensively on the professions, summed up the difficulties of such research when he wrote:

> History is first and foremost a tangled net of events. Each event lies in dozens of stories, determined and overdetermined by the causes flowing through them, yet ever open to new directions and twists. Indeed, given happenings may be seen as parts of different events within different stories. Because people and groups construct their future by interpreting their causal environment, the very knowledge of the past itself shapes the future, even though aggregate regularities and structural necessity simultaneously oblige it . . . direct cause interacts with structural determination and intention to produce a succession of futures. . . . The writer

---

[2] Passmore, J. (1974). The objectivity of history. In Gardiner, P. (ed.). *The philosophy of history*. Oxford: Oxford University Press, p. 152.

[3] Geertz, C. (1973). Thick description: towards an interpretive theory of culture. In Geertz, C. *The interpretation of cultures: selected essays*. New York: Basic Books.

[4] Denzin, N. K. & Lincoln, Y. (eds.). *Handbook of qualitative research*. London: Sage, p. ix.

[5] Burn, A. R. (1954, 1981). Introduction. In *Herodotus: the histories*. London: Penguin, pp. 10–12.

must disentangle the threads of determinants, structures, and intentions, then reweave them into an analysis and then recount that analysis in some readable form — arduous tasks indeed.'[6]

This book has sought to take up that challenge.

DATA COLLECTION PROCEDURES

Data was collected through two main instruments: the oral history interview and documentary research using the Institute of Public Relations (IPR) archive. In addition, field notes were taken during interviews and visits and a research diary was kept throughout the collection process.

Sampling

Sampling of interviewees was carried out by snowballing. Altogether, 67 interviews were carried out (see Appendix B). Priority was determined by the age of the interviewee and their importance or renown in the field, for example, those who had held office at the IPR. All interviewees were asked to recommend other sources. Included in the sample were two journalists who had written critically about public relations in the 1960s, one film documentarist with knowledge of aspects of the publicity world, the two children of a particularly eminent figure in public relations (one of whom was in public relations himself), the son of a deceased researcher into public relations, a relevant source from the National Union of Journalists (NUJ), two senior employees of the IPR, and an academic responsible for drawing up early curricula for a public relations degree. Of these it is worth highlighting the contributions of Katherine Whitehorn, journalist, and Michael Frayn, author and journalist. Selected because of their historical contribution to the emerging critique of public relations in the 1960s, they provided fulsome and uninhibited responses that were much appreciated. The vast majority of the public relations practitioners interviewed had experience of public relations from the 1950s. Only two had prewar and a handful had wartime experience in the field. Only 13 of those interviewed were women,

---

[6] Abbott, A. (1998). *The system of professions: an essay on the division of expert labor.* Chicago: University of Chicago Press, p. 319.

reflecting the fact that women did not enter the occupation in any numbers until the late 1960s and early 1970s following the growth of consumer markets in which, it was felt at the time, women would naturally be more expert. Ten interviewees were still practising public relations. The sample was biased in favour of those who had been active members of the IPR and, within that category, 13 had been president. Two had held high office in the International Public Relations Association and another two in the Public Relations Consultants' Association. Two former editors of the institute's journal were interviewed as were two of its executive directors (chief administrators). All sources were British, except the son of the renowned American historical figure Ivy Lee. Overall, the degree and quality of access was excellent and, in six instances, correspondence developed producing further insights and opportunity for cross-checking.

Initial contact with former practitioners was facilitated by the fact that many of the key informants who had retired had kept up their subscriptions to the IPR. Considerable effort was made to trace key informants who were no longer members of the IPR and the intervention and personal recommendation of those already interviewed were often important elements in achieving an interview. However, a number of very useful informants had already died, leaving those who remained to shape the history. As Cutlip pointed out, in relation to histories of American public relations, there is always the danger that, in relying on oral history accounts, those with the most resilient genes and constitutions are liable to greater and possibly disproportionate representation in history.[7] Because many of the interviewees were in their 70s and 80s, these sources were subject both to memory losses and post hoc rationalisation. For this reason, the documentary research was invaluable in triangulating the project and providing evidence that could support or counter claims made in interviews.

Within the IPR archive, most attention was given to the published journals of the institute. All journals were read from 1948–1999, but most emphasis in data analysis was given to the formative period, which was determined to be from 1948 to around 1970. The reading was primarily historical because it was important to construct a clear timeline, but a second, more sociological, reading was tackled to elucidate key themes.

---

[7] Cutlip, S. M. (1994). *The unseen power: public relations: a history*. Hillsdale, New Jersey: Lawrence Erlbaum Associates, p. 190.

Interview Guide

The guide (see Appendix B) fell into three main areas: autobiographical career history, view of the development of the professionalisation processes, and opinions about the scope and function of public relations. Questions were open to allow interviewees to expound freely on their experiences.

REDUCTION OF DATA: CODING PROCEDURES EMPLOYED

Interview transcripts and journals were coded during a process of reading and rereading. Key concepts and important individuals were indexed on cards. Themes were brought together via the use of diagrams and the tabulation of key quotes. The process of constructing this data bank was useful in the early stages of making sense of the raw data. Some examples of loose categories tabulated initially were: truth promotion, proselytising/evangelism, manners, common sense, propaganda, myths and mentors. These categories formed the basis for analysis of occupational values and beliefs and provided the context for understanding the motivations and assumptions of public relations practitioners. However, the categories were not adequate as a complete organising tool and instead were integrated into an historical narrative that combined primary and secondary sources of data. At this stage, it was possible to begin to foreground the concept of professionalisation and to concentrate on issues of social legitimacy, jurisdiction, ethics, regulation, and education. Each of these main themes required further separate readings of journals and transcripts.

ANALYSIS AND THEORISATION

A variety of theoretical sources were used in analysis to assist conceptualisation of themes within the historical narrative. For example, philosophical literature was employed to analyse professional codes of ethics.

OVERALL LIMITATIONS OF THE STUDY

The scope of the research is limited in the sense that the focus on professionalisation naturally excludes those who did not concern themselves with the professional project, such as those in the Government Information Services (GIS).

The sheer volume of original material forced a concentration on some themes more than others, so this book is necessarily only a partial history. The focus on professionalisation provided some limits, but even so it was necessary to be frugal. More emphasis has therefore been given to what are seen as the formative years, although, where possible, connections have been made to present-day practice or issues.

APPENDIX B

Interviewees

G. C. B. Andrew
Corelli Barnett
Honorary Professor Sam Black*
Joyce Blow
Pat Bowman
Rosemary Brook
Denis Buckle
Michael "Tim" Buckmaster*
Sybil Buckmaster
Francis Butters
Alan Campbell-Johnson*
John Cole-Morgan
Kenneth Cook
John Crisford
John Dennison
Derek Dutton
Peter Earl
Alan Eden-Green
Nigel Ellis
Dick Fedorcio
Michael Frayn
Prince Yuri Galitzine
Eric Gould
Tim Halford
Roger Hayes
Janet Hewlett-Davies

Professor John Horden
Colonel Hornby
Henry James
Sheelagh Jefferies
Richard Kelsall
Ellis Kopel
John Lavelle
Geoff Lewis
David Linton
Herbert Lloyd
Ian Macphail
Michael MacAvoy
Ken Matthews
Margaret Nally
Warren Newman
Gerard Noel
Phyllis Oberman
Nora Owen
Stephen Peet
Professor Ben Pimlott
Geoffrey Philips
Michael Rice
Linda Rogers
Basil Saunders
Bill Simpson
Harvey Smith

Tony Spalding
George Speakman
Mervyn Thomas
Margaret Thomson
Honorary Professor Tim
   Traverse-Healy*

Peter Walker
Reginald Watts
Jon White
Katherine Whitehorn
Nancy Wise
Alan Wood

*Signifies those interviewed more than once.

APPENDIX C

Interview Guide

1. Please tell me something about your career and how you got into PR.
2. What sort of work did you do? Which organisations/clients?
3. Were you involved with professional bodies? If so, what were they like?
4. Who were the most influential practitioners? And who were the heroes and villains of your era (if any) and why?
5. How, why, and when did public relations start in the UK? How did the occupation develop and grow?
6. Who went into PR and why?
7. Do you think public relations is a profession?
8. What do you think the effects of PR are on society in general?
9. When did women move into the occupation and why?
10. What have been the most important changes in PR and why?
11. Why has there been so much discussion about the definitions of PR?
12. Who else do you think I should talk to?

Author Index

Subject Index